New Management
in Human Services

New Management in Human Services

Paul R. Keys and Leon H. Ginsberg, Editors

National Association of Social Workers, Inc.
Silver Spring, MD 20910

Library of Congress Cataloging-in-Publication Data

New management in human services.

    Includes bibliographics and index.
    1. Human services—United States—Management.
2. Social work administration—United States. I. Keys, Paul R. II. Ginsberg, Leon H. III. National Association of Social Workers.
HV91.N46 1988   361.3′068   88-28922
ISBN 0-87101-161-1

Printed in the United States of America

Cover design by Dan Hildt

Interior design by Ellen C. Dawson

Contents

▲

Foreword

▲

THE PRIMARY PURPOSE of the National Association of Social Workers (NASW) is to promote effective social work practice in the United States. Consequently, it is most appropriate that NASW publish *New Management in Human Services*. Management clearly plays a significant role in the delivery of services. If social workers are to provide effective services, then we must manage the delivery of those services effectively. Because social workers have tended to concentrate on the connection of services from the line worker to the client, there has been a paucity of literature on the management of services. We must remedy the gap in the literature to increase the effectiveness of social work services.

In developing this book, the first NASW has published on management, Paul Keys and Leon Ginsberg sought contributions from many different social workers in different levels of management. Several of the contributors are practitioners who currently manage large, complex agencies. Others are academics who have had experience in managing programs in schools and in agencies. All bring extensive experience in managing and in writing about management to this book. The authors also represent different constituencies; therefore, they offer the reader information on managing diverse programs. In addition to general management theories and education that apply to managing any level of any program in the human services, chapters address management in the nonprofit sector, in alternative programs, and in public service.

Besides serving as an excellent test to prepare social work students for future management positions, we believe *New Management in Human Services* will serve as a useful refresher for current practitioners. We hope that it will stimulate social workers to develop increasingly effective ways of managing social work services.

SUZANNE DWORAK-PECK, ACSW
President

MARK G. BATTLE, ACSW
Executive Director

October 1988

Preface

▲

IN DEVELOPING THIS BOOK, the editors and authors planned to bring some of the most effective and current management approaches to the operations of social work agencies and programs. The objective was to provide theories that bridge the gap between the traditional business emphasis on the bottom line and cost-effectiveness and the people and values orientation of social work. These modern approaches, which incorporate the best from the two seemingly dichotomous orientations, then could be used to improve social work services to clients and to advance the profession.

Theoreticians and managers increasingly have come to believe that social work programs need well-informed and conceptually sound management by social workers and those sympathetic to the goals of social work who are committed to the values of the profession and to the clients the profession serves. Policymakers, consumers of services, and the general public have demanded social work programs that are managed effectively as a result of the increasing role social work services play in the American economy and the daily lives of American citizens. Social workers also have recognized the need for improved management.

While the growth in social services has precipitated a demand for more effective management, a coincidental growth in more sophisticated management theories has occurred. However, the most current management theories do not always find their way in a timely fashion into social work education and theory. The primary goal of this book, therefore, is to demonstrate how these new approaches to management can be applied effectively in social work organizations.

The idea of applying management theory, which is derived primarily from disciplines such as business and public administration, to social work certainly has been attempted before the publication of this book. Over a decade ago in Colombia, Leon Ginsberg taught courses that incorporated the idea. In addition, most of the texts currently used to teach social work administration—which this book is designed to complement, not replace—are based on management theories or approaches.

viii

The approaches used by the authors in *New Management in Human Services* differ from those in most current texts in several ways. First, the approaches are those currently used and discussed in the United States, whereas the theories in other texts precede today's popular concepts by many years. Second, the authors address several Japanese management theories that have been credited for the recent boom in the Japanese economy. These theories, unfortunately, often are misinterpreted by Americans because of the different contexts for Japanese and American management. In this book, the authors describe how social workers can use derivations of the Japanese theories successfully. Third, the theories emphasized here tend to be empirically based. That is, they are based on observable phenomena and research. In contrast, many of the earlier theories were a priori, based on someone's ideas about what management is or should be, rather than on real management experiences.

While the book was being edited and typeset, several events reinforced the editors' viewpoint that management constantly must adapt to new and different experiences and expectations. In recent months, after most of the articles were written, the world's stock markets experienced several declines; "posturing" for the 1988 elections became a daily issue; and Thomas Peters and Robert Waterman, currently the most influential management theorists, both published new books that extended their earlier theories. The fact that everything about management remains in a state of change is one of the most important modern principles. The authors contend that the fundamental management skill is assessing and dealing with people in a changing environment. All the other knowledge and techniques are useful only if one understands workers and the environment sufficiently to apply the correct approaches to the right circumstances at the right time.

This book reflects the desire of the National Association of Social Workers (NASW) to improve social work practice and the standing of the profession through many means, including the improvement of social work management. The editors are indebted to President Suzanne Dworak-Peck and Executive Director Mark Battle (a modern management theorist) for their support and assistance, to Publications Director Linda Beebe for her constant assistance as both a modern manager of publications and executive editor of this book, to Shanti K. Khinduka, former chair of the Publications Committee, for his assistance and support, to Wendy Almeleh for her skill and patience in editing the book, and to the NASW editorial staff for their superb production work. Robert

T. Maslyn, social work leader, federal official, and convenor of the National Network for Social Work Managers, has created a climate of renewed interest in the managerial elements of the profession. Finally, the editors are greatly in debt to the authors, who represent a broad professional, geographical, and ethnic spectrum, for providing comprehensive information on the new management in human services.

1

Management of Social Services: Current Perspectives and Future Trends

Richard L. Edwards and Burton Gummer

ALL MANAGERS, whether in business, government, or the voluntary social services, must set goals; select the means for accomplishing those goals; acquire funds and physical facilities; hire people with the necessary skills; design mechanisms for assigning, monitoring, and coordinating work; determine whether the organization is accomplishing what it has set out to do; and introduce changes when needed. The ways in which these tasks are carried out, however, depend on the goals pursued; the means available for accomplishing those goals; and the social, political, and economic context within which the work occurs.

The positions of a product manager in a home appliance firm, the first secretary in an American embassy, and the director of an urban child welfare agency are comparable in the scope of their operations, the resources for which they are responsible, and some common tasks. For instance, all of these managers probably have had to introduce computerized information and reporting systems to subordinates and to deal with staff resistance to innovations.

Despite this common problem and the strategies for dealing with it, the difficult problems that each type of manager faces are idiosyncratic to the organizations in which the managers work. Thus, the product manager will look for ways to relieve the subordinates' fears that a computerized information system will mean the loss of jobs (a realistic

1

concern, given the company's cost-conscious climate). For the foreign service officer, a computerized information system will present monumental security problems, as well as inhibit staff willingness to engage in informal, exploratory discussions of sensitive issues. The social agency director may be preoccupied with the cavalier fashion in which software designers eliminated whole categories of information that, although essential to his or her work as the agency's chief executive officer, cannot be inputted into the system because the categories do not "compute." All of the managers face the same task—the implementation of an innovation—but the special circumstances of their situations are sufficiently different to consider business, governmental, and social work management as three separate fields of practice.

Social work managers face special problems and need special administrative strategies for addressing them. In this chapter, the unique aspects of social work management are discussed and current thinking about strategies for administrative practice in social agencies are reviewed. Additionally, ways in which recent developments in management practice might be adopted profitably by social work managers are described.

ORGANIZATIONAL CONTEXT

The specifics of any administrative practice are determined by the nature of the environment of an organization, its goals, and the ways in which it pursues them. Social service agencies, regardless of their auspices, size, or goals of service, have enough common features to justify treating them as one organizational type with common management problems. Although none of the following characteristics is exclusive to social agencies, taken in combination, the characteristics make the social agency unique among organizations. These characteristics are politicized funding, goals with strong value and ideological components, multiple constituencies with multiple expectations, underdeveloped and indeterminate technologies, and heterogeneous administrative and service personnel. Moreover, these factors form a seamless web of influences on social agencies, making it difficult to examine one in isolation from the others.

Social agencies, unlike businesses that receive income from the sale of products but like other nonprofit and public sector organizations, are budget driven (Drucker, 1973; Sarri & Hasenfeld, 1978). Their budgets, moreover, are generated by a political process. The politics of funding may be explicit and above board, as in the budgetary processes of state and federal governments (Wildavsky, 1979), or subtle and covert, as is the case with United Way agencies and private foundations (Kramer & Grossman, 1987; Potuchek, 1986). The political nature of funding is related, in turn, to two other characteristics of social service organizations: (1) disputes over agency goals and (2) the underdeveloped nature of service technologies.

Social agencies pursue goals over which there are serious ideological disagreements. Some, like distributive justice for the poor, racial and ethnic minorities, and other oppressed groups, have been a source of contention since the founding of the republic. Others, like changing mores of sexual behavior, marital relations, gender roles, and child rearing, are of recent vintage, stemming largely from the revolution in personal and family life-styles that began in the 1960s. Although proponents of both sides of these controversies invoke scientific research and professional expertise, they use these arguments for support rather than illumination. Thus, responses to issues such as whether teenagers should be given contraceptive devices or abortions without the knowledge or consent of their parents or whether gays and lesbians should be allowed to adopt children ultimately will be determined by a process in which power and influence, rather than knowledge and expertise, are the deciding factors.

When a consensus has been reached about goals and a public policy has been mandated, as in the case of the need for permanency planning for children in foster care (Costin, 1979; Fanshel & Shinn, 1978) and the Adoption Assistance and Child Welfare Act of 1980 (P.L. 96–272), then the issue is the best way to achieve the goals. Funding sources, however, must decide which of the competing proposals for accomplishing the goals that have been submitted by agencies will be most effective and hence which ones they should support. Their initial response is to follow what Potuchek (1986) called the *merit model.* According to this model, "a funding organization should evaluate an application for funds by first assessing the *need* for the services proposed in that application and then evaluating the *effectiveness* of the proposed program for meeting those needs" (pp. 421–422; italics in original).

The difficulty in demonstrating the effectiveness of a service, however, has existed since the inception of the profession largely because of the underdeveloped nature of the technological base for social work practice. Technologies provide the means for accomplishing goals. For an activity to be worthy of the name *technology,* it has to meet certain criteria (Perrow, 1967); foremost among them is the high probability of producing the intended results. In this sense, much of social work practice is less technology than a collection of insights gathered from experience, intuition, and trial-and-error experiments that suggest ways for approaching problems but do not guarantee solutions in a majority of cases.

Lacking reliable, objective criteria for evaluating the potential effectiveness of a particular proposal, funders must use other devices. When people agree about goals but disagree about means, Thompson and Tuden (1959) argued, they are likely to use *judgment*, as opposed to *rational calculation*, as the means of deciding. Moreover, to enhance the quality of their judgments, they adopt formal or informal rules that mandate representation by all interested parties, the broad dissemination of information, discussion and debate, and abiding by the will of the majority. In short, they create a *political arena* for decision making. Moreover, the politicalization of funding decisions can be expected to intensify as competition for declining public—particularly federal—dollars increases among social agencies and between social service sector and other recipients of public funds (Gruber, 1983).

Another feature of social service organizations is the existence of diverse interest groups, each with a stake in, and many with influence over, agency activities. In general, organizations develop in one of two ways (Meyer, Scott, & Deal, 1981). In the first, technological innovations (for example, the silicon chip) foster the development of rational bureaucratic structures to coordinate the technical work efficiently. In the second, social processes emerge (such as changing attitudes toward adolescent sexual behavior stemming from an increase in teenage pregnancies) that define certain rules and programs, and the organizations incorporate these programs and conform to these rules as rational and legitimate. Social agencies develop along these lines, and, as products of their communities, are tightly linked to the values, attitudes, beliefs, and resources of the community.

According to Martin (1980), the social agency's constituencies are the general public; legislative and regulatory bodies; local funding and regulatory bodies; employee unions, professional associations, and licensing and accreditation bodies; sources for referral of clients; the personnel resource pool; and clients, both individuals and organized associations. Each group controls in various degrees important resources such as money, skilled personnel, sanction by the community, and clients. If a group controls a resource that is unavailable elsewhere (for example, an accreditation body that is responsible solely for determining eligibility for third-party insurance payments), the agency is placed in a power-dependent relationship; that is, it must be responsive to the group's wishes, which curtails its ability to act independently. The existence of powerful external interest groups also means that social agencies are required to pursue many, frequently competing, goals. The interests of the general public, funding sources, employees, and clients often are different and occasionally antagonistic (Perrow, 1978). Nevertheless, social agencies must develop *goal structures* (a euphemism for the melange of contradictory purposes that agencies frequently must pursue) that accommodate their constituencies (Martin, 1980; Sarri & Hasenfeld, 1978).

The final feature of social service organizations is the heterogeneous mix of professions and occupations involved both in their administration and in the provision of services. Before the 1960s, social work and social services were virtually synonymous, and the typical social agency was administered and staffed by social workers. However, the antipoverty programs initiated during the administration of Lyndon B. Johnson often viewed social work and social agencies as part of the problem and thus employed different types of personnel and alternative service strategies. The spate of programs developed since then spurred the development of new service specialties (drug and alcohol counseling, gerontology, rehabilitation of the physically handicapped, child care, and employee assistance) that put an end to social work's hegemony over the field (Turem, 1986).

A similar development has occurred in the management of social agencies. Public expenditures for health, education, and social services in 1950 increased from $23.4 billion to $492.2 billion in 1980 (Bixby, 1983), of which nearly two-thirds ($314 billion) was spent on social programs alone. As the scope of the welfare state expanded, concern with its proper management became a major issue. Although social work is attempting to respond to demands for trained managers to administer the increasingly large and complex agencies that are responsible for income transfers and services for children, the mentally and physically disabled, and the elderly, the presence of the profession in middle- and upper-management positions has declined steadily since the 1970s (Gummer, 1979; Patti, 1984). Managers who are trained in business and public administration have made significant inroads in positions traditionally held by social workers.

Social work managers are considered to be out of step with the growing conservatism that makes cost containment the sole criterion of the effectiveness of programs. Ideologies aside, social workers are seen as having neither the technical skills nor the personal traits needed to manage large organizations. They are viewed as being preoccupied with consensual decision making, concerned with process rather than outcome, and overly identified with the recipients of services at the expense of the interests of society at large. This perception of social workers has serious consequences for the profession's future, Turem (1986) suggested, "especially for a profession that may be losing control of its own work place" (p. 20).

THE SOCIAL WORK MANAGER: ROLES AND FUNCTIONS

Social work managers must respond to several environmental, organizational, and programmatic factors. Additionally, social work managers need to perform certain functions and roles that are considered essential for effective managerial practice in social agencies.

Most analyses of managerial behavior first identify important tasks and then group similar tasks into categories of management roles. Patti (1977), for example, studied social work managers' activities during a typical workweek. He found these activities to be, in descending order of the amount of time spent on each activity, supervising; information processing; controlling; direct practice; planning; coordinating; extracurricular (professional development and community service); representing; evaluating; budgeting; staffing; negotiating; and supplying.

The emphasis that managers in the Patti study gave to particular tasks varied with the auspices of the managers' employing organization. Thus, managers of public agencies spent more time coordinating the work of others than did those in voluntary agencies. This task also was associated with the size of organizations, because the public agencies in this study generally were larger and structurally more complex (with more hierarchical levels and functional divisions) than were the voluntary agencies. The managers of voluntary agencies spent more time than those managers in public agencies representing the agency to the community, which could be expected, given their greater reliance on multiple sources of funding and the contributions of volunteers, and more time in direct service activities. Experience suggests that managers in voluntary agencies must keep a hand in practice to maintain credibility among subordinates in organizations with norms that define (rightly or wrongly) clinical expertise as an important component of managerial competence.

The amount of time that managers spent in various activities differed by their administrative level as well. Executive-level managers spent comparatively less time in supervisory activities than did departmental or program heads and first- and second-line supervisors. Nevertheless, managers at all levels engaged in supervision-related activities for significant portions of their workweeks. Executive-level managers and administrative support staff spent three times as much time on planning as did first-line supervisors—a finding that confirms the idea that there is greater emphasis on analytical and conceptual work at upper management levels (Jaques, 1976). Managers in executive-level positions spent an average of two hours a week on budgeting activities, compared with the one-half hour spent by those at the departmental and supervisory levels. Finally, the time spent on negotiating and representing was greatest among those at the highest administrative levels (Patti, 1977, pp. 10–15).

Managerial Styles

The activities that an individual manager emphasizes and the manner in which he or she performs them make up the manager's style. Managerial style is influenced greatly by the nature of the organization (size and auspices) and the manager's hierarchical position, but there also is room for personal and other factors. Managers' social and psychological characteristics, as well as their professional and philosophical orientations to their work, play an important part in shaping how they define their roles and the distinctive ways in which they perform them.

Berg (1980) developed a model of the leadership style of agency executives that is based on the managers' inclinations to be *proactive* or *reactive* and the extent to which they identify with their professions. The proactive executive is "guided by the motivation to actively influence and shape the external environment of the organization as well as its internal structure in order to fulfill the organization's mission" (Hasenfeld & English, 1974, p. 155). The reactive executive is devoted primarily to maintaining the status quo and to avoiding risk-taking situations or circumstances. The level of identification with professional values and beliefs influences the manager's perception of the agency and its processes. Managers who are highly identified with their professions "will be more responsive to professional interests and concerns, and will be more likely to place a higher priority on those dimensions of agency practice that reflect these concerns" (Berg, 1980, pp. 25–26). Combining these factors produces a matrix of four leadership styles (Figure 1).

Local managers concentrate on their subordinates' socioemotive needs. They focus on the dynamics and operations of the agency, identify

Figure 1.
Dimensions of Leadership and Leadership Style

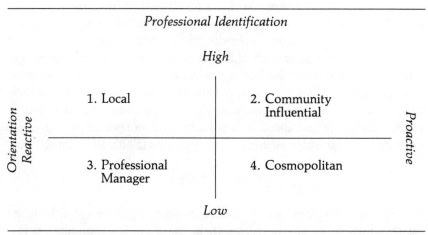

Professional Identification

High

	1. Local	2. Community Influential
	3. Professional Manager	4. Cosmopolitan

Orientation Reactive ... *Proactive*

Low

Reprinted by permission of publisher, Family Service America, from Berg, W. E. (1980). Dimensions of leadership and leadership style. *Social Casework, 61,* 26.

with the agency's reference groups, and are highly committed to the agency's norms. This type of manager is concerned primarily with the professional aspects of agency practice.

Cosmopolitan managers are task-oriented leaders. Because of their strong focus on an agency's external relationships and their identification with external reference groups, they are committed minimally to the agency's norms. Their chief concern is with the attainment of goals.

Professional managers are task oriented, but they focus on internal agency operations. Because they identify with external reference groups of professional managers, their commitment to the agency's norms is minimal. They also are concerned with operational efficiency.

Community managers, like local managers, are socioemotive leaders, but they are oriented externally to local and national professional service groups. Their commitment to the agency's norms is mixed, because they subscribe to norms of professional practice but not to those prescribing idiosyncratic agency procedures. They identify with external professional leadership groups and focus on the attainment of goals.

Analyses of Styles

These analyses of social work management styles reflect the current belief that management is a multifaceted activity that depends on individual, organizational, and environmental factors for the particular form it takes. The simple question—What is the best way to manage?—has been replaced by a complicated one—What are the organizational and managerial tasks that must be performed by a manager in a particular organizational location, at a certain hierarchical level, at one point in the organization's history, and under specified external political, social, economic, and cultural conditions? The search for the best way has been replaced by efforts to build contingency models that identify the different management tasks that must be performed to achieve an organization's purposes. The challenge to modern organizations, then, is to develop managers and management teams with sufficiently broad repertoires of skills to deal with the tasks that must be accomplished.

RECENT TRENDS IN MANAGEMENT THEORY AND PRACTICE

Social work managers often look to the more established fields of business and public administration for the latest developments in management thinking and practice, particularly because they often are criticized for being weak in the statistical, analytical, and computer technologies that play such an important role in business management (Shapira, 1971; Turem, 1986). Ironically, just as schools of social work are beginning to upgrade their capabilities in these "hard" management areas (Edwards, 1987), the business management field has shifted markedly from quantitative techniques toward the "soft" human relations aspects of organizations and management.

The fascination with quantitative approaches to management began in the 1950s. Since then, business schools have stressed the acquisition of skills that enable their graduates to engage in sophisticated quantitative, statistical, and financial analyses and to use increasingly complex computerized information systems. The curricula of business schools have commonly included more management science content than any other subject matter on the assumption that the acquisition of specific management skills is sufficient preparation to be a successful manager. The well-trained manager, many argue, can manage anything, without regard for the specific program content or technology of the organization to be managed.

However, faced with increased competition, especially from Japanese businesspeople, the American business community has begun to question some of its assumptions about what leads to success. The search is on for new management techniques that will, once again, make the United States competitive in a world where productivity is the name of the game. A number of new management books have appeared (many on the best-seller list) that are replete with prescriptions for success (Blake & Mouton, 1981; Blanchard & Johnson, 1982; Deal & Kennedy, 1982; Kotter, 1982; Ouchi, 1982; Pascale & Athos, 1981; Peters & Austin, 1986; Peters & Waterman, 1982; Siu, 1980). Details about these new management approaches and how useful they are for the management of social work organizations are discussed in this section.

The search for ways to increase productivity is one of the central forces behind recent developments in management practice. The question is: How to improve productivity? There are many answers to this answers. During the 1940s and 1950s, the answer was strategies for improving motivation, with a heavy reliance on executive leadership. By the 1960s, there was a shift to goal- or results-oriented strategies, with an underlying philosophy of accountability. The better known of these strategies are Management by Objectives, Program Planning and Budgeting System, zero-based budgeting, and Managing by Exception (Mali, 1981, pp. 28–29).

The 1960s also were a time of dramatic increases in social welfare expenditures; by the end of the decade, there was a growing concern over "uncontrollable" social spending. By the mid-1970s, the mood in the United States became increasingly conservative, and many businesspeople, including some in the Nixon administration, argued that social service programs should be run by business-trained managers. Thus, the management of social service programs became influenced increasingly by notions of "bottom-line" accountability adopted from business (Keys & Cupaiuolo, 1987). However, research in the late 1970s questioned the value of the quantitative emphasis that had come to dominate management training in business schools (Pfeffer, 1977, 1981). Coupled with the increasing concern about the ability of American industries to compete with those of other nations, a number of authors began to explore the reasons for the presumed superiority of foreign competitors. In addition, researchers began to search for characteristics that distinguished the most successful American businesses from their less successful counterparts. These explorations resulted in the publication of a body of work that makes up the "new management."

CHARACTERISTICS OF THE NEW MANAGEMENT

The new approaches to management can be divided into two categories: (1) those related to an organization and (2) those related to an individual manager. Included in the organizational category are the Japanese approach to management and a variety of approaches to changing an organization's culture. The Japanese management style—labeled *Theory Z* by Ouchi (1982)—contains the following elements: lifetime employment, infrequent evaluations and promotions, nonspecialized career paths, implicit control mechanisms, collective decision making, collective responsibility, and a holistic concern. In contrast, American business organizations are characterized by short-term employment, frequent evaluations and promotions, specialized career paths, explicit control mechanisms, individual decision making, individual responsibility, and segmented concerns (Ouchi, 1982, pp. 48–49).

Japanese Style

A major philosophical tenet of the Japanese management approach is a mutual commitment between the organization and the individual, as well as a commitment to the general development of the individual. In contrasting Japanese and American management approaches, Smith and Doeing (1985) suggested that the primary difference between organizations in Japan and the United States is the extent of the involvement of individuals with the organization. The Japanese model is predicated on a significant investment in the total individual. According to Smith and Doeing (1985), this type of investment

> requires many years in order to pay dividends. Thus, the primary virtue required is that of patience. In order for the Japanese method to work, patience must be shown in regard to: (1) length of employment, (2) career development, (3) tolerance for mistakes, and (4) the development of the holistic person. The organizational model utilized in the U.S. emphasizes immediate results. It has a low tolerance level for incompetence and a high tendency to reward competence. This creates a considerable amount of competition, not only between individuals but also among organizations themselves. In sum, the typical U.S. organization has tended to be more interested in the short-run. (pp. 3–4)

Quality Circle

An important feature of the Japanese management approach is the quality circle. A quality circle consists of a small number of employees who regularly meet to identify, analyze, and formulate solutions to organizational problems. Arbose (1980) identified the basic characteristics of quality circles as follows: voluntary participation, training of participants in statistical analysis and problem-solving techniques, the participants' selection of problems for consideration; regular meetings (at least one hour per week) held on company time, and the participants' regular presentation to the top management of ideas and suggested solutions to problems.

In Japan, where more than one million quality circles involve more than 10 million workers (Middleman, 1984, p. 33), quality circles are a highly structured approach to participatory decision making. Middleman (1984) suggested that upper-level managers in U.S. companies have been attracted to quality circles primarily because these managers are convinced that quality circles are a participative management approach that is not expensive and does not require major changes in an organization. Gregerman (1979) indicated that quality circles may be expected to produce a return on an investment of as much as 800 percent. Employees' ideas that were generated in quality circles have resulted in many testimonials about the annual savings that various organizations have experienced. Gryna (1981), however, studied 11 companies and found that despite the major benefits attributed to quality circles of improved employees' attitudes and behavior, actual cost savings were modest.

Work Teams

Perhaps the major advantage of the Japanese approach is the creation of work teams whose members share a common purpose. Those who are involved in doing the work also are involved in planning how the work will be done and for what purpose (Smith & Doeing, 1985). Because there are obvious cultural differences between Japan and the United States, some have questioned whether the Japanese approach to management can be effectively implemented in U.S. organizations. Nevertheless, a growing number of U.S. organizations, mostly in the business sector but including some in the public sector, have implemented elements of the Japanese approach, especially quality circles (Contino & Lorusso, 1982; Middleman, 1984; Ouchi, 1982). Further, some similar management approaches are being used in Sweden that are of particular interest because the Swedish culture is not as radically different from our own as that of the Japanese.

Swedish Approach

One notable Swedish experiment with new management approaches has involved Volvo's Kalmar automobile assembly plant (Gyllenhammar, 1977; Hellriegel, Slocum, & Woodman, 1986; Jonsson, 1982; Lohr, 1987). By organizing its Kalmar plant into work teams, Volvo has been successful in increasing productivity, quality control, and profits. Each work team is responsible for the complete assembly of cars, in contrast to the traditional assembly line approach of other automobile industries. In the Volvo Kalmar plant, managers generally have been promoted from the shop floor and thus have first-hand experience with the automobile manufacturing process. All major decisions must be processed and approved by a joint labor–management committee. The system of work teams has resulted in happier workers and sharply increased productivity. When asked about their preferences, 90 percent of the Volvo workers stated that they preferred the team system to the assembly line (Lohr, 1987).

Another Swedish automobile manufacturer, Saab, has had similar successes (Huse & Cummings, 1985, pp. 9–10). The Saab Scandia plant was experiencing problems with high turnover rates, unplanned work stoppages on the production line, and overall low-quality work. Saab managers, union officials, and workers joined in a problem-solving group to generate new ideas for addressing these problems. One of the group's recommendations that was adopted was the creation of production groups and development groups. Each production group assumed responsibility for scheduling, planning, and monitoring its own work and, ultimately, for productivity and standards of quality. The development groups were responsible for coordinating the work of from two to 10 production groups and comprised a supervisor, a planner, a production technician, and elected representatives from the production groups. Three years after the groups were established, the company noted dramatic improvements in productivity and morale. Unplanned production stoppages decreased from 6 to 2 percent, required extra work and adjustments because of poor quality decreased by about 50 percent, and turnover was reduced to about 20 percent from a previous high of 73 percent in some units. These improvements led to substantial savings, as well as to the increased quality of the products. Saab has used the approach developed at its Scandia plant as a model for redesigning older and newer plants.

The management approach used at Volvo, Saab, and other Swedish organizations generates positive results because it creates a working environment that is conducive to high morale by providing workers with more variety in their jobs, greater responsibility for quality, and a more active role in decision making. None of these features is particularly new or revolutionary. What is different, however, is the organizations' commitment to them, which apparently has a significant effect on the organizational culture.

Organizational Culture

The corporate or organizational culture has become a major topic of interest in recent years. Deal and Kennedy (1982) defined *corporate culture* as "a cohesion of values, myths, heroes, and symbols that has come to mean a great deal to the people who work there" (p. 4). They pointed out that every business—in fact, every organization—has a culture:

> Sometimes it is fragmented and difficult to read from the outside—some people are loyal only to their bosses, others are loyal to the union, still others care only about their colleagues . . . . Whether weak or strong, culture has a powerful influence throughout an organization; it affects practically everything—from who gets promoted and what decisions are made, to how employees dress and what sports they play. (p. 4)

Deal and Kennedy (1982) argued that a major reason for the success of the Japanese management approach is its ability to maintain a strong and cohesive culture, both within and among individual businesses and throughout the country. They stated that although the homogeneity of values that characterizes Japan does not fit the American culture on a national scale, the Japanese approach, nevertheless, can be effective when applied to individual U.S. organizations.

Deal and Kennedy (1982) developed profiles of nearly 80 U.S. companies. From these profiles, they drew several conclusions about the importance and characteristics of organizational culture.

Organizational Beliefs

The most successful companies tended to be characterized by a "clearly articulated set of beliefs" (Deal & Kennedy, 1982, p. 7). Of the companies they studied that had such beliefs, two-thirds had qualitative beliefs or values and one-third had widely understood financially oriented goals. The qualitative beliefs were exemplified by such phrases as "IBM means service," "Progress is our most important product" (General Electric), and "Better things for better living through chemistry" (DuPont). Companies with clear value systems expended a great deal of energy in communicating their philosophy throughout the organization. Their values tended to emphasize the importance of people—both customers or clients and employees. These companies took seriously what their customers and clients had to say and tried in a variety of ways to merge the employees' interests and the company's interests.

These values are considered the bedrock of the corporate culture and "provide a sense of common direction for all employees and guidelines for their day-to-day behavior" (Deal & Kennedy, 1982, p. 21). When an organization's values are strongly held and generally shared, they command attention and serve as guides to individual and collective behavior; when the values are weak, they often are ignored.

Corporate Heroes

The successful companies had corporate "heroes." Such heroes, Deal and Kennedy (1982) suggested, are pivotal figures in a strong culture:

> The hero is the great motivator, the magician, the person everyone will count on when things get tough. They have unshakable character and style . . . Heroes are symbolic figures whose deeds are out of the ordinary, but not too far out. They show—often dramatically—that the ideal of success lies within human capacity. (p. 37)

Organizational or corporate heroes reinforce the basic values of the culture in several ways. They make success attainable and human, provide role models, symbolize an organization to the outside world, preserve what makes an organization special, set a standard of performance, and motivate employees. An organization can make heroes out of both managers and workers, but it needs to give them recognition.

Rites and Rituals

Deal and Kennedy (1982) discussed the importance of rites and rituals, which they described as "culture in action," arguing that "without expressive events, any culture will die" (p. 63). Such events may be informal, as in various kinds of play and joking during company time, or formal elements of day-to-day operations, such as ceremonies that focus attention on particular individuals or units. In either case, these activities are essential aspects of the organizational culture; they teach people to act in the organizational context and are avenues for rewarding those whose behavior is consistent with the organization's values.

Communication Networks

Communication networks are another crucial element of the organizational culture. Every culture has an informal communication network that is the primary means of communication within an organization. Such a network is important, Deal and Kennedy (1982) stated, "because it not only transmits information but also interprets the significance of the information for employees" (p. 85). In a social work agency, for instance, the executive director may issue an official memorandum stating that a supervisor has resigned to accept a position elsewhere and indicating how much that person will be missed. However, the informal communication network may quickly spread the word that the particular supervisor had consistently failed to produce statistical reports on time and that the resignation had been demanded after repeated warnings. This unofficial truth reinforces the basic values, beliefs, and behavioral expectations of an organization.

McKinsey Framework

Another view of the organizational culture that has done more to focus attention on the new management than any other single effort is Peters and Waterman's (1982) study of "excellent companies." While working for McKinsey and Company, a prominent management consulting firm, the authors became interested in how large corporations could become more innovative. They identified seven components— the *McKinsey 7-S Framework*—that must be considered for the effective management of an organization. These components are structure; strategy; style; systems; staff (people); skills; and shared values (culture). The framework can be a useful diagnostic tool, as well as a key for managers who are attempting to change their organizations. The 7-S framework also suggests that real change in organizations is a function of at least seven factors instead of the two—(1) structure and (2) strategy— that frequently have been the focus of organizations' efforts to change. After studying a variety of organizations, Peters and Waterman concluded that innovative organizations are especially good at responding to changes in their environments. As they noted, when the environment changes, these companies change too:

> As the needs of their customers shift, the skills of their competitors improve, the mood of the public perturbates, the forces of international trade realign, and government regulations shift, these companies tack, revamp, adjust, transform, and adapt. In short, as a whole culture, they innovate. (p. 12)

Their interest in innovation led Peters and Waterman to undertake a study of excellence—to learn what characteristics were shared by highly regarded companies. They identified and studied 62 American companies that they defined as excellent performers over a 20-year period. Their research convinced them that the excellent companies, were, above all,

> brilliant on the basics. Tools didn't substitute for thinking. Intellect didn't overpower wisdom. Analysis didn't impede action. Rather, these companies worked hard to keep things simple in a complex world. They persisted. They insisted on top quality. They fawned on their customers. They listened to their employees and treated them like adults. They allowed their innovative product and service "champions" long tethers. They allowed some chaos in return for quick action and regular experimentation. (p. 13)

Peters and Waterman identified several attributes that characterize the excellent, innovative companies.

A Bias for Action

Although the excellent companies may be analytical in their approach to decision making, they are not paralyzed by that fact; they place a premium on experimentation.

Close to the Customer

The excellent companies strive to learn from the people they serve and stress quality, service, and reliability.

Autonomy and Entrepreneurship

The excellent companies permit and nourish many leaders and innovators in the organization. They encourage practical risk taking and support "good tries."

Productivity through People

The excellent companies treat their rank-and-file personnel as the root source of quality and productivity. They foster an attitude of respect for the individual and a view of every worker as a source of ideas, and not just a pair of hands.

Hands-on, Value-Driven Approach

The excellent companies have a clearly articulated value system, and managers maintain a close, personal connection with all phases of the operation.

"Stick to the Knitting"

The excellent companies generally stay close to businesses they know; they do not expand into businesses that are far from what they know and do best.

Simple Form, Lean Staff

The excellent companies tend to have simple structural forms and are not top heavy with executives and managers.

Simultaneous Loose–Tight Properties

Although the excellent companies are almost fanatical about their core values, they tend to push autonomy down as far as possible; they are both centralized and decentralized.

Organizational Norms

Blake and Mouton (1981) suggested another approach to managing the organizational culture. They argued that attitudes about productivity "arise from the norms of the organizational groups in which we hold memberships." (p. 17). Furthermore, they noted that norms, which they defined as "any uniformity of attitude, opinion, feeling, or action shared by two or more people," (p. 17), may promote productivity or restrict output. To enhance productivity, it is first necessary to understand that behind any definition of productivity are the people whose actions generate productive results. Thus, it is people—workers, super-visors, and managers—who get the work done, not machines or other forms of capital. In most group situations, there are pressures to con-form to the group's norms. The manager's task, Blake and Mouton in-dicated, is to study prevailing norms and develop strategies to modify them toward norms of greater productivity. They stated that the key factor is to involve those whose behavior is regulated by prevailing norms in studying what those norms are and exploring alternatives that might better serve an organization.

Effectiveness of Individual Managers

In addition to suggestions for changing organizational structures, the new-management literature looks at how individual managers can become more effective. In his research on high-level managerial work, Kotter (1982) studied 15 "general management" executives who held positions with multiple functional responsibilities in a variety of cor-porate and business settings. The executives' jobs were demanding in terms of both decision making and implementation. The factors that contributed to making the general manager's job difficult included the organization's diversification and growth, technological developments, governmental regulations, and international competition. In addition, Kotter noted that

> informational contexts, characterized by major uncertainties, great diver-sity, and high volume—in combination with human contexts, character-ized by large numbers of people, diverse orientations, and dependent relationships—almost always posed serious intellectual and interpersonal problems for the incumbents. (p. 30)

The general managers tended to be motivated and ambitious, en-joyed status and power, and had few conflicts about using or dealing with power. They were emotionally stable, even tempered, personable and good at developing relationships, and tended to be optimistic. Intellec-tually, they appeared to be above average, but not "brilliant." However, they tended to have reasonably strong analytic and intuitive skills.

In addition to sharing many personality traits, the general managers in Kotter's study had substantial knowledge of the business in which they were involved, as well as in the companies in which they were employed, including the specific products, competitors, markets, customers, technologies, unions, and governmental regulations associated with their respective industries. They also tended to have extensive networks of relationships with people throughout their companies and industries. These relationships involved "bosses, peers, and subordinates inside the corporation as well as customers, suppliers, union officials, competitors, and government people outside the firm" (p. 39).

Kotter concluded that the notion of the "professional manager" who can step into any business and run it well is a myth. He found that the successful general managers were both specialists and team players who depended on detailed knowledge of their industry, technology, product, market, and competitors, rather than managerial generalists. Kotter argued that extensive knowledge of the business and the organization for which one is responsible is essential for effective managerial decision making under complex conditions:

> Such knowledge can help guide one in sorting through enormous quantities of potentially relevant information and then in making sense of that information. Under relatively simple conditions, common sense can serve as a guide, and/or the relevant knowledge can be learned in a short period of time. Neither is probably possible under conditions of great complexity. (p. 41)

Kotter found that the general managers also depended on their large, informal networks of relationships to keep them informed and help them make and implement important decisions. He observed that the way the general managers approached their jobs did not seem professional; in fact, their behavior might be characterized as inefficient by proponents of rational management. Given the nature of the general managers' jobs, however, their behavior is logical. A primary feature of the general manager's job is the ability to complete tasks through a large and diverse group of people, including staff not reporting directly to him or her, subordinates, outsiders, subordinates of subordinates, and bosses. Because general managers may have little direct control over most of the people whose activity is essential to the successful operation of the organization, they must depend on more than formal management tools to accomplish organizational goals. Thus, they make use of a wide range of informal strategies and tactics that are reflected in their day-to-day job behavior.

Orientation to People

Kotter's perceptions of what it takes to be a successful top-level manager were echoed by Peters and Austin (1986), who argued that two of the most important aspects of managerial success are "pride in one's organization and enthusiasm for its works" (p. xvii). Peters and Austin suggested that organizations tend to get bogged down in techniques, devices, and programs that are developed in response to increasing complexity but that deflect attention from people—both employees and customers or clients. For organizations to be successful, they must institute a form of leadership that represents the "operationalization of paradox." The paradox is seen in leaders who

> are tough as nails and uncompromising about their value systems, but . . . care deeply about and respect their people . . . . The best bosses are—in school, hospital, factory—neither exclusively tough nor exclusively tender. They are both: tough on the values, tender in support of people who would dare to take a risk and try something new in support of those values. They speak constantly of vision, of values, of integrity; they harbor the most soaring, lofty and abstract notions. At the same time they pay obsessive attention to detail. No item is too small to pursue if it serves to make the vision a little bit clearer. (p. xviii)

Peters and Austin stated that managers should instill a strong customer/client orientation throughout their organizations and stress the value of innovation. Managers should ensure that their personnel take exceptional care of customers or clients through a continuous effort to provide superior-quality service. Furthermore, they should stress constantly the need for and support of innovation. The organizations that succeed, Peters and Austin contended, are adaptive. That is, they are in touch with the outside world, are able to sense change and adapt to it, not through detailed analyses of data, but through "constant contact with and reaction to people . . . [by] every person in the organization" (p. 7). Peters and Austin suggested that organizations can do so, in part, through a management approach they call "management by wandering around."

A major managerial problem in American organizations is that many managers are out of touch with their employees and their customers or clients. To remedy this situation, managers need skill in leading, the essence of which is coaching, or developing those with whom they work. Managers who are skilled in management by wandering around are able to listen, to teach, and to facilitate. Listening is crucial for gaining information, firsthand and undistorted, from employees, customers/clients, suppliers, and others, and is a form of caring. Teaching is crucial for the transmission of values that underlie the organizational culture. Facilitating is important because it represents a way for a manager to be of direct help; often, projects are delayed because of bottlenecks that a manager can relieve immediately—but only if he or she is available. These three roles generally are performed by a manager simultaneously, often during brief, informal visits with personnel at various levels in an organization. The management-by-wandering-around strategy provides managers with opportunities to listen and learn, support efforts at innovation, reward high-quality work, and reinforce key organizational values.

"One-Minute" Management

Still another approach to increased productivity is contained in one of the smallest of the new management books, *The One Minute Manager* (Blanchard & Johnson, 1982). This book makes up for its small size by the extravagance of its claims. The magic prescription promulgated by the authors involves three management techniques: (1) one-minute goal setting, (2) one-minute praising, and (3) one-minute reprimanding. In *one-minute goal setting*, managers inform others of their responsibilities and accountabilities. Goal setting is based on the premise that 80 percent of the important results in an organization come from 20 percent of its goals. Consequently, one-minute goal setting is done only on that 20 percent; that is, the key areas of responsibility. Typically, individuals are expected to set three to six one-minute goals on which they will work at any one time. Goal-setting also involves identifying the performance standards that will be expected. Goal statements of no more than 250 words are written on one page and usually can be read in less than a minute.

One-minute praising represents an organizational philosophy that accents the positive. When the manager "catches people doing something right" (Blanchard & Johnson, 1982, p. 40), he or she makes it a point to tell them what they did right and share how good the manager feels about what they did. This approach stresses positive reinforcement in frequent small doses; it does not wait for an annual performance appraisal to let people know they are doing well. In using the *one-minute reprimand*, the manager determines the facts when it appears someone has made a mistake and then tells the individual precisely what he or she has done wrong and shares how the manager feels about it—angry, annoyed, frustrated, and so forth. This reprimand generally takes no more than 30 seconds and is followed by a few seconds of silence to allow the individual to think about what has been said. Then, the manager reminds the individual how much he or she is valued and well regarded, indicating that the person's performance is being criticized, not the individual.

Although the one-minute approach has a gimmicky quality, it nevertheless is consistent with other contributions to the new management literature. Underlying this approach is the importance of people within the organization or, as Peters and Waterman (1982) expressed it, "productivity through people." Furthermore, *The One Minute Manager* underscores the importance of the organizational culture and value system as well as of establishing measurable goals.

APPLICATIONS TO SOCIAL WORK MANAGEMENT

Some common elements run through the new management literature. They include the focus on the organizational culture; the emphasis on the mission of the organization and clarification of goals; the orientation to customers/clients; the need for long-range strategic planning, as well as the attainment of short-term goals for services and improved quality; communication from top to bottom, and vice versa; the involvement of organizational members in decision making, with special attention to issues of productivity and quality control; and the emphasis on efforts to ensure the well-being of organizational members and their commitment to goals of the organization.

Much of what is in the recent management literature is not new, however, especially the material on small-group processes and human interactions (Middleman, 1984). What is new is the packaging. Many of the new management concepts are consistent with the values of the social work profession, and their implementation, on a selective basis, would be in keeping with these values. However, those who attempt to introduce (or, in many instances, reintroduce) some or all of these elements into social agencies must consider the agencies' special organizational and programmatic features. Furthermore, top-level managers must be committed to changing the ways in which these organizations are managed. This commitment requires serious attention to the organizational culture and the development of systematic and comprehensive strategies for change, rather than simply grafting on a few new techniques or gimmicks taken from the popular management literature. It also requires that managers adopt a proactive stance about change.

One significant feature of social work organizations that must be recognized in planning for change is politicized funding. Social work organizations must have funds to function and they must obtain the necessary funds in a highly politicized competitive environment. Funding for social services is essentially a zero-sum game, because few, if any, slack resources are available to deal with organizational problems.

To compete successfully for funding, social work organizations must have a strong and widely accepted image in the community (Jansson &

Simmons, 1986) so they can establish a claim on a domain of service. Thus, managers of social work organizations need to understand the importance of the organizational culture in building the identity and mission of their organization (Schein, 1985). A first step in managing the organizational culture is to specify a set of clearly articulated values. In a social work organization, these values should reflect the values of the profession and emphasize the importance of people, both clients and staff.

Efforts should be made to involve people at all levels of the organization in meaningful decision making, as well as in the articulation of the values of the organization. Such efforts might include the adoption of a formal program of quality circles or the establishment of a less formal system of work groups. Regardless of the format, these groups should provide organizational members with regular opportunities to analyze the quality of their work and a forum for suggesting improvements.

Attention to organizational values inevitably will lead to the recognition that social work organizations often experience conflicts over goals. Such conflicts are a permanent feature of social agencies, given the controversial nature of many social service programs and the deep ambivalence of the American public toward social welfare in general. Because multiple constituencies are a fact of life for social work managers (Martin, 1980), attempts must be made to recognize the competing demands made by these constituencies, and the staff should be involved in considering how to address them. The working team can play an important role by providing a forum for discussing these problems.

It is important to build a consensus about goals at the smallest possible organizational level. Two key elements in achieving such a consensus are communication and participation. Communication means more than just telling; it means creating understanding (Kirkpatrick, 1985). Participation means involving all those who are concerned about and will be affected by the change. The successful organizations in Japan and Sweden (Jonsson, 1982; Lohr, 1987; Ouchi, 1982), as well as those excellent American companies studied by Peters and Waterman (1982), all emphasize communication and participation. They provide many examples that can be adapted for use in social work organizations.

Social work organizations also are characterized by low levels of technological development, which often make it difficult to evaluate the effectiveness of organizational activities. Thus, many attempts to evaluate the effectiveness of services fall into the trap of measuring the means, rather than the ends. Goals frequently are stated in quantitative rather than qualitative terms, and the emphasis is on processes rather than

than outcomes. How many interviews, how many placements, how much case recording, and how much money is spent too often become the focus of evaluative efforts. The real issue—the effectiveness of the service in solving or resolving the client's problem—often gets lost in the maze of operational statistics. Thus, social work organizations can be more effective if they take a clue from the new management and get back to the "basics." Workers need to be committed to agency programs, even when concrete evidence of qualitative effectiveness is lacking or hard to come by. Managers must serve as role models; they must be committed to excellence and insist that everyone else in the organization has such a commitment.

Communication and participation are important because of the mix of professions and occupations involved in the administration of social agencies and in the provision of services. It is essential for social work managers to be knowledgeable about the business they are in and to be skilled at building networks of relationships (Kotter, 1982). They must be adept practitioners of organizational politics, understanding the nature of organizational power and being skilled at working with coalitions (Gummer & Edwards, 1985).

CHALLENGES

A number of demanding challenges face today's social service organizations at every level of the social service enterprise. At the level of services, social workers are under greater pressures than ever before to demonstrate the usefulness and effectiveness of their services. These pressures have intensified since the social services evolved into the larger "human services" field, with a growing number of providers competing for funds and service mandates. At the managerial level, the old business-as-usual practice of selecting managers from senior service workers who have no special preparation for their new roles is no longer acceptable. Social workers must compete with a variety of other professionals for the control of social agencies. Finally, the social policy environment within which social services exist has been and will continue to be an increasingly hostile one.

In this chapter, the challenges to social work have been approached from one perspective: how to incorporate management innovations into the operation of social agencies. The incorporation of these innovations, of course, is not a panacea for all the ills that beset social welfare programs, but it is an essential first step. If social workers are to provide the kinds of services that they see are needed by their clients and if they are to advocate for the public policy legislation and budgets to support these services, they first must regain or solidify their control over their organizational base. To do so, they must present themselves as knowledgeable and competent managers, second to none. Without such expertise, they run the risk of being left adrift in a sea of bureaucratic and political sharks. Although some individuals may be able to outswim sharks, most people would rather have a nice big organizational ship to protect them.

REFERENCES

Arbose, J. R. (1980). Quality control circles: The West adopts a Japanese concept. *International Management, 35,* 31–39.

Berg, W. E. (1980). Evolution of leadership style in social agencies: A theoretical analysis. *Social Casework, 61,* 22–28.

Bixby, A. K. (1983). Social welfare expenditures, fiscal year 1980. *Social Security Bulletin, 46,* 9–17.

Blake, R. R., & Mouton, J. S. (1981). *Productivity: The human side.* New York: AMACOM.

Blanchard, K., & Johnson, S. (1982). *The one minute manager.* New York: William Morrow.

Contino, R., & Lorusso, R. M. (1982). The theory Z turnaround of a public agency. *Public Administration Review, 42,* 66–72.

Costin, L. B. (1979). *Child welfare policy and practices.* New York: McGraw-Hill.

Deal, T. E., & Kennedy, A. A. (1982). *Corporate cultures: The rites and rituals of corporate life.* Reading, MA: Addison-Wesley.

Drucker, P. (1973). On managing the public service institution. *The Public Interest, 33,* 43–60.

Edwards, R. L. (1987). The competing values approach as an integrating framework for the management curriculum. *Administration in Social Work, 11,* 1–13.

Fanshel, D., & Shinn, E. B. (1978). *Children in foster care.* New York: Columbia University Press.

Gregerman, I. B. (1979). Introduction to quality circles: An approach to participative problem-solving. *Industrial Management, 21,* 21–26.

Gruber, M. L. (1983). The intractable triangle: The welfare state, federalism, and the administrative muddle. *Administration in Social Work, 7,* 163–177.

Gryna, F. M. (1981). *Quality circles: A team approach to problem-solving*. New York: American Management Association.

Gummer, B. (1979). Is the social worker in public welfare an endangered species? *Public Welfare, 37*, 12–21.

Gummer, B., & Edwards, R. L. (1985). A social worker's guide to organizational politics. *Administration in Social Work, 9*, 13–22.

Gyllenhammar, P. G. (1977). *People at work*. Reading, MA: Addison-Wesley.

Hasenfeld, Y., & English, R. A. (Eds.). (1974). *Human service organizations*. Ann Arbor: University of Michigan Press.

Hellriegel, D., Slocum, J. W., & Woodman, R. W. (1986). *Organizational Behavior*. St. Paul, MN: West.

Huse, E. F., & Cummings, T. G. (1985). *Organizational development*. St. Paul, MN: West.

Jansson, B. S., & Simmons, J. (1986). The survival of social work units in host organizations. *Social Work, 31*, 339–343.

Jaques, E. (1976). *A general theory of bureaucracy*. London: Heinemann Educational Books.

Jonsson, B. (1982). The quality of work life—The Volvo experience. *Journal of Business, 1*, 119–126.

Keys, P. R., & Cupaiuolo, A. (1987). Rebuilding the relationship between social work and public welfare administration. *Administration in Social Work, 11*, 37–46.

Kirkpatrick, D. L. (1985). *How to manage change effectively*. San Francisco: Jossey-Bass.

Kotter, J. P. (1982). *The general managers*. New York: Free Press.

Kramer, R. M., & Grossman, B. (1987). Contracting for social services: Process management and resource dependencies. *Social Service Review, 61*, 32–55.

Lohr, S. (1987, June 23). Making cars the Volvo way. *New York Times*, pp. D 1 ff.

Mali, P. (1981). *Management handbook: Operating guidelines, techniques and practices*. New York: John Wiley & Sons.

Martin, P. Y. (1980). Multiple constituencies, dominant societal values, and the human service administrator: Implications for service delivery. *Administration in Social Work, 4(2)*, 15–27.

Meyer, J. W., Scott, W. R., & Deal, T. E. (1981). Institutional and technical sources of organizational structure: Explaining the structure of educational organizations. In H. D. Stein (Ed.), *Organization and the human services: Cross-disciplinary reflections* (pp. 151-179). Philadelphia: Temple University Press.

Middleman, R. R. (1984). The quality circle: Fad, fix, fiction? *Administration in Social Work, 8,* 31-44.

Ouchi, W. G. (1982). *Theory Z: How American business can meet the Japanese challenge.* New York: Avon Books.

Pascale, R., & Athos, A. G. (1981). *The art of Japanese management.* New York: Simon & Schuster.

Patti, R. J. (1977). Patterns of management activity in social welfare agencies. *Administration in Social Work, 1*(1), 5-18.

Patti, R. J. (1984). Who leads the social services? The prospects for social work leadership in an age of political conservatism. *Administration in Social Work, 8*(1), 17-29.

Perrow, C. (1967). A framework for the comparative analysis of organizations. *American Sociological Review, 32,* 194-208.

Perrow, C. (1978). Demystifying organizations. In R. C. Sarri & Y. Hasenfeld (Eds.), *The management of human services* (pp. 105-120). New York: Columbia University Press.

Peters, T., & Austin, N. (1986). *A passion for excellence: The leadership difference.* New York: Warner Books.

Peters, T. J., & Waterman, R. H., Jr. (1982). *In search of excellence: Lessons from America's best-run companies.* New York: Warner Book.

Pfeffer, J. (1977). Effects of an MBA and socioeconomic origins on business school graduates' salaries. *Journal of Applied Psychology, 62,* 698-705.

Pfeffer, J. (1981). *Power in organizations.* Boston: Pitman Books.

Potuchek, J. L. (1986). The context of social service funding: The funding relationship. *Social Service Review, 60,* 421-436.

Sarri, R. C., & Hasenfeld, Y. (1978). The management of human services—A challenging opportunity. In R. C. Sarri & Y. Hasenfeld (Eds.), *The management of human services* (pp. 1-18). New York: Columbia University Press.

Schein, E. H. (1985). *Organizational culture and leadership.* San Francisco: Jossey-Bass.

Shapira, M. (1971). Reflections on the preparation of social workers for executive positions. *Journal of Education for Social Work, 7,* 55-68.

Siu, R.G.H. (1980). *The master manager.* New York: John Wiley & Sons.

Smith, H. L., & Doeing, C. P. (1985). Japanese management: A model for social work administration? *Administration in Social Work, 9*(1), 1-12.

Thompson, J. D., & Tuden, A. (1959). Strategies, structures, and processes of organizational decision. In J. D. Thompson, P. B. Hammond, R. W. Hawkes, B. H. Junker, & A. Tuden (Eds.), *Comparative studies in administration* (pp. 195–216). Pittsburgh, PA: University of Pittsburgh Press.

Turem, J. S. (1986). Social work administration and modern management technology. *Administration in Social Work, 10*(3), 15–24.

Wildavsky, A. (1979). *The politics of the budgetary process* (3rd ed.). Boston: Little, Brown.

2
▲

Applying Modern Management Concepts to Social Work

Leon H. Ginsberg

THE LITERATURE ON MANAGEMENT is surpassing the old standards of popular publishing—diets and child rearing—in the competition for bookstore space and sales. Recently, one of the national, shopping mall-based chains displayed over 100 titles, ranging from a thick guide on manners for executives to several works on successful selling (Augustine, 1986; Blanchard & Lorber, 1985). The popular shortcut books on managing and dealing with children seem to exchange places; for example, *The One Minute Manager* (Blanchard & Johnson, 1983) begat *The One Minute Father* (Johnson, 1983), *The One Minute Mother* (Johnson, 1983), and similar books for teachers and other groups. By way of balancing the score, *Parent Effectiveness Training* (Gordon, 1970) was followed by *Leader Effectiveness Training* (Gordon, 1980). The mass marketing of literature through stores in shopping malls is, itself, a characteristic of the new American management. Business issues currently are prominent in the popular culture. A 1987 film was about stock brokers and a best-selling novel of 1987–88 was Wolfe's *Bonfire of the Vanities* (1987).

Before the explosion in the management literature, a teacher could tell students that successful book publishing involved defining a scheme for solving some common problem, such as maintaining one's ideal weight, raising children without trauma to them or their parents, nurturing a fulfilling and happy marriage, or achieving a happy sexual relationship. Diet, sex, marriage, and child rearing were and continue to be

American preoccupations. But currently, management seems to be gaining ground as a concern. Perhaps the popularity of management stems from the competition among the millions of baby boomers, who are in their prime managerial years, or it may be a result of the recent troubles in the U.S. economy, which have led to widespread unemployment for the first time in the memories of most Americans. Even that phenomenon resulted, in part, from the new competition that the United States faces from the economies of other nations that were long-term beneficiaries— Japan, Korea, Singapore, and Taiwan, for example.

For whatever reasons, management has become the preoccupation of the nation. In addition to books, there has been a proliferation of magazines about business and management other than the venerable *Wall Street Journal, Forbes,* and *Fortune.* Additionally, millions of dollars worth of audiotapes are sold each month to people who want to enhance their knowledge of and hone their skills in managing while they drive to visit customers or commute to work. Videotapes of the same sort are used by individuals and businesses in every part of the country. A major industry has arisen around the management and motivation seminars conducted by some of the people who write the books and create the tapes. There is a frenzied rush to improve the performance of managers, compete in world markets, and generally perform more ably in many enterprises. Management consulting and training has become a multibillion-dollar business.

Social work has not escaped the pressure to improve its management. For many years, it has been clear that many management practices apply equally well to profit-seeking and nonprofit organizations. Governmental agencies have recognized the crucial need to stretch their resources—to do the most with whatever they have. Furthermore, many social workers, after completing their education, which often includes a single course on management, have felt it necessary to supplement their training with some of the expensive seminars, tapes, and films offered by commercial outlets.

The significance of modern management concepts and information for social work should be understood in terms of the nature of modern social welfare. Although social welfare is not discussed often in the profession—perhaps because it is so fragmented—it has become one of the giant industries in the United States, and its expenditures are hundreds of billions of dollars. Clearly, the wise management of social welfare is as necessary as the wise management of any other resource-laden industry.

Social work, which historically has borrowed the best teaching from such fields as political science, psychology, and sociology, can improve itself and the skills of its practitioners by using the teachings of the best modern management theorists for its purposes. That effort, in the tradition of social work knowledge development, is the subject of this chapter.

TRADITIONAL VERSUS MODERN SOURCES

Traditional approaches to directing organizations have focused on the roles ostensibly played by those who administer organizations. One of the largest selling and most traditional texts, Koontz, O'Donnell, and Weihrich's *Essentials of Management* (1986), is organized around the functions of planning, organizing, staffing, leading, and controlling and contains a condensation of the 1930s concept of planning, organizing, staffing, directing, coordinating, reporting, and budgeting that was developed by Gulick and Urwick (1937). Crow and Odewahn's (1987) *Management for the Human Services* also focuses on the roles of managers. The 10 roles on which it concentrates were taken from Mintzberg (1973).

The validity of early twentieth-century theories such as Frederick Taylor's (1947) scientific management and later ideas such as the human relations approach to management have been debated in management texts and courses. These theories, which were advanced for their times because they made use of empirical methods to determine the ideal approaches to management, were developed before the invention of the microchip and the computer, television, jet air travel, satellite communications, and the discovery of atomic energy.

Thus, many of the traditional management theories were devised between World War II and the 1980s—when the United States was the world's richest country and was the sponsor of the redevelopment of Asia and Europe. Currently, the world's wealth is much more evenly distributed. Modern technology, research, and theory building come from all over the world, not just from the United States. The era of continuing U.S. prosperity is either over or, at least, has been interrupted. It was not until the late 1970s and early 1980s that U.S. social work managers had to cope with budgeting in light of revenue shortfalls and reductions. The problem until then was to determine the allocation of budgetary increases.

Management theories currently have a number of distinguishing characteristics. For example, they draw on worldwide experiences, especially those that have affected Asia. They are based on empirical findings, especially those developed by Peters and Waterman (1982). They are rooted in the management context and the realization that effective management must relate to the times and circumstances in which it is practiced. Rather than relying on fixed roles and definitions, management theories are behaviorally oriented, suggesting principles of performance for managers of high-quality organizations. In its own way, modern management is the conceptual equivalent, in its major departures from the past, of the technological changes of the late twentieth century. Peters and Waterman's *In Search of Excellence* (1982), which is based on research on what the authors considered to be the best-run companies in the United States, is perhaps the best regarded of the modern theoretical works. The follow-up book *A Passion for Excellence* (Peters & Austin, 1986) had some of the same virtues and received similar criticisms as *In Search of Excellence*. The most important criticism of the books was that some of their examples fell apart and some of the businesses that were considered excellent declined shortly after the books were published. Nevertheless, Peters and Waterman's theories remain good. It is doubtful that the companies these authors originally cited as excellent failed because they followed the principles of excellence. Other factors contributed to the failures, including discoveries of the innovative ideas of the excellent companies by other companies that then capitalized on those ideas.

PRINCIPLES OF EXCELLENCE

Perhaps the most spectacular success–failure story involved People Express airline, which competed well against other airlines for several years before it was absorbed into a larger airline. People Express had the virtue of centralized operations (Newark, New Jersey) and proved there was a market for travelers who did not want to buy all the services that most airlines provided. Originally, People Express charged for checking luggage and for snacks and meals and apparently had less-than-efficient reservation and information systems. However, it had begun to cope even with this last problem by installing a sophisticated computer system shortly before it was absorbed. For its time, People Express was an excellent example of the application of the eight principles of an excellent corporation defined by Peters and Waterman: a bias for action; be close to the customer; autonomy and entrepreneurship; productivity through people; a hands-on, value-driven approach; "stick to the knitting"; simple form, lean staff; and simultaneous loose–tight properties.

Domino's Pizza was another example that Peters and Waterman gave of an excellent company. However, it may not be as competitive in its field as it was when they studied it, partly because Pizza Hut and other large pizza franchises have adopted some of Domino's programs such as making rapid home deliveries. That fact does not suggest that the original ideas were poor; rather, it may prove their virtue.

Although Peters and Waterman's eight basic principles were written for businesses, they have ready application and significance for voluntary and public social welfare organizations as well. Although the ends are different, in that businesses necessarily focus on earnings and agencies focus on other kinds of indicators of success, the eight principles are means to ends that are appropriate for any kind of organized endeavor.

A Bias for Action

Peters and Waterman (1982), both of whom have written new books (Peters, 1987; Waterman, 1987) found that the best organizations are those that act instead of think about acting, planning for action, or studying possible activities. This principle—a *bias for action*—is important for social workers. Social workers probably have even a greater need for action perhaps because action so often is stifled by organizations that tend to be immobilized. One consequence of community priority studies and planning projects is that planning and study rarely lead to action. Organizations that identify and quickly act on an obvious need and an advantageous change in their programs often succeed more dramatically and for the longer term than do those organizations that continue to determine what action to take, if any. All actions are not necessarily beneficial, however, nor should an organization squander its resources on frivolous projects that have little possibility of success. However, taking an occasional risk or acting without complete information—because complete information is never available—often makes good sense for a social work manager.

Studying and assessing needs often is less effective than simply trying out an idea because research may generate misleading results. Often a pilot study or a small demonstration program that tries new ideas or programs will succeed more readily and more permanently—with later modifications—than will a perfectly designed attempt based on an ideal planning effort. Some of the most successful social agencies—that meet their community's needs and build their own strength—have been those that identified and attempted to respond to new needs, such as assisting clients with acquired immune deficiency syndrome (AIDS), dealing with the growing problem of homelessness, and finding different ways to serve national and international migrants in the United States. Sometimes simply allowing a worker to try a new approach or service to a new community is an excellent way to determine whether the activity is worth more effort and agency resources. Successful organizations and their managers have a bias toward acting on a community's needs, on opportunities, and on new developments.

Peters and Waterman found that actions pay rewards to an organization, even though some actions have negative results. Innovative actions seem to keep employees motivated and optimistic. Customers, and, in the case of social agencies, clients, seem to respond positively to innovative and constantly changing organizations. For example, the director of a youth corrections facility that reevaluated and changed its comprehensive treatment approach every few years indicated that simply modifying the approach seemed to keep the staff and the youths involved and focused on treatment, although he had no evidence that one treatment approach was significantly better for the whole institution than any other. The author's experience as a director of activities for a community agency substantiates the virtue of action. The agency had two objectives for large-scale youth programs. The first was a winter vacation camp for one week in December and the second was a three-week day camp in the summer. For the winter vacation camp, postcard surveys were sent to parents to assess the need for the project. The bulk of the responses indicated that such a program was not needed. When summer approached, the author mailed an announcement of the summer day camp with details on costs, the site, and the program, rather than conducting a survey. The response was sufficient for the program to be held that summer, and the camp has continued operating for 25 years. A study or a long period of planning might have doomed the program, whereas action brought it to fruition.

Be Close to the Customer

Organizations are becoming more aware of the importance of being responsive to the needs of their customers. Successful manufacturers often seem to be those that can best assess and meet the demands of their customers. At times, that ability is more important than the quality of the products they manufacture. IBM, for example, continuously monitors the use of its products by its customers and responds promptly and effectively to the need for service (Peters & Austin, 1986; Peters & Waterman, 1982).

The principles of excellence are as important in social work management as they are in the management of manufacturing, financial, and sales organizations. In the proprietary practice of social work, they are even more crucial. However, the concepts and language have to be better identified with and adapted to social welfare organizations. For instance, the principle of being close to the customer is easy to understand when it is applied to an organization that sells products. The example of the IBM staff staying close to customers by frequently visiting the offices of customers who purchase their equipment and quickly responding to customers who need help is reasonable. However, what if the service is Aid to Families with Dependent Children (AFDC), food stamps, or the secure incarceration of offenders against the law? In those circumstances, social work managers must understand that clients are not always customers. A number of other groups are the "customers" of the social workers who provide those services. Thus, the social work manager needs to determine who is purchasing the agency's services. Is it the agency's board of directors, the state legislature, or the federal government? This consideration does not mean that the manager should not be close to and concerned about the *recipients* of service, who are the clients. However, the real customers—the people who buy the service and pay the bills—may well be others. Therefore, the manager must stay close to members of the agency board or the state legislature or the federal government officials who supervise the program and who purchase the services that are provided.

Autonomy and Entrepreneurship

Excellent organizations also prize autonomy and entrepreneurship among their employees. They allow workers to try new ideas and programs. They listen carefully to and are supportive of innovative ideas. Excellent organizations often are short on discipline and long on imagination and creativity. Managers in these organizations support the workers' search for new and better ways to serve clients. The workers may spend less time than their counterparts in more traditional organizations carrying out orders or following policy manuals or procedural guides. Head Start, crisis intervention, case management, family day care, partial hospitalization, employee assistance programs (EAPs), and workfare are all innovative social work programs that started with workers who were allowed to develop their ideas on the basis of their observations of people's needs.

Furthermore, the best organizations often pick the best innovative ideas from their smaller counterparts and build on them. Even some large corporations find their best ideas in the smaller organizations and among the customers with whom they work. Modern hotel chains are patterned, in many ways, on the innovative lodging designs of Holiday Inn, a chain of motels that was first established in Memphis, Tennessee. Before the development of the Holiday Inn corporation, there was a vast distinction between *motels*, which usually were owned locally, located away from downtown areas, and oriented to motorists, and *hotels*, which were large, downtown structures, some of which belonged to national chains. Some of the giant international hotel operations, such as Hilton and Sheraton, appear to have emulated Holiday Inns in their current practices, for example, by locating outside center cities and building smaller hotels with accessible parking.

Social agencies are different from businesses in that they try to avoid competition and duplication. If money is being made in the soft cookie industry, other companies justifiably get into it and do all they can to sell their versions of the product. However, if one agency is providing high-quality alcoholism treatment to everyone who needs it at a fee that is based on the clients' ability to pay, other agencies will not enter that field and try to compete because that would scatter the few resources available for helping people who abuse alcohol. However, autonomy and entrepreneurship still can be fostered within organizations and within the constraints of the planned, nonduplicative ideal of the human services industry by allowing workers to find their own ways to deal with the problems and agency's clients.

Agencies frequently seek out and pay for the best possible social workers they can find but then try to place those social workers in the tight constraints of agency discipline. Workers are required to practice in precisely the same ways as their peers and under the close supervision that often is found in social work programs.

An imaginative agency gives capable workers the freedom to find new ways to serve through groups, through consulting with community agencies, through sponsoring programs with related agencies and professionals, and through instituting programs in churches and other related institutions that may have better access to clients. An effective organization not only will find good social workers who have some initiative but will give them the opportunity to demonstrate their abilities through independent and innovative activities.

Of course, the agency remains accountable for the ways in which it expends its resources. Accountability is addressed frequently in the current literature on social work management (Carter, 1983) and is a reality that managers of voluntary as well as public agencies must confront regularly. Those who manage, it often seems to observers of new approaches, are immobilized by the need to be accountable to such a degree that they stifle the imaginations and productivity of their employees.

Productivity through People

A related principle of excellence is productivity through people, which states that excellent organizations make their mark by effectively using the talents of people. The organizations do so by keeping employees happy, letting them know that they count, using their ideas, and giving them some role in managing and profiting from the company. This principle follows McGregor's (1960) notion of *theory Y organizations*—those that believe people can be counted on to help and that rely on their people for assistance and ideas. So many organizations treat employees as if they were human forms of machinery or hardware and thus fail to get the best out of their workers. Rewarding employees, recognizing them, and perhaps helping them benefit financially when the agency benefits financially are all means used by excellent companies in their work with their employees.

Managers of large organizations can personalize their relationships with employees and improve their employees' morale by maintaining direct contact with them. In one large state government organization with which the author is familiar, the state director interviews all final candidates for positions. These candidates are recommended through the chain of command after a careful screening process, based on preestablished criteria and an internal merit system. The final interview and official selection are made by the top manager. This manager rarely rejects the recommendations he receives. However, his final selection communicates to the whole agency staff that he cares about all the employees and that they are ultimately responsible to him for their employment. Such an action gives him an opportunity to meet everyone at least once and helps him retain the loyalty of a large number of employees.

In another large state government organization, the director sends a personal letter to each employee on the anniversary of the employee's appointment to a position in the agency. Employees know, of course, that the director's letters are prepared from a schedule, although they are personally signed. However, the action communicates to them that the top management knows when they first started working and considers each anniversary of their appointment significant. Some large agencies have a similar program for their employees' birthdays. Birthdays and beginning dates of employment are important milestones for employees, although they are essentially symbolic and have no special organizational meaning. Furthermore, employees recognize that the management cares enough to pay attention to something that is primarily of interest to them as people.

Symbols of position are important to some managers and staff at other levels in organizations. In some federal government agencies, careful attention is given to the size of offices and furnishings so that people of the same rank are treated equally and better than those who are subordinate to them. These and other noneconomic rewards for staff, such as service pins, patches for uniforms, and recognition in employee newsletters, often mean much more than employees are willing to admit.

Hands-On, Value-Driven Approach

Peters and Waterman (1982) noted the value of the hands-on, value-driven approach to management. They stated that organizations must know their values and work to pursue them. Effective managers, they suggested, remain close to the organization and work to make sure that the values of the organization are pursued.

If that value in social work practice involves helping clients become independent, then everything needs to be assessed through a screen of moving clients from dependence to greater independence. If the value involves improving clients' mental health functioning, then that value becomes the screen through which the organization measures its success. Whatever the values—social work agencies pursue many different kinds of values in many different ways—the manager's focus should remain on the achievement of those values.

Stick to the Knitting

In presenting the principle "stick to the knitting," Peters and Waterman (1982) caution businesses to avoid diversifying into fields they do not understand. The same principle may be applied readily to social agencies, even though social agencies may need to change their direction, particularly when the nature and degree of the social problems in their communities change.

Thus, an agency that is doing well should not abandon its successful activities for others that may seem attractive but that may not promise success. There are many such examples. An effective agency that provides direct services may find itself hopelessly underused by the community when it tries to convert to a planning, advocacy, or standard-setting agency. Similarly, an agency that is effective at organizing services and planning for the resolution of human needs may be lost when it attempts to provide direct services. In another example, a health care organization may be tempted to provide mental health services but encounter many problems when it tries to add a service that is so different from the immunizations, family planning, and other public health programs it has provided. An agency that provides day care services to preschool children may have difficulty operating an afterschool program for school-age children. None of these examples means that an agency should never change its roles or add functions. Instead, efforts to do so should be studied carefully, all the implications should be analyzed, and existing, successful services should not be dropped before the new effort proves successful.

Simple Form, Lean Staff

Another principle of excellence is that organizations should have a simple form and a lean staff. The more complex one makes an organization and the more layers one encounters, the more problems one is likely to have in accomplishing anything. Supervisors who supervise supervisors who supervise yet lower-level workers may unnecessarily complicate an organization. At times, it seems as if social work organizations reward key staff by giving them more people to supervise or more power over others. In fact, an excellent organization tends to minimize supervision and maximize goal-related work by all staff members.

Keeping the staff lean and small makes good sense not just to save money, but to avoid the complications of a larger staff. Many managers have discovered, to their surprise, that a larger staff does not really enhance the functions of the organization but, instead, makes it more difficult to achieve their agency's objectives. There is some evidence that hiring additional people complicates the manager's job because he or she must find ways to occupy them.

When the author first became commissioner of welfare in West Virginia, he found that a number of dedicated people were working hard at jobs that no longer seemed necessary. Perhaps the jobs continued without their being evaluated or, perhaps, there may have been more employees than useful work for them to do. In one situation, an employee was preparing a detailed monthly report on a small program. The report may have been needed in the past but it no longer was. Therefore, the report-writing position was eliminated and the employee was moved to a job in the same city serving clients, with no reduction in salary. However, the new position was in a local office, rather than state headquarters, a fact that the employee initially resented. In social work programs, focusing on the operational, client-serving levels and reducing the concentration of resources at the headquarters levels is consistent with modern management concepts. Many positions in headquarters are simply not needed. Sound management often requires one to appraise carefully the need for the people who surround the top levels of the organization.

Simultaneous Loose-Tight Properties

The last of the eight principles of excellence is that an organization must have both loose and tight properties. That is, there must be a strong hand running the organization and a strong central direction and dedication to objectives within it, but the organization must give its workers the opportunity to work independently and exercise some autonomy.

Many organizations go too far in one of the two directions. For example, the author recalls an organization that was so anxious to have professional social workers that it hired as many as it could and let the social workers work wherever they wanted. It was in those wonderful days in the 1960s, when there were too many social work jobs and not enough social workers to fill them. However, the organization made an obvious error in turning over its direction to the needs of potential staff, rather than in meeting its own needs. By the 1980s, the agency faced the same problems and successes as others in social welfare. There were now more social workers to employ and fewer dollars with which to employ them. The more formal and structured patterns of the modern era meant that the agency had to define its needs carefully and create positions based on them, while eliminating those positions that no longer were needed. The early loose patterns were balanced by tighter arrangements.

A combination of enough looseness to provide for flexibility and imagination within the staff and enough control to make the organization fit together is a critical principle. Being able to control, let go, take command, and delegate are all parts of effective, modern management.

Peters and Waterman's principles of excellence are the most widely used of the modern management concepts that are prevalent in U.S. businesses today. A careful study of the principles, along with conscientious applications to social work management, can improve the functioning of most social agencies.

Although the principles discussed by Peters and Austin (1986) and Peters and Waterman (1982) were developed with profit-making businesses in mind, it is useful for social work managers to think of their enterprises in some of the same terms. More and more social welfare positions are becoming business related and businesslike. Many social workers now engage in full- or part-time private practice. Others serve proprietary hospitals and nursing homes. An increasing number are employed by businesses to operate EAPs or work with agencies that contract with businesses to provide such services. Even the voluntary, nonprofit, and governmental social work programs, however, have many of the attributes of businesses. They must balance their expenditures and resources, deploy personnel advantageously, change their operations in light of changing needs and conditions, take action when it is needed, relate effectively to customers, and pursue the activities they know how to do best. Therefore, modern management concepts are highly relevant to social work managers, as well as to their counterparts in business and industry.

REFERENCES

Augustine, N. R. (1986). *Augustine's laws*. New York: Viking Penguin.

Blanchard, K., & Johnson, S. (1983). *The one minute manager*. New York: Berkley.

Blanchard, K., & Lorber, R. (1985). *Putting the one minute manager to work*. New York: Berkley.

Carter, R. (1983). *The accountable agency*. Beverly Hills, CA: Sage.

Crow, R. T., & Odewahn, C. A. (1987). *Management for the human services*. Englewood Cliffs, NJ: Prentice-Hall.

Gordon, T. (1970). *Parent effectiveness training: The tested new way to raise responsible children*. New York: McKay.

Gordon, T. (1980). *Leader effectiveness training*. New York: Bantam.

Gulick, L., & Urwick, L. (1937). *Papers on the science of administration*. New York: Institute of Public Administration.

Johnson, S. (1983). *The one minute father.* New York: Morrow.

Johnson, S. (1983). *The one minute mother.* New York: Morrow.

Koontz, H., O'Donnell, C., & Weihrich, H. (1986). *Essentials of management* (4th ed.). New York: McGraw-Hill.

McGregor, D. (1960). *The human side of enterprise.* New York: McGraw-Hill.

Mintzberg, H. (1973). *The nature of managerial work.* New York: Harper & Row.

Peters, T. J., (1987). *Thriving on chaos: Handbook for a management revolution.* New York: Alfred A. Knopf.

Peters, T., & Austin, N. (1986). *A passion for excellence: The leadership difference.* New York: Warner Books.

Peters, T. J., & Waterman, R. H., Jr. (1982). *In search of excellence: Lessons from America's best-run companies.* New York: Warner Books.

Taylor, F. (1947). *Scientific management.* New York: Harper & Row.

Waterman, R. H., Jr. (1987). *The renewal factor: How the best get and keep the competitive edge.* New York: Bantam Books.

Wolfe, T. (1987). *Bonfire of the vanities.* New York: Giroux, Farrar & Strauss.

3

MBA, MPA, MSW:
Is There a Degree of Choice for
Human Service Management?

Anthony A. Cupaiuolo and Marc L. Miringoff

THE RELATIVE MERITS of the master of business administration (MBA); master of public administration (MPA); and master of social work (MSW) programs in the preparation of managers of human service organizations are examined in this chapter. Such a review is particularly timely, given the pervasive interest in improving the teaching and practice of management, regardless of profession or academic discipline. Both the popular literature and more scholarly endeavors are resoundly touting theories and techniques that propound participatory and human relations approaches to management and that deemphasize autocratic and purely quantitative perspectives. It is particularly important, therefore, to consider where each of the three degree programs stands with respect to current and evolving management pedagogy and the consequent implications for what they can contribute to management of the human services.

Although this assessment is intended to be as objective as possible and to point out what each discipline can and cannot offer, it would be naive and misleading to suggest that the inherent value of a degree could play a more significant role than the political power of a particular profession in determining which type of academic training is most suitable for a given position. As Mosher (1963) pointed out, once a given profession becomes dominant in a particular agency, that profession will seek to control the personnel process of that agency. For example, to build a career in the highway bureau, an aspiring administrator would need to be an engineer, but in a policy analysis operation, one would need a doctorate in economics (Ellwood, 1985).

In addressing how the three different graduate degrees prepare their graduates for human service management, it is useful to think in terms of the professional identity that each degree helps to mold. According to Denhardt and Nalbandian (1982), as noted in Durant and Taggart (1985), the development of professional identity has both substantive and psychological components. The substantive aspect consists of the knowledge needed for professional competence, while the psychological aspect involves the normative issues of what can and should be done with that knowledge. This psychological dimension also might be viewed as the product of the socialization that all professional students experience. *Socialization* consists of learning the roles, values, attitudes, and expectations that members of a profession tend to hold in common. It would appear, then, that even if there were substantial similarity in the content of the management curricula of the three degrees, the professional identities formed by each degree might be different because of the differential socialization process. Consequently, how the three disciplines apply their knowledge of management might vary substantially.

One other caveat is in order. Any discussion of the management of an organization's activities should differentiate between maintenance management and service management. *Maintenance management* comprises activities like budgeting, personnel administration, and record keeping; *service management* includes activities that are related directly to the quality, substance, and effectiveness of the agency's product, such as casework or child care. Although maintenance functions are essential to the survival of any formal organization, as Miringoff (1980) pointed out, they do not, per se, assure that an organization will carry out its service function effectively to benefit the individuals, groups, or communities that are its clientele. A human service organization requires both efficient, expeditious maintenance management and effective service management if it is to be a viable entity and meet its obligation to its clients.

In considering how each discipline prepares its graduates for the management of human service organizations, then, it is necessary to keep in mind the distinctions between maintenance management and service management. It is certainly conceivable that a particular discipline might do a better job of training managers for one function than for another function.

MBA DEGREE

MBA programs have experienced unprecedented growth in recent years. In 1986, 71,000 men and women received the MBA degree—a nearly 30 percent jump from 1980, more than a threefold rise from 1970, and almost a fifteenfold increase from 1960, when only 4,814 MBA degrees were awarded. In addition, some 200,000 students were pursuing MBAs in 1986 (Byrne, 1986).

Not everything, however, has been rosy for the institutions and schools that offer the MBA degree. Schools have been criticized for failing to educate MBAs about new technology (Turner, 1987). Additionally, some institutions, like the prestigious Harvard Business School, have been criticized for overemphasizing quantitative skills to the neglect of people skills (Bean, 1986). Furthermore, it would seem that demographics alone (the emergence into adulthood of the baby-boom generation) will cause a decline in the growth of MBA programs and probably even a decrease in the absolute number of students and the elimination of some programs.

Given the proliferation of MBA programs and the veritable hoard of graduates produced by them, it is certainly reasonable to examine and consider how the MBA degree might be useful for management of the human services. After all, if the major corporations that undergird the economy of the country are snatching up MBAs as fast as they can, should not public and not-for-profit social agencies do likewise? The school of thought that argues that management is management regardless of the context would unhesitatingly answer yes. Those who hold the opposing view, however, assert that there are significant differences in the goals, structure, and personnel of the public and private sectors (*see, for example,* Cupaiuolo and Dowling, 1983). In their view, there is only limited transferability of knowledge and skills from the corporate to the public sector, especially to public welfare and human services programs in general. The limited transferability would apply as well to the not-for-profit sector to the extent that its goals and operations are more similar to the public sector than to the corporate sector. Rather than trying to answer a priori whether knowledge of and skills in management transcend the context in which they are applied, the authors will look at what constitutes the MBA curriculum and will discuss it with reference to management in the human services.

MBA Curriculum

MBA programs are generally offered by degree-recommending schools or colleges reporting to a central administration of a university. The American Assembly of Collegiate Schools of Business (AACSB) is responsible for accrediting undergraduate and graduate education programs in business administration and accounting. Although it is impossible to describe the MBA curricula of all the more than 650 schools in which they are offered, one finds a common denominator in the criteria of AACSB. For both undergraduate and graduate education, AACSB (1986–87) requires that students be offered a common body of knowledge in business education encompassing the following areas:

(a) a background of the concepts, processes and institutions in the production and marketing of goods and/or services and the financing of the business enterprise or other forms of organization;
(b) a background of the economic and legal environment as it pertains to profit and/or nonprofit organizations along with ethical considerations and social and political influences as they affect such organizations;
(c) a basic understanding of the concepts and applications of accounting, of quantitative methods, and management information systems including computer applications;
(d) a study of administrative processes under conditions of uncertainty including integrating analysis and policy determination at the overall management level. (p. 29)

In addition to meeting these core requirements, the MBA program is expected to be broad in nature and aimed at general competence for overall management. Business schools have a certain flexibility and freedom in how they translate the common body of knowledge into specific course work. In the main, however, they include courses in accounting, finance, economics, organizational behavior, quantitative analysis, statistics, management information systems, marketing, business law, human resources management, and general management. Depending on the particular specialization, an MBA student can take courses in many other subjects, ranging from collective bargaining to taxation to international business operations.

Utility for Management of the Human Services

In assaying the utility of the MBA degree for the management of human service organizations, consider Miringoff's (1980) distinction between maintenance management and service management. The MBA degree seems to be more appropriate for maintenance management than for service management. For example, one area in which there is unanimity about the value of the MBA degree is finance. MBA students learn a great deal about raising, allocating, and expending funds. Large human service agencies, whether public or not-for-profit, certainly should value the MBA degree as a qualification for such positions as budget director, comptroller, or chief financial officer. Depending on the specialization, other positions for which the MBA might be applicable include human resources manager (personnel director) and director of management information systems; both of these positions generally are found only in large, complex, multidimensional organizations.

The MBA degree per se would seem to have little or no relevance for services management if one believes that to manage a particular "product," it is necessary to understand that "product." Although some argue that good managers can manage anything, there is an increasing consensus that one cause of the decline of American private enterprise is that too many American business executives are financial or legal experts and are often ill informed about the products their companies manufacture and sell. W. Edwards Deming, the American quality control expert whose assistance to the Japanese after World War II raised him, in their eyes, to the level of a deity, was appalled by the idea of the interchangeable manager (Halberstam, 1986, p. 314). He believed that successful managers had to be fully acquainted with a wealth of factors that affect their products. Perhaps the issue can best be summarized in the words of Red Auerbach, the key person behind "Celtic pride" and commitment to excellence in basketball through team play. Auerbach (Webber, 1987) responded to the *Harvard Business Review's* question about whether managing the Celtics is like managing any other business by asserting: "People say that I could run any other business . . . that I should take over the Red Sox or manage the Patriots, but that doesn't make sense. My knowledge of the product isn't there" (p. 90).

It is the authors' contention that the MBA holder who does not already have relevant experience or education in human services is not well prepared for the service management component of a human service organization. MBA students do not learn about the delivery of income maintenance, mental health, and child welfare services and are not likely to learn much about the organizations that provide such services. Almost all the examples they are given about managing an organization and its personnel come from the private sector, which is not surprising because that is what the majority of students want and what the faculty are best equipped to provide.

The failings of the MBA degree are not related solely to a lack of focus on human services and the organizations that deliver them. It can be assumed that the MBA socialization process is at best irrelevant to the human services and at worst even inimical to them. It appears that for some people, money is a motivating factor for getting an MBA degree. Such a materialistic ethic even has the business schools worried. Approximately 25 percent of a typical incoming MBA class enters from investment banking or consulting, and probably twice that many go into these fields after graduation (Byrne, 1986). The Harvard Business School, among others, is trying to deemphasize the financial aspects of managing and to stress manufacturing and marketing (Byrne, 1986). Although new graduates may not find manufacturing and marketing to be as lucrative as investment banking and consulting, their expertise is needed for the long-term benefit of individual companies and the economy in general. Attempts are also being made to instill in students a sense of business ethics and skills in working with people. For the most part, however, little in the current business school culture supports the humanitarian and altruistic values that underpin human service organizations.

MPA DEGREE

The MPA degree is the most difficult of the three degrees to describe, principally because it has come under many different influences historically and because its institutional locus is so diversified. DeYoung and Watts (1986) reported on the distribution of public administration programs regarding institutions in 1983 (p. 94) (Table 1).

Just as the institutional locus of public administration programs varies greatly, so do the orientations and focal points of these programs; therefore, it is difficult to render general observations about the nature and utility of the MPA degree (Ellwood, 1985). For example, some programs that are located in political science departments tend to treat public administration as a subfield of political science and hence emphasize political processes. Separate public administration programs are likely to concentrate on general administration and management, but a small number of the more prestigious schools, such as Harvard University's John F. Kennedy School of Government, emphasize policy analysis or methods for identifying the "correct" policy; such programs build

Table 1.
Institutional Locus of Public Administration Programs, 1983

Institutional Locus	%	Number
Separate professional school of public administration/affairs (PA/A) reports directly to the central university administration	13.98	26
Separate departments of PA/A in a large unit, such as a social sciences division or college of arts and sciences	34.41	64
Professional school of PA/A combined with another professional school (such as business administration)	5.38	10
Department of PA/A combined with another department (such as business administration)	8.60	16
PA/A program within a political science department	37.63	70

SOURCE: DeYoung, T., & Watts, B. (1986). The institutional environments of public administration programs. Paper presented at the Ninth National Conference on Teaching Public Administration, Pace University, New York.

a curriculum around quantifiable analytical and optimization techniques. A few large public administration schools, such as the Maxwell School of Public Administration of Syracuse University, offer comprehensive programs in which students may select a traditional political science approach to public administration, an administration approach, or the public policy approach. Finally, there are generic management programs that, although not MPA programs per se, provide some training that is relevant for public service. Typically, such programs are found in a business school that has a separate public service track. A few universities, Yale being the most notable, have developed a core curriculum in generic management that is supposedly applicable to both the private and public sectors.

Before looking at the relevance of the MPA degree for the management of human service organizations, it is worth comparing the trend in MPA enrollments with that of MBA enrollments. Although business schools have experienced unbridled growth, such has not been the case for public administration programs. Enrollments in public administration programs that are members of the National Association of Schools of Public Affairs and Administration (NASPAA) increased by 124 percent between 1973 and 1979, rising from 12,800 to 28,250; however, the enrollments declined by 25 percent from 1979 to 1983, falling to a total of 21,128 (Ellwood, 1985, p. 28). The decline in interest in public administration programs reflects the generally antigovernment ideology of the Reagan Administration, which has sought to "privatize" governmental programs and operations and to reduce the number of federal employees.

MPA Curriculum

As should be clear by now, MPA programs differ widely in their objectives and emphases. However, NASPAA promulgates standards, for the common components of the curriculum of programs in public administration and affairs, regardless of their orientation. According to NASPAA (1986), each student should be provided with a basic understanding of public policy and the ability to deal with

■ political and legal institutions and processes
■ economic and social institutions and processes
■ organization and management concepts, including human resource administration
■ techniques of analysis, including quantitative, economic, and statistical methods. (sec. 3.21)

There is, obviously, a similarity between these criteria and the prescribed curriculum for MBA. The major difference is the emphasis of MPA on "political and legal institutions and processes," which provides students with an understanding of the public sector context or how the government works. For the most part, the other components of the core curriculum suggest courses that engender the skills needed to manage effectively in government.

Utility for Management of the Human Services

Much of what has been said about the strengths of MBA programs for managing human service organizations also can be said about MPA programs. Certainly, MPA graduates, especially those who have completed programs in which management was emphasized, have the potential to assume leadership positions in staff or support departments, such as personnel or finance. Although they may not have as strong a background in accounting as do their business school counterparts, MPA graduates have a superior knowledge of government, political processes, and the civil service, which better prepares them for most management positions in federal, state, and local human services agencies, such as public welfare and mental health. Keys and Cupaiuolo (1987) observed that managing public welfare programs requires a working knowledge of budgeting, administrative law, computer science, and quantitative methods for decision making to recognize what these disciplines cannot provide answers to just as much as what they can offer. These fields of study typically are found in public administration programs.

How well MPA graduates are likely to manage the service function in human services agencies is likely to depend on their previous experience or training in human services per se. A number of public administration programs offer a specialization in human services. It can be assumed that graduates of such programs have substantive knowledge of services, as well as generic management skills, and, therefore, that they would be well qualified to manage programs such as income maintenance and Medicaid. This assumption does not suggest, however, that they are ideally suited to supervise clinical or casework services, which entails a knowledge of psychodynamics and the casework process.

The development of an underlying ethos for MPA programs has been an evolutionary process. Historically, much emphasis was placed on the public administrator serving as an effective manager who operates from a value-neutral perspective and efficiently implements policies established by elected executives and legislators. Even though value neutrality is impossible to achieve, it still was proferred as an ideal worth pursuing. Currently, there seems to be little support for such a one-dimensional view of the public administrator as a value-free technocrat. According to Astrid Merget (1986), NASPAA president, the MPA ethos can be described as follows:

> What distinguishes an MPA is defined less in academic substance and in practical skill but more in a professional ideology. That ideology affirms the role of government as a proactive translator of policy into action; as an agent for improving social welfare; and as a champion of social justice. Embedded in that ideology is the conviction that politics is a noble profession: politics as the act of deliberation transforms conflict into consensus. (p. 4)

To the extent that Merget's articulation of the MPA ethos is adhered to by the public administration profession and is inculcated in MPA students, it would seem that the MPA socialization process results in a value orientation that is congruent with the values that should characterize human service delivery systems.

MSW DEGREE

Students of management or administration in schools of social work have always been few in number. Usually, over three-quarters of the students in schools of social work receive training that is fundamentally clinical. The curriculum has been based on an ever-expanding body of practice theory and courses that are derived and borrowed from psychology, sociology, and psychiatry. Then, there has been the "other track."

In the 1960s, the "other track" was usually community organization designed to train students for careers in community action programs, community mental health, and the many other programs of community involvement and participation that existed during that period. Sometimes it was group work, a method closer to that of the clinician that was derived from the settlement movement. Sometimes it was social policy; several schools, such as the Florence Heller Graduate School for Advanced Studies in Social Welfare, Brandeis University, and the School of Social Service Administration, University of Chicago, created programs exclusively in that area. But even during the 1960s, only a small minority of students were involved in any of these programs.

The 1970s was a period of consolidation in social programs, and management/administration became the dominant mode of study in the second track. Some schools created generic programs called macro practice, which combined courses in community organization, group work, social policy, and administration. But administration came to dominate because there were few jobs in the field for those trained specifically in community organization or in social policy. At present, some schools have no second track, although courses in social policy are required for all students, and, all told, about 15 percent of all social work students major in management or administration.

MSW Curriculum

Social work education has been dominated by a perspective that stresses the one-to-one relationship. It is this orientation that immediately differentiates professional training in social work from that of the MBA or the MPA degree. The emphasis is on the intrinsics of human interaction for its own sake, and it is this interaction between the professionally trained social worker and his or her client that constitutes the route to the desired outcome. The task is defined, shaped, and bounded by the interaction itself. The MBA or the MPA student is trained to seek outcomes of another sort—those that lie in the market, the organization, or the structure of government. This fundamental difference in perspective creates the dilemma for those who teach management in schools of social work: How does one create a curriculum that allows the student to move freely in two worlds that often demand roles, skills, and approaches that are different and sometimes contradictory?

The most obvious approach is to allow the worlds to exist side by side without touching. Hence, management students draw from a generic content that they share with the clinical students. But when clinical students begin, later in their training, to specialize in subjects such as working with substance abusers or family treatment, the management students turn to "administration." The administration track often consists of courses in the theory and practice of administration, drawn from sources similar to those used in the MBA or MPA programs, supplemented by courses in writing grant proposals, program evaluation, and sometimes organizational analysis. This approach, however, often leaves the fundamental questions untouched: How is the purpose of the curriculum for management of the human services different from that of the MBA or MPA curriculum? Does the management in social work curriculum have something unique to offer?

Utility for Management of the Human Services

As was noted earlier, a common assumption is that managers can manage anything, from insurance agencies to automobile plants to public transportation to income maintenance programs to family services. From the perspective of a well-integrated curriculum for management of the human services, this statement is only partially true. Although the difference between two kinds of management processes, (1) service management and (2) maintenance management, has been described, another distinction must be considered—that of two kinds of human service organizations: (1) the planning organization and (2) the delivery organization.

The *planning organization* does not deliver a service directly to clients. In the public sector, its purpose is usually to plan policies; to achieve fiscal and program accountability; and to monitor, process, and integrate the different levels of government. In the private sector, the planning organization has similar aims: to raise funds, to achieve program and fiscal accountability, and to coordinate efforts. The *delivery organization* interacts with clients; it delivers the services. Such an organization is usually part of a network of accountability that includes one or more planning organizations. The management of these two organizations is vastly different.

The planning organization requires little service management. Its perspective is more distant than that of the delivery organization, more abstract, and concerned more with aggregates than with individuals. In such an organization, the principles learned in the MPA curriculum seem applicable and are, as was indicated, a central part of the MSW curriculum. Generic management skills, strong organizational analytical skills, and a broad-based knowledge of the specific services involved and their social objectives could constitute a core of training that would result in the effective management of many human service planning organizations.

The management of human service delivery organizations is more difficult, since the two worlds of management and social work are farther apart. A manager in an essentially clinical setting, functioning either in a middle-level or executive position, surely requires much of what is offered in a social work curriculum. In this type of organization, the intangibles play a far greater role. The morale, the sense of purpose, even the expressed affect of the staff, over time, can influence and even determine the quality of the services that are provided; thus, the commonality gained from shared socialization is more vital. The MBA or MPA graduate would have as difficult a time assuming a position of major authority in a human service delivery organization as would the social worker who attempted to run Howard Johnson or the U.S. Department of Transportation.

In addition to a knowledge of the intangibles of the human service organization and a socialization into the human service profession, a manager trained through the MSW curriculum is taught a perspective that is in concert with the current human relations approach referred to as the "new management theory." As Keys and Cupaiuolo (1987) noted, "a certain irony exists in the notion that the decades old management philosophy of social work . . . is highly compatible with the Theory Z approaches and the general thrusts of Japanese style management theories now receiving increased attention in American business (p. 56). Hence, the current emphasis on the participation, cooperation, and decision making of workers and the focus on individual motivation, human interaction, group dynamics, the outcome of tasks, and the process of affective exchange closely mirror the philosophical and conceptual bases of social work education. Basic courses such as human behavior and social environment, social work practice, social group work, and many advanced courses that cover the theory and techniques of working with individuals and families all contribute to a general human relations approach to working with people that is easily accessible to the would-be manager.

CONTINUUM OF DEGREES

It is the authors' contention that the MBA, the MPA, and the MSW are a kind of continuum of degrees for management in the human services. The MBA can contribute skills and knowledge from the realm of finance, but its orientation and purpose are distinct limitations. The MPA can contribute more, particularly in the public-sector planning organizations that constitute the vast network of governmental organizations in this country's decentralized social welfare institution. The MSW contributes skills and knowledge that are appropriate to human service-delivery organizations in which clients interact with the institution.

Yet, the realm of academic training and that of reality do not always mix. The human services, particularly at the planning level in local, state, and federal governments, often are managed by people with no training in management and little sympathy for or identification with the purposes of social work. Although much needs to be done to fashion relevant curricula appropriate to these levels of government, equal attention must be directed outside academia to ensure that the managers of human service organizations are selected primarily because of their commitment to and competence in carrying out the responsibilities of those organizations.

REFERENCES

Accreditation Council Policies, Procedures, and Standards. (1986–87). St. Louis: American Assembly of Collegiate Schools of Business.

Bean, B. A. (1986, March 24). Remaking the Harvard B-school. *Business Week*, pp. 54–58.

Byrne, J. (1986, March 24). The battle of the B-schools criticized for failing to educate MBAs about new technology. *Business Week*, pp. 61–70.

Cupaiuolo, A., & Dowling, M. (1983). Are corporate managers really better? *Public Welfare, 41,* 12–17.

Denhardt, R., & Nalbandian, J. (1982). Teaching public administration as a vocation: A call for theorists. *Southern Review of Public Administration, 6,* 151–161.

DeYoung, T., & Watts, B. (1986). *The institutional environments of public administration programs.* Paper presented at the Ninth National Conference on Teaching Public Administration, Pace University, New York.

Durant, R. F., & Taggart, W. A. (1985). Mid-career students in MPA programs: Implications for pre-service student education. *Public Administration Review, 45,* 301–308.

Ellwood, J. W. (1985). A morphology of graduate education for public service in the United States. Unpublished manuscript, National Association of Schools of Public Affairs and Administration, Washington, D.C.

Halberstam, D. (1986). *The reckoning.* New York: William Morrow.

Keys, P. R., & Cupaiuolo, A. A. (1987). Rebuilding the relationship between social work and public welfare administration. *Public Administration in Social Work, 2,* 47–58.

Merget, A. (1986, January). President's report. *Public Enterprise* (newsletter of the National Association of Schools of Public Administration), p. 4.

Miringoff, M. L. (1980). *Management in human service organizations.* New York: Macmillan.

Mosher, F. C. (1963). *Democracy and the public service.* New York: Oxford University Press.

Standards for professional masters degree programs in public affairs and administration. (1986). Washington, DC: National Association of Schools of Public Administration.

Turner, J. A. (1987). U.S. business schools criticized for failing to educate MBAs about technology. *Chronicle of Higher Education, 35.*

Webber, A. M. (1987). Red Auerbach on management. *Harvard Business Review, 65,* 84–91.

4

A Curriculum Model for Social Work Management

Wilburn Hayden, Jr.

UNDERPINNING THE PRACTICE of modern social work management is the theoretical linkage of knowledge, values, and skills that assures the effective delivery of services by social work organizations. Such a theoretical linkage is equally necessary for practice and for teaching. Historically, the curriculum on management—and in higher education in general—evolved from a pragmatic collection of courses and instructional objectives. These courses and objectives are what the instructors or administrators of the discipline deemed to be essential content. Seldom has a theory of curriculum been used to create or guide the curriculum and instruction.

The teaching of social work management should be based on a curriculum theory to assure that students master the knowledge and values that are basic to professional practice. The curriculum model presented in this chapter was developed from the curriculum theory of Ausubel (1960, 1963, 1967, 1968; Novak, 1977). Ausubel's theory is defined first, and then the curriculum model as defined by Ausubel's theory for teaching modern social work management is illustrated.

The knowledge, values, and skills in the curriculum model are the result of the author's conceptualization of modern social work management as developed in the literature (Austin, 1986; Crow & Odewahn, 1987; Edwards, 1987; Egan, 1985; Gortner, Mahler & Nicholson, 1987; Radin & Benton, 1986; Schaefer, 1987; Slavin, 1985; Turem, 1986; Weiner, 1982; Wholey, 1986). Although there is no one true conceptualization of modern social work management, Ausubel's theory (as you would expect from a curriculum theory) is such that it can be used with any conceptualization or discipline. Thus it is far more significant to understand the curriculum theory and model than to accept the conceptualization. Therefore, each educator will have to conceptualize knowledge, values, and skills before utilizing this theory.

AUSUBEL'S CURRICULUM THEORY

Two key principles define *Ausubel's curriculum theory: (1) progressive differentiation* and *(2) integrative reconciliation*. Both of these principles are integrating threads of the curriculum theory in relation to Ausubel's theories of teaching and learning. These principles guide curriculum planning in such a way that the key concepts (knowledge and values) of a discipline become a stable part of the learner's cognitive structure and result in psychological meaning (the development of skills) for practice.

Progressive Differentiation

According to Ausubel, concepts are first introduced in a general, inclusive form and then subsuming concepts are progressively elaborated on in greater and greater detail. "In other words, the sequence of the curriculum is organized so that each successive learning is carefully related to what has been presented before" (Joyce & Weil, 1972, pp. 206–207). In a simplistic way, the curriculum is an extension of the sequencing described in Ausubel's theories of teaching and learning. It is the building of the combination of prescriptions of meaningful learning, the subsumption process, cognitive development, advance organizers, and pedagogy into a structured series of intended outcomes of learning (Ausubel, 1960). As a concept, progressive differentiation does not require the placing of a specific concept at the top or bottom of a conceptual hierarchy. As Novak (1977) noted:

> The choice does not mean that the idea of progressive differentiation has no value; the sequence of examples, the kind of examples or exercises chosen, and relative emphasis given to specific topics or concepts may be substantially different if instruction is based on one conceptual hierarchy rather than another. The central point is that efficient learning of concepts requires explication of relationships between concepts and progressively greater development of the most salient concepts. The specific sequence

of experiences provided to achieve concept differentiation is only one of an almost infinite variety of learning sequences. This process is well illustrated by children as they acquire concepts. (p. 88)

Progressive differentiation is based on two assumptions, according to Ausubel and Robinson (1969):

(1) . . . it is less difficult for human beings to grasp the differentiated aspects of a previously-learned more inclusive whole from its previously-learned differentiated parts, and (2) . . . an individual's organization of the content of a particular subject-matter discipline in his own mind consists of a hierarchical structure in which the most inclusive ideas occupy a position at the apex of the structure and subsume progressively less inclusive and more highly differentiated propositions, concepts, and factual data. (p. 168)

Ausubel's (1968) expository description of progressive differentiation is as follows:

If the human nervous system as a data processing and storing mechanism is so constructed that both the acquisition of new knowledge and its organization in cognitive structure conform *naturally* to the principle of progressive differentiation, . . . optimal learning and retention occur when teachers deliberately order the organization and sequential arrangement of subject matter along similar lines . . . new ideas and information are learned and retained more efficiently when more inclusive and specifically relevant ideas are already available in cognitive structure to serve a subsuming role or to furnish ideational anchorage. Organizers . . . exemplify the principle of progressive differentiation and serve this function in relation to any given topic or subtopic where they are used. (p. 153)

Progressive differentiation in the development of a curriculum is accomplished by using a hierarchical series of courses or by dividing the knowledge of the discipline into hierarchical arrangements of concepts that are covered in the courses or curriculum units in descending order of inclusiveness. Within the hierarchies are the advance organizers (concepts that are clear, relevant, and inclusive and that precede the material to be learned), followed by their corresponding units of detailed, differentiated material, sequenced in descending order of inclusiveness. In this way, not only does a relevant and inclusive subsumer provide ideational scaffolding for each curriculum unit (course) of differentiated subject matter, but both the ideas within each unit and the various units in relation to each other are also progressively differentiated (Ausubel & Robinson, 1969, pp. 68–69).

Integrative Reconciliation

Integrative reconciliation is "the explicit attempt to point out significant similarities and differences and to reconcile real or apparent inconsistencies between successive ideas presented in a sequentially organized learning . . . material" (Ausubel & Robinson, 1969, p. 171).

In the learning and teaching process, organizers are designed to further the principle of integrative reconciliation. They explicitly point out the ways in which previously learned related ideas in the cognitive structure are either basically similar to or essentially different from new ideas and information in the learning task. As Ausubel (1968) explained:

> Thus, if an organizer can first delineate clearly, precisely, and explicitly the principal similarities and differences between the new subsuming concepts and principles to be learned, on the one hand, and similar established ideas in cognitive structure on the other, it seems reasonable to postulate that the enhanced discriminability of the new anchoring ideas would enable the learner to grasp later the more detailed ideas and information in the learning passage itself with fewer ambiguities, fewer competing meanings, and fewer misconceptions suggested by the established ideas than would otherwise be possible; and that as these clearer, more discriminable, and less confused differentiated new meanings interact with their subsumers and with analogous established meanings during the retention interval, they would also retain their identity longer. This is the case both because the differentiated material is learned in a clearer, more stable, and more discriminable fashion in the first place, by virtue of the greater discriminability of the new anchoring ideas under which it is subsumed, and because more discriminable subsumers are themselves more stable and hence better able to provide continuing secure anchorage. (p. 157)

Novak (1977) illustrated the role of integrative reconciliation in the curriculum according to Ausubel's theory, as follows:

> To achieve integrative reconciliation more surely, we must organize instruction so that we move "up and down" the conceptual hierarchies as new information is presented. We might do well to start with the most general concepts, but we need to illustrate early how subordinate concepts are related, and then move back through examples to new meanings for higher order concepts. (pp. 90–91)

Careful development of instructional objectives and the explicit presentation of these objectives are necessary for learners to achieve integrative reconciliation. The use of appropriate cognitive bridges in moving from one concept to another is also essential (Novak, 1977).

The idea of integrative reconciliation, together with that of the progressive differentiation of concepts, is important for understanding Ausubel's theory of curriculum. As Novak (1977) pointed out,

Ausubel's learning theory focuses on the role of concepts (subsumers) for effecting meaningful learning. His additional stress on progressive differentiation of concepts, superordinate learning, and integrative reconciliation further lends relevance to curriculum and instructional planning. If learning is to be meaningful, then new knowledge to be learned must have relevant anchoring concepts available in the learner's cognitive structure. Because an enormous array of information is to be learned in any discipline, only the most general, most inclusive concepts are likely to provide anchorage in a wide variety of learning situations. (p. 137)

The curriculum is so structured that major concepts are introduced early and thus serve to facilitate the meaningful learning of a wide array of information, as well as of new subsumed concepts. The planning of a curriculum that is consistent with Ausubel's theory depends on the primary and difficult task of identifying concepts within the discipline and organizing them into some hierarchical or relational scheme. The following section takes on this task.

THE CURRICULUM MODEL

In developing the curriculum model, one must organize the key concepts of modern management so that each successive learning of concepts is related to what has been presented before. One starts with the most-inclusive key concepts and subsumers under the less-inclusive concepts or variables and subheadings. The key concepts and their subsumed variables and subheadings are organized in such a way that they are linked by an inherent logic that should parallel the structure of ideas that is being built up in the learner's mind. Figure 1 is the model that results.

The models start with the social work core, which should be the most inclusive concepts for modern social work management. These concepts (which may be organized into courses) are part of the existing knowledge base for the learner—the foundation for learning modern social work management—and become part of the learner's existing cognitive structure. Meaningful learning results when this relationship is established as one moves the learner from the core through the key management concepts.

How the model is translated into courses is dictated by the readiness of the learners, the significance and desired degree of mastery of concepts, the instructor, the choice of the content to be covered, and the credit ratio of the course work to the requirements of a course. The concepts that are related or linked to each other may be taught in a single course or in parallel courses offered during the same term. Thus, one may teach community and organizational structures and the problem-solving framework in a single course or in parallel courses, but one would *not* teach skills and theories of management in the same courses or parallel courses.

The following is an example of how the model's key concepts might be organized into courses over three semesters:

Semester 1
    A. Human behavior and the social environment:
                                    3 semester hours
    B. Values and the history of social welfare and services:
                                      3 semester hours
    C. Research and evaluation: 3 semester hours
    D. Theories of management: 3 semester hours
Semester 2
    E. Community and organization structures: 3 semester hours
    F. Fields of practice: 3 semester hours
    G. Electives or concentration: 3 semester hours
Semester 3
    H. Roles and settings for practice: 3 semester hours
    I. Skills for management: 3 semester hours
    J. Electives or concentration: 3 semester hours
Semester 4
    K. Block field placement: 9 semester hours

This systematic ordering of the content of courses is based on how people learn from a theoretical cognitive perspective. It provides for the progressive differentiation of concepts and notions that enhance the integrative reconciliation of the content of the courses. The movement from course to course is progressive from the most general, inclusive elements to the more and more detailed, specific elements. As the learner moves through the courses, he or she acquires new information, which is received and associated with the concepts in his or her cognitive structure. The new meaning that results is perceived as relevant and subsumable under the content of the previous courses, because the concepts in the new courses are continuously being related back to the general, inclusive elements of the earlier courses. This arrangement provides the learner

Figure 1.
Curriculum Model for Teaching Modern Social Work Management Based on Ausubel's Theory

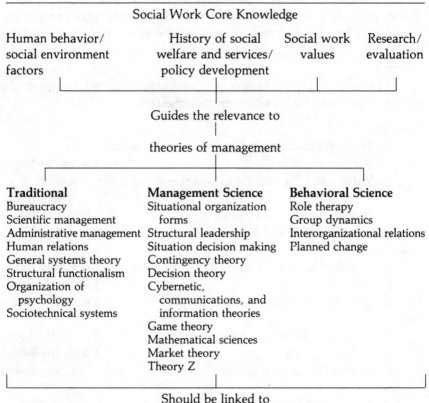

Social Work Core Knowledge

| Human behavior/ social environment factors | History of social welfare and services/ policy development | Social work values | Research/ evaluation |

Guides the relevance to

theories of management

Traditional
Bureaucracy
Scientific management
Administrative management
Human relations
General systems theory
Structural functionalism
Organization of
   psychology
Sociotechnical systems

Management Science
Situational organization
   forms
Structural leadership
Situation decision making
Contingency theory
Decision theory
Cybernetic,
   communications, and
   information theories
Game theory
Mathematical sciences
Market theory
Theory Z

Behavioral Science
Role therapy
Group dynamics
Interorganizational relations
Planned change

Should be linked to

Community Structure
a. The community as a concept
b. Characteristics of communities
c. Dynamics of social change
d. Essential community functions
e. Different concepts of community
f. Structure
g. Concepts of power
h. Leadership

Organizational Structure
a. Importance of the organizational context: Voluntary associations, service agencies, and planning
b. Essential elements: Budget, design, and program planning, personnel, and time phasing
c. Analysis of change capability: Power, conflict, communication, and group activities
d. Theoretical perspectives
e. Aspects of formal organizations
f. Overview for planning and coordinating: Service delivery, coordination, social planning

Figure 1. (Continued)

Related to
|

The Problem-solving Framework
a. The community and organizational contexts
b. Problem-solving process
c. Problem analysis
d. Needs assessments
e. Causal factors
f. Policy developments
g. Strategies
h. Evaluation
i. Issues

|

Separated by
|

Fields of Practice
a. Administration
b. Planning
c. Locality development
d. Community organization
e. Social action

|

Determines practice
|

Roles	**Skills**	**Settings**
a. Consultant/analyst	a. Communication	a. Government
b. Advocate	b. Reflection	b. Public welfare agencies
c. Planner/developer	c. Information	c. Mental health agencies
d. Administrator	d. Entrepreneurial	d. Health agencies
e. Broker	e. Management	e. Aging agencies
f. Organizer	f. Conflict resolution	f. Youth agencies
g. Coordinator	g. Decision making	g. Other
h. Supervisor		
i. Others		

Outcome
|

Modern social work managers

with strong anchors for the ideas and notions that are being taught. The outcome is the mastery of the essentials of modern social work management organized through concepts that were related to and consistent with a systematic ordering of knowledge for practice.

Teaching a Concept

Power is a major concept in modern management that emerges and is used in many different ways by managers at various levels in the field. An agency executive director views and uses power as the basis for his or her authority, for relationships with members of the board of directors or staff, and for negotiating with other agency directors or community leaders. A community organizer will use power as the basis for managing changes in a community. He or she has to understand the formal and informal power wielded by members of a community to be able to organize the members of various groups to advocate for the community's position in the decision-making power structure in the community.

According to Ausubel's theory, the concept of power should be presented and linked throughout the curriculum so that it has logical and psychological meaning. The courses in the curriculum go from the general to the specific to the utilization of all that has been learned for practice. The following example depicts this flow of information about power as it may be presented and learned each semester.

Semester 1

Course A:	What is the impact of the settlement housing movement in the late nineteenth and early twentieth centuries on the acquisition of power by community members?
Course B:	Is the value orientation of the right to self-determination a basis for using power to create change?
Courses C and D:	What evidence exists to support power as a concept for change (and at what probability level)?

Semester 2

Course E:	How does the problem-solving process generate activity for the use of power for change?

Course F: What determines the level of informal or formal power that is needed for a social action activity to be a success?

Course G: How may power be used in other areas to bring about change?

Semester 3

Course H: What levels of power are appropriate for an organizer to be effective in a particular setting?

Course I: At what point does the use of power lead to conflict?

Semester 4:

Fieldwork: How effective and competent is the organizer in utilizing power to bring about change?

As can be seen, the general questions that the student is required to answer are presented in Semester 1. As the learner moves through the courses each semester, the answers to previous questions develop the base for understanding and answering questions in the courses that follow. During the final semester, the learner is expected to put into practice or answer the question: Which roles are appropriate for me to adopt that will have the greatest impact on my use of power to create change?

Significance for Modern Management

Social work management requires more cognitive development for skillful practice than does clinical practice, which is more dependent on the affective domain. Ausubel's theory is classified in the information-possessing category (Block, 1971; Hilgard & Bower, 1975; Hirst, 1966; Johnson, 1967; E. Maccia, G. S. Maccia, & Jewett, 1963; Moore, 1974). This branch of curriculum theory focuses on the acquisition of knowledge to master a subject. The concern for mastery makes Ausubel more useful than other curriculum theories for ordering the knowledge needed for effective management practice.

Few students enter the management curriculum with the background knowledge that is necessary to learn and retain knowledge for the effective and competent management of practice. Through the organization and linkage of modern management concepts, Ausubel's theory provides a framework for assuring that the student's development for learning and attention to the subject matter are structurally integrated into the learning process. By introducing new or less familiar concepts at a relevant time, the teacher is preparing the learner for the more complex, more specific, and less abstract materials that follow. Ausubel and Robinson (1969) referred to this process as the use of advanced organizers to facilitate learning. The use of advance organizers with respect to modern management concepts is a significant factor in making Ausubel's theory the framework for the curriculum. Ausubel developed advance organizers as a way of compensating for the inadequate buildup of material by the learner who lacks background knowledge and of enabling the advanced learner to perform at or beyond expected levels. Numerous studies (for example, Ausubel, 1963) have supported the use of advance organizers.

The dependence of the theory on the logical sequence of learning and retention is another factor that supports its use. The theory requires that the knowledge and values of the discipline be conceptualized in an inherent logic that draws on and mobilizes the relevant subsuming concepts that can be established or already exist in the learner's cognitive structure so that the new material becomes familiar and meaningful (Ausubel, 1963, pp. 85–86). Thus, the curriculum for modern management will be developed on the basis of a theory whose effectiveness in the teaching and learning process has been tested.

REFERENCES

Austin, M. J. (1986). Community organization and social administration: Partnership or irrelevance? *Administration in Social Work, 10*(3), 27–39.

Ausubel, D. P. (1960). The use of advance organizers in the learning and retention of meaningful verbal material. *Journal of Educational Psychology, 51*, 267–272.

Ausubel, D. P. (1963). *The psychology of meaningful verbal learning.* New York: Grune & Stratton.

Ausubel, D. P. (1967). *Learning theory and classroom practice.* Toronto: Ontario Institute for Studies in Education.

Ausubel, D. P. (1968). *Educational psychology: A cognitive view.* New York: Holt, Rinehart, & Winston.

Ausubel, D. P., & Robinson, F. G. (1969). *School learning: An introduction to educational psychology.* New York: Holt, Rinehart, & Winston.

Block, J. H. (1971). *Mastery learning: Theory and practice.* New York: Holt, Rinehart, & Winston.

Crow, R. T., & Odewahn, C. A. (1987). *Management for the human services.* Englewood Cliffs, NJ: Prentice-Hall.

Edwards, R. L. (1987). The competing values approach as an integrating framework for the management curriculum. *Administration in Social Work, 11*(1), 1–13.

Egan, G. (1985). *Change agent skills in helping and human services settings.* Monterey, CA: Brooks/Cole.

Gortner, H. G., Mahler, J., & Nicholson, J. (1987). *Organization theory: A public prospective.* Homewood, IL: Dorsey.

Hilgard, E. R. , & Bower, G. H. (1975). *Theories of learning.* Englewood Cliffs, NJ: Prentice-Hall.

Hirst, P. (1966). Educational theory. In J. W. Tibble (Ed.), *Story of education.* Boston: Routledge & Kegan Paul.

Johnson, M., Jr. (1967). Definitions and models in curriculum theory. *Educational Theory, 17,* 127–140.

Joyce, B., & Weil, M. (1972). *Models of teaching.* Englewood Cliffs, NJ: Prentice-Hall.

Maccia, E., Maccia, G. S., & Jewett, R. (1963). *Construction of educational theory models.* Columbus: Ohio State University Foundation.

Moore, T. W. (1974). *Educational theory: An introduction.* Boston: Routledge & Kegan Paul.

Novak, J. D. (1977). *A theory of education.* Ithaca, NY: Cornell University Press.

Radin, B. A., & Benton, B. B. (1986). The new human services manager. *New England Journal of Human Services, 6,* 13–19.

Schaefer, M. (1987). *Implementing Change in Service Programs* (Vol. 49). Beverly Hills, CA: Sage.

Slavin, S. (1985). *An introduction to human services management* (2nd ed.). New York: Haworth.

Turem, J. S. (1986). Social work administration and modern management technology. *Administration in Social Work, 10*(3), 15–24.

Weiner, M. E. (1982). *Human services management: Analysis and applications.* Homewood, IL: Dorsey.

Wholey, J. S., Abramson, M. A., & Bellavita, C. (1986). *Performance and credibility: Developing excellence in public and non-profit organizations.* Lexington, MA: Lexington Books.

5

Data Processing and Social Work Management

Leon H. Ginsberg

LITTLE HAS CHANGED the organization and operations of business and industry in the late twentieth century as much as the development of computer technology and automatic data processing. Many business functions that were impossible even to conceive just a few years ago now are central to the daily lives of most people in industrial nations. Airline reservations and the myriad combinations of fares, which no agent or clerk could reasonably be able to identify and apply with the use of paper manuals and guidebooks, now are instantly and accurately available on computer screens. Food stores use scanners to detect and charge for each grocery item and to identify each item on the cash register tape. Fast-food chains employ people with little training who are able to take and calculate orders simply by matching keys with pictures of the food items that are ordered. Machines calculate the price and the change and even admonish the clerks to repeat courteous phrases to their customers.

U.S. businesses and industry have grown in new and dramatic ways because of computer technology. At the same time, computer technology has developed to accommodate the new demands of management. The symbiotic growth of business and technology, both of which have responded to the growth in the population, is probably the most important development of the late twentieth century.

Of course, business and industry are large, generic terms in this context. That is, to discuss economic changes and their enhancement through the development of computer technology intelligently, one must consider such generally nonprofit fields as health care, education, and social welfare as industries.

COMPUTERS AND THEIR SOCIAL WELFARE APPLICATIONS

Computer technology in social welfare has been significant for decades. In fact, many large public social welfare agencies began using computer applications with their programs at the same time as did the for-profit businesses. Computers and social welfare services are a natural partnership. Computers are effective for the efficient storage and instantaneous recall of large bodies of information, and many state departments of social or human services have kept data on their huge caseloads of clients on computer systems. Several publications in the recent social work literature discuss ways in which computers can be used in teaching and practice (Born, 1987; Schoech, 1985; Slavin, 1982).

Researchers at the U.S. Department of the Army recently issued a challenge to social work educators and practitioners to make use of the available technology because of the natural association of social work tasks and computer capabilities (Parker, Chynoweth, Blankinship, Zaldo, & Matthews, 1987). They point out that social workers

- write reports and progress notes;
- pull and read numerous files;
- take case histories and develop diagnoses;
- tap into local area resource networks;
- keep in touch with professional developments; and
- provide facts and figures to contribute to agency accountability process. (p. 57)

Each of these tasks, which are of special interest to managers, is made easier by the use of computer technology.

The various ways in which computer technology can be applied to the operations of agency programs as well as some of the guidelines that managers may follow in determining when and how to use automated data processing are described in this chapter.

Economic Assistance Applications

As computer systems have become more sophisticated, they have also become available for assistance in dealing with the actual services that are provided. For nearly a decade, some states have used computer programs to take clients' applications for such assistance as food stamps,

AFDC, and Medicaid. These programs, which are complicated by the federal and state policies under which they operate, require a large number of specific pieces of information from clients that agency workers traditionally asked of clients and recorded on paper application forms. Today, workers in many states simply ask the questions required of the social welfare programs after being prompted to do so by computer programs and key the clients' answers into the computer. The computer then dutifully records and compares the answers to the requirements for the program and determines whether the client is eligible for the assistance and the amount of aid to which the client is entitled. The computer then actually writes the check or orders the food stamps to be mailed or mails the medical assistance identification card. It also reminds the agency when and how to check up on the client's future eligibility and, if the client is no longer eligible, sends a letter notifying the recipient that help will no longer be provided. The computer system specifies why the client is being removed from the rolls and explains the client's right to appeals and the procedures for doing so. In some states, the notice is written in Spanish for Spanish-speaking clients.

The U.S. Department of Health and Human Services has been promoting such a system—called the Family Assistance Management Information System (FAMIS) for use by all the states. The federal government provides extra financial support for states that use an approved system of that sort because it assumes that eligibility and payments are more accurately determined with such programs than they might be with more traditional methods.

Enforcement of Child Support

Federal–state programs also make extensive use of computer systems to enforce child-support laws. These systems are designed primarily to locate absent parents who are not paying for the care of children who are receiving assistance. Regional parent-locator systems help track parents who have moved to other states. The insertion of a social security number can help locate a parent who is employed or receiving unemployment assistance anywhere in the country.

Social Service Applications

Many state and local agencies make extensive use of automated systems in fields such as child welfare. Children who are victims of abuse or neglect, for example, are followed from their homes into diagnostic and treatment programs or foster care or back to their families; with the addition of appropriate services, through computer systems. Some systems calculate and write the checks to foster families or group homes for the children's care. Others alert the workers and the courts to establish and follow through on court appearances. Still others maintain a register of child abusers, so they can be monitored, as well. Some of the more sophisticated systems also keep records on the foster homes and group homes, prepare licenses for them, and remind the agencies to correct the deficiencies found in these homes.

Adoption agencies use computer systems to maintain registers of children who are available for adoption and of potential adoptive parents. They also try to match the children with potential parents through automated programs that select the relevant characteristics of each and determine how they might connect with one another.

In fields such as mental health, developmental disabilities, and vocational rehabilitation, computer systems keep track of clients, work to ensure that they are receiving appropriate case management services, and plan for future aid to clients. They also keep records on vendors of group or foster care for adults and automatically arrange for the payment of fees to providers of such care.

Social workers who are engaged in private practice as individuals or groups often make extensive use of computer systems for record keeping and financial management functions, including billing clients or third parties who are responsible for the clients' fees.

Quality Control

Public and voluntary social agencies typically are concerned with maintaining the high quality of their services. Public agencies that receive federal support—notably those that operate AFDC, food stamps, and Medicaid services—are required to implement quarterly quality control actions that necessitate the use of automated systems. Under these systems, the agency draws a computer-generated random sample of its cases. Those cases are studied intensively by a special quality control staff and the results are forwarded to federal offices that draw a computer-generated sample of that sample and study those cases further. A series of statistical tests is applied to the two samples to determine the nature and extent of the agency's errors. From those activities, the agency is assigned an error rate, which can be the basis for fiscal penalties imposed by the federal government.

These quality control methods were adapted from similar efforts in industry, especially manufacturing. They involve complex statistical calculations and other methodologies that are based on the use of automated systems.

Agencies in other fields also use these quality control approaches to ensure the effective performance of their workers and to determine the impact of their policies and programs. Programs in mental health, child protective services, and others that provide noneconomic assistance measure themselves through comparable programs.

Generally, computer systems are a major aid to the management of social welfare programs of all kinds. The ways in which those systems may be applied are continuing to evolve.

Use in Voluntary Agencies and Private Practice

It is not only in the financial assistance, protective services, and other predominantly public functions that computer applications are found. Parker et al. (1987) cited a number of examples of computers being used for such direct practice activities as home assessments of marital interactions, marital counseling, assistance to families with exceptional children, and systems psychotherapy. There are several examples of computers being used in geriatric services.

Parker et al. also pointed out that there are many useful computer programs for self-help activities, such as relaxation and nutritional guidance, as well as for the subtle approaches to therapeutic interventions by social workers. Although the objective of the Parker et al. article is to persuade social work education programs to make more and better use of computer technology, an equally strong case can be made for extending the use of computers through agency management. If social work education programs help alert their students to the possibilities of computers and if managers aggressively work to introduce computers into their daily activities, the field and the profession are likely to become modernized in ways that will improve services to clients through several routes.

Voluntary agencies and private practitioners also can become more efficient with even lower levels of computer use than those that bring technology into the therapeutic process. For example, intake interviews or clients' histories can be handled and clients' records can be constructed and updated through computer systems. In addition, as is being done in many settings, financial statements to clients, bills to third-party payers, and reports to purchase-of-service contractors all can be handled expeditiously with computers.

DIRECT MANAGEMENT APPLICATIONS

Traditionally, social work managers have used computer systems for more direct management functions. Many agencies use or contract for automated accounting systems that help monitor budgets and expenditures and provide information on which managers may act. Computer systems have also proved helpful in designing office configurations, in managing fund-raising appeals, and in maintaining membership lists.

Perhaps the largest single use of computers, however, is *word processing*, which is simply the use of modern machines for typing. Computer systems make it possible for professional and support staff to complete perfectly typed letters, reports, and other documents in a fraction of the time it would take typists to do so on ordinary typewriters. Word processing programs allow for the instantaneous correction of errors, the moving of text from one place to another, the automatic identification of spelling errors, and the use of such attractive features as the justification of righthand margins that are complicated and tedious with typewriters but simple on computers. Another important function of word processors is the ability to produce dozens of individualized letters, all appearing to be typed personally for the recipient only, in a few seconds. Many managers and members of their support staff have discovered that the use of word processors or computers for word processing, despite some initial anxiety about what appears to be a major change, is simpler and much less tedious than is the use of more traditional office equipment.

Many managers have discovered how to use the computer's more sophisticated capabilities. Some managers, who have branch offices or colleagues with whom they must communicate frequently, connect *modems* to the computer to communicate with each other's computers over telephone lines. Thus, a director of a state agency who wants to get a message to all the agency directors in the country can do so instantaneously and in writing by using a network of computers connected by modems or other devices.

Some agencies also have found it useful to provide staff development and training through computer programs. There are catalogs full of computer-based "canned" software programs—booklets and computer diskettes sold as a package. Some programs teach people how the agency operates; others, often tied to the automated systems used by the agency, teach employees how to work with those systems; and still others correct the spelling, writing style, and punctuation of manuscripts. Through these training and instructional programs (some of which are called *computer-assisted instruction* programs), social workers, support personnel, and others learn at their own pace without the cost of instructors, time set aside for classes, and other more expensive means of developing staff capabilities.

Computers also are useful in preparing brochures and proposals. Most computers have the capacity to prepare graphics as well as text so that charts, cartoons, and other illustrations may be incorporated into printed materials. The printers that are adaptable to computers, in many cases, can replace the large printing presses traditionally used for preparing agency materials through systems called *desktop publishing* (Kleper, 1987). Therefore, many agencies now prepare their interpretive materials, annual reports, letterheads, and other documents in their own offices with their own staff and equipment.

Literature searches also are expedited by computer programs. Many libraries are tied to systems that can instantly identify a large number of books and journal articles on many subjects. For example, the *Abstracts* section of *Social Work Research and Abstracts*, published by the National Association of Social Workers (NASW) is available as a computerized data base through BRS Information Technologies.

SELECTING A COMPUTER SYSTEM

Some managers find it possible—especially in smaller agencies—to automate many of their activities simply by purchasing a few computers, printers, and software programs. Managers or other staff members, if they have or take the time to obtain some computer knowledge, may do well on their own with such functions as word processing, record keeping, and accounting. Selecting a computer system in such cases often is complicated. There are many different kinds of computers, most of which are incompatible with one another and can use only software programs that are made especially for them. Although a few years ago the whole field seemed to be moving toward machines and programs that were *IBM compatible,* which means that the machines, although not produced by IBM, can interact with IBM products and use programs designed for IBMs, that movement may not continue in the future. At this writing, some companies were finding that a variety of computers, such as the Apple Macintosh, could compete with the IBM or IBM compatibles for many office tasks. The kinds of machines and software they use continue to develop and change rapidly.

Townsend (1984) gave wise advice when he told potential computer purchasers to expect their machines to be obsolete before they are unpacked from their original cartons. The editors of this book, both of whom have been using computers for several years, suggest that managers shop for computers and find the system that is most desirable in terms of price, capacity to do what is needed, available software, and the existence of a local repair service. Many computers built by small companies or whose manufacturers are now defunct still can perform the necessary tasks and can be serviced locally in most medium-sized cities. The computer field changes so rapidly that it is impossible to choose a system that will remain the most desirable for more than a few years. For example, five years ago, the OP/M operating system was the most desirable but today it is MS-DOS. A prudent manager might well choose to buy a system that is a bit out-of-date at a large financial saving because the latest, more desirable-seeming system might well be worth half its current price in a matter of months.

STAFFING OR CONTRACTING FOR SERVICES

In some larger and more complicated social agencies, managers and staff members are not able to install or program their own computer programs and equipment. Therefore, they must either develop an internal data processing staff or contract with a computer services company.

Some large agencies find it possible and useful to employ a permanent computer staff. People are needed to develop programs, modify existing programs, add new functions, arrange for the repair and replacement of equipment, and generally meet the data processing needs of the organization. However, computer service specialists command large salaries and are in demand throughout business, industry, and the government. Therefore, social agencies, which often pay lower salaries and provide little upward mobility, find it difficult to recruit and retain computer specialists, especially computer programmers, who know how to code computers to achieve the tasks specified by managers. For these reasons, many agencies often find it useful to contract for services. Although the hourly cost of doing so may be much more expensive than the hourly salaries of full-time computer specialists employed by agencies, the total costs, after considering the expense of support services, fringe benefits, and year-round salaries may be less than for hiring a full-time staff.

In practice, most agencies with sizable computer operations employ a full-time staff as well as contract from time to time with specialized organizations or individuals for specific projects. Some social welfare applications, including several described at the beginning of this chapter, require specialized knowledge and experience. It is a rare computer staff that can develop any kind of program without help.

When contracting for computer services, most managers have found it essential to know exactly what they want and how they want to apply computer methods to their agencies. Some managers find it helpful to employ consultants to draw up specifications for the desired services if their staff is unable to perform the task. Then the agency takes competitive bids from computer companies and chooses the best offer.

It should be noted that the "best" offer for leasing contracts for any type of service is not necessarily the cheapest. That is, credence must be given to such factors as the experience of the bidders in conducting similar projects and their knowledge of the task to be accomplished, which is determined by reading the bid. A low bid from bidders who may not know how to do what they say they will do is not a bargain, many administrators have discovered.

Some agencies have found it beneficial to arrange for incremental payments for services on the basis of achieved efforts. In so doing, they avoid paying for computer systems that are inefficient, that are only partially completed, or that do not work at all.

At times, a computer plan is based on transferring a computer system from one agency to another, conceivably at significantly less expense. When such a transfer is possible, it can be an efficient way to obtain a system. However, most managers have found that transferring even a highly comparable system requires some modification. Sometimes, too, the system cannot be transferred. Therefore, before agreeing to a transfer plan, the receiving manager should be reasonably assured that the system can be moved to the new agency.

The computer or *information systems* industry, as it is now commonly called, is highly competitive and, in some cases, lucrative. The equipment or *hardware* is less expensive and more powerful than might have been supposed in the 1960s, when the technology was beginning to be common. Some small hand-held computers that cost less than $100 are able to do more and have more capacity than whole university computing centers in the 1960s. Increasingly, the costs are small and the potential profits are large.

Managers who seek computer services will be confronted by many individuals and organizations that are anxious to provide services, from giant corporations, for whom computer services are a sideline and that serve their clients through the unused capacity of their large computers, to individuals who work out of their homes and contract for time with companies that own computers. Some individuals or small partnerships are able to earn adequate incomes by serving the computer programming and systems design needs of a handful of clients—at high profits to themselves and at relatively low cost to their clients. Managers should check references carefully and speak to others who have had actual experience with the bidders for the services. They also should follow the general rules of effective purchasing, as they do when purchasing furniture, renting office space, or leasing equipment.

It also is essential for managers to involve supervisory and line staff in determining what they need in the way of systems. Such employees often have a good understanding of what the agency needs and how it can be achieved. They also will have to work closely with the computer specialists the agency uses to program the computer to achieve what the agency wants and avoid what it does not want.

Supervisory and line staff also can look critically at a proposed program. What features might improve the performance of the agency and what features might burden it? Managers who are unfamiliar with the details of their agency's work may be attracted to a system that does more than the agency needs to have done. Computer systems can achieve any level of complexity, generate any number of management reports, and automate almost any function. However, the costs of designing and implementing systems that do more than one wants can be burdensome financially as well as demoralizing for a staff that does not see any purpose in carrying them out. Reports that are not read and computerized activities that cost thousands of dollars to design and carry out but that replace simple, routine tasks that workers can complete in seconds are some examples of unnecessary services. On the one hand, thoughtful supervisory and line staff can help managers avoid such pitfalls. On the other hand, managers should be alert to staff members who are resisting automation of their work. Major changes in some agencies are a source of serious concern for some staff members who may fear they will be unable to use new systems or that their positions will be eliminated because of the systems that are being implemented. Involving the staff members in the design of the system and providing them with training in how to use it should help alleviate such anxieties.

It should be clear that not all agencies use computer programs. Some are satisfied to keep their records exclusively on paper because they can meet their management needs without using modern technology. By the next century, however, it will be a rare organization of any kind that does not use automated data processing in some aspects of its work.

COMMITMENT TO AUTOMATED SYSTEMS

Management has become modern in a variety of ways, especially in the use of computer systems to replace some functions and enhance others. Working with the agency staff to design the most appropriate system for the agency is also an important part of using automated data processing. Care is also important in selecting the procedures for assigning systems design work within the agency or contracting for outside consultants.

Managers must be committed to using automated systems in their agencies and should have a clear understanding of how they will do so before they commit the necessary resources. In the current management context, few means are as likely to destroy the credibility of a manager than the purchasing of thousands of dollars worth of computer capability and then failing to use it. One is better off postponing such a step until there is a clear plan and timetable for implementing the use of automation in the agency.

REFERENCES

Born, C. E. (1987). Microcomputers and field instruction. *Journal of Social Work Education, 23*, 69–74.

Kleper, M. L. (1987). *The illustrated handbook of desktop publishing and typesetting.* Blue Ridge Summit, PA: Tab Books.

Parker, M. W., Chynoweth, G. H., Blankinship, D. A., Zaldo, E., & Matthews, M. (1987). A case for computer applications in social work. *Journal of Social Work Education, 23*, 57–68.

Schoech, D. (Ed.). (1985). *Computers in human services.* New York: Haworth.

Slavin, S. (1982). *Applying computers in social service and mental health agencies.* New York: Haworth.

Townsend, R. A. (1984). *Further up the organization.* New York: Alfred A. Knopf.

6
▲

Collective Bargaining in the Social Services

Milton Tambor

DESPITE THE GROWTH of social work unionization and the increasing involvement of social workers in the collective bargaining process, the field of labor relations is largely ignored in social work. The actual training of social work supervisors and administrators in labor relations is limited. In social work education, the curricula on management and planning do not include information on labor relations. The result, as Shaffer and Ahearn (1981) indicated, is that the impact of unionization and collective bargaining on the delivery of services and on models for practice is simply not addressed.

Within the profession, NASW has formulated standards of personnel practices related to tenure, promotions, salaries, hours of work, leaves, layoffs, retirement, and insurance benefits. NASW's *Standards for Social Work Personnel Practices* (1971) supports the collective bargaining process as a way of solving employer–employee problems and hence of bringing about employment conditions that will be conducive to the best possible services to clients. However, in contrast to the American Nurses Association and the National Education Association, NASW has not expanded its organizational purpose to include

---

Much of the material in this chapter was originally published as Chapter 7 in *Social Workers and Labor Unions* by Howard Jacob Karger (Contributions in Labor Studies, No. 26, Greenwood Press, Inc., Westport, CT, 1988), pp. 83–96. Copyright © by Howard Jacob Karger. Used with permission.

collective bargaining and union representation. There is also no evidence that NASW intends to consider acting as a bargaining agent. Any such major organizational change is not likely in the near future, because NASW is a membership organization encompassing both social work administrators and practitioners. The consequence is that collective bargaining is of secondary interest to the professional organization.

This chapter attempts to begin to bridge the labor-relations gap in social work. The scope of collective bargaining is described and the bargaining process and the provisions included in the labor agreement are outlined. Areas in which further research and education are needed are suggested.

SOCIAL WORK UNIONIZATION: GROWTH AND DISPERSION

According to reports of the Bureau of Labor Statistics for 1986 (Adams, 1987), 17.5 percent of the U.S. labor force were union members. The proportion of the organized labor force peaked at 35 percent in 1945 and has been declining since 1954. Much of that decrease has been attributed to structural changes in the U.S. economy. Specifically, manufacturing jobs, for which union representation has been strong, have been reduced sharply, while lower-paid nonunion jobs in the service sector have been expanded greatly (AFL-CIO, 1985).

In the public sector and among specific occupational groups, however, the trend has been reversed. In the past 20 years, the unionization of federal, state, and local government employees has grown dramatically. Of these approximately 16 million employees, 6 million, or nearly 36 percent, are represented by unions ("It Pays to Belong to a Union," 1987). Among protective services occupations, including the police and fire fighters, and within professional specialty groups, such as teachers and nurses, the unionization rate is also above 30 percent (Adams, 1987). The unionization of social work has occurred in the context of the increased unionization of human service professionals in the public sector.

Although no precise figures are available on union membership among professional social workers, estimates range from 22 percent to 33 percent of an approximately 250,000-member social service work force (Galper, 1980). In Canada, it is estimated that a majority of social workers are covered by bargaining agreements and that in British Columbia, the proportion is above 90 percent (Levine, 1975). In public welfare departments, where many U.S. social workers are employed, the percentage is as high as 69 percent (Stieber, 1973). The American Federation of State, County, and Municipal Employees (AFSCME), the largest AFL-CIO union, with a membership of 1.1 million, represents 50,000 social service workers in city, county, and welfare departments and 10,000 in voluntary agencies (according to a telephone interview with the director of research, AFSCME, August 14, 1987). The Social Service Employees Union (SSEU), with a membership of 650,000 (Medhoff and Freeman, 1984), represents more than 20,000 social service workers concentrated in California, New York, the New England states, and Pennsylvania (Galper, 1980). In smaller numbers, social workers belong to Local 1199 of the National Union of Hospital and Health Care Employees, United Office and Professional Workers of America, Communication Workers of America, American Federation of Teachers (AFT), and United Automobile Workers and are members of faculty labor organizations and independent staff associations.

As an occupational grouping, social workers are located in both the public and private nonprofit sectors within a diverse range of institutions, including hospitals, schools, mental health clinics, public welfare departments, and voluntary agencies. Furthermore, in contrast to nurses and teachers, most bargaining units—those employee groups represented by the union for collective bargaining—are not confined exclusively to professional social workers. As a result of a mutuality of labor interests, human service unions often represent other service and support workers in addition to professional social workers. The dispersal of social workers in heterogeneous bargaining units among a multiplicity of employer institutions in different international unions and labor organizations may explain why there has been no complete study of social work unionization. As a result, much of the experience of social service unions is communicated in local union and international newspapers. Leftist political organizations, activist groups, and such radical social work journals as *Catalyst* also report on issues related to the practices of social work trade unions.

CURRENT EMPLOYMENT CONDITIONS

Significant changes in the nature of social work practice and in the working conditions affecting social workers have increasingly been noted by students of social work labor patterns. The standardization of professional tools, increasing pressure toward greater productivity and a lesser influence in policy-making decisions are cited by some as indications of a decline in professional autonomy and status in social work (Tudiver, 1982; Wagner & Cohen, 1978). Some critics call this trend the "industrialization" of social work practice and believe it is reflected in the erosion of craft elements related to professional judgment and skills and the emergence of repetitive and mechanistic work (Fabricant, 1985). The introduction of *Taylorism*, or scientific management, into social services, according to some observers, has distorted the nature of human service work and is designed only to reduce costs (Patry, 1978). For social workers, the dismantling of human service programs under the Reagan Administration has also resulted in greater job insecurity, higher unemployment, a decline in real wages, and the displacement of both higher degreed and lower degreed social service workers from their jobs (Ratner, 1985).

For social workers who must cope as individuals with the worst of these employment conditions, the prognosis is not good. Their job stress increases as their control over their jobs decreases, and they experience a sense of powerlessness and impotence in the workplace (Sherman & Wenocur, 1983). With its emphasis on individualism, personal excellence or pathology, and the service ethos, professionalism provides no solace; it only contributes further to a sense of alienation (Arches, 1985). In such a case, the individual social worker is likely to take a leave of absence, pursue another career, or quit.

CONTRIBUTIONS OF UNIONS

Unionization provides a vehicle for both defending professional autonomy and improving working conditions. As an organization of employees, the union is built on mutual support. Workers act together as agents of change on the basis of their own interests within their work settings. By advocating actively for themselves as workers, social workers in unions believe they can be more effective in helping their clients gain a greater measure of power and control over their lives (Sherman & Wenocur, 1983; Tambor, 1973).

In a study of unions and their impact on the economy, Medoff and Freeman (1984) emphasized the union's important role in providing workers with a means of communicating with employers and forcing employers to respond to workers' concerns. The "collective voice–institutional response" function of the union is responsible not only for increasing wages and fringe benefits for union members but for greatly reducing the probability that workers will quit their jobs. According to these economists, union work forces are more stable than are nonunion work forces, even when compensation is the same. There is no evidence to suggest that social service unions perform any different functions. Therefore, union representation not only improves the welfare of social workers in areas of economic and job security, but may improve the quality of services to clients by promoting a greater continuity in the delivery of such services.

Besides negotiating job security and bread-and-butter issues, social service unions—along with labor organizations representing nurses and teachers—seek to expand their bargaining scope to include policy- and decision-making processes in agencies. As a union leader quoted in Weitzman (1975) explained, "to the professional—the teacher or case worker— things like class size and case load size become as important as the number of hours in a shift is to the blue collar worker" (p. 201). The interest of social service unions in bargaining about the organization's mission and standards of service is attributed to the professional's concern with job satisfaction, the centrality of professional judgment, and identification with clients (Lefkowitz, 1972).

COLLECTIVE BARGAINING LAWS

Managers need to understand the legal basis for unions. Collective bargaining in the social services is based on state and federal statutes covering employees in the public and private sectors. Public employees have full bargaining rights in 22 states ("Making the Union Work," 1987). Comprehensive bargaining laws are in effect in Alaska, California, Florida, Hawaii, Illinois, Iowa, Michigan, Minnesota, Montana, Nebraska, the New England States, New Jersey, New York, Ohio, Oregon, Pennsylvania, and Wisconsin. In five other states—Delaware, Kansas, South Dakota, and Washington—full bargaining rights are denied only to state employees. In states without bargaining laws, union representation is often limited to the protection of employees' rights: utilizing existing civil service procedures or initiating legal action through the courts.

In the voluntary sector, depending on how the agency is funded and affected by interstate commerce, social workers may be covered under the National Labor Relations Act (NLRA). Private health care institutions, such as hospitals, health maintenance organizations, nursing homes, extended care facilities, or other institutions caring for the sick and aged, are now also covered by the Wagner Act as amended in 1974. In other cases, social workers may fall under state statutes modeled after the Wagner Act or may be treated as public employees under state laws.

Under comprehensive state bargaining laws and the NLRA, employees have the right to select a labor organization as their exclusive bargaining representative. A union files a petition demonstrating that at least 30 percent of the employees in an eligible unit are interested in forming a union on the basis of cards signed by workers authorizing the union to be their representative with the employer. When a union has a majority of the signed authorization cards in an appropriate unit, it can request voluntary recognition from the employer; if that recognition is granted, bargaining can proceed immediately. In nearly all cases, the National Labor Relations Board (NLRB), a state employment commission, or a quasi-judicial body conducts a secret-ballot election to determine whether the majority of the workers want that labor organization to be their bargaining agent. Before the election, the employer and union usually sign a consent agreement that defines the appropriate unit of eligible employees and specifies how the election is to be held. Supervisors with authority to hire, fire, or discipline normally are excluded from a bargaining unit of line staff.

These laws prohibit the employer from interfering or coercing employees in the exercise of their rights to join a labor organization. They similarly prohibit a union from restraining employees in the exercise of their rights to refrain from union activity. On certification, the employer is obligated legally to bargain with the union. Disputes about the election, the composition of the bargaining unit, and the failure to bargain can be litigated in formal hearings conducted by state employment relations commissions and the NLRB.

HOW UNIONS ARE ORGANIZED

In 1926, social workers in New York City hospitals and agencies organized the Association Federation of Social Workers and demanded collective bargaining with the Federation of Jewish Philanthropies (Fisher, 1980). The issues that prompted those social workers to form a labor organization included regular salary increments; caseloads; health insurance; salary scales related to training, experience, and job requirements; and the standardization of procedures for promotions. Several years later, in response to deep salary cuts and payless vacation days, the association conducted a two-hour work stoppage. Subsequently, salaries and benefits were restored.

Sixty years later, these same working condition issues still generate union interest and union organizing. In one community mental health agency, the impetus for an organizing drive was a unilateral reduction in hours and arbitrary layoffs. In another agency, the seeming unfairness of merit salary increases and possible favoritism in awarding promotions became key organizing issues. Sometimes, the distribution of salaries and salary increments, not low pay per se, may be the central concern. New workers, for example, may be hired at higher salaries than current employees are paid, or sharp disparities in salaries between administration and line staff may exist. For one agency director, being a male and the primary breadwinner was sufficient reason for determining salary differences (Tambor, 1979).

In one workplace, what the staff members considered to be an unfair discharge of a fellow employee demonstrated to them that the agency's grievance procedure, with decision making residing exclusively with the agency board, could not provide for due process. Rather, they thought that a union grievance procedure incorporating final and binding arbitration by a neutral third party was a critical element in the protection of their jobs ("Community Mental Health Organizing," 1977). In the local and state employment sectors, the size of caseloads, the lack of pay equity, low salaries, poor physical working conditions, the downgrading of services, and the absence of a career ladder and training may be major organizing issues. Lesser importance may be attached to job security and promotions when state and local civil service rules provide some protection.

Doubts regarding the legitimacy of personnel practices also can spark union interest. When an agency board announced to the staff personnel committee that other priorities compelled the agency to suspend further discussion on revising personnel practices for six months, the staff committee recognized their powerlessness and formed a union. In the public sector, workers may confront a civil service system that restricts bargaining to certain subject matters or allows for only a meet-and-confer mechanism that falls far short of collective bargaining.

During the initial phase, a core organizing group emerges. Members of this committee begin to articulate the grievances and concerns of the staff. As the process unfolds, they assume responsibility for developing communication networks, arranging for meeting and meeting places, planning agendas, and chairing meetings. They may request information from other unionized social workers in the community and invite representatives of several different international unions to attend staff organizing meetings before a union is chosen to be the petitioner in a representation election. The primary considerations in the selection of a labor organization involve the union's experience in that service sector; resources; reputation; and influence, both locally and nationally; and its commitment to democratic processes.

Because a representation election is dependent on signed authorization cards from the majority of the employees in a bargaining unit—those workers having a "community of interest" in the performance of their work—the definition of an appropriate bargaining unit is most important. Broad bargaining units that encompass professional, paraprofessional, and clerical workers generally increase the collective strength of all workers. The fragmentation of bargaining units or the exclusion of eligible employees from union representation dilutes that strength. In some cases, the size and diversity of the work force, the separate interests of employee groups, or local statutes and regulations may mandate separate occupational bargaining units.

The success of a union organizing campaign usually can be linked to the effectiveness of the organizers. Effective organizers project credibility in the workplace through their job performance, knowledge of the agency, and rapport with co-workers. They know how to listen to and be responsible for the way co-workers experience their working conditions. If some workers are fearful, the organizer must acknowledge the potential for tension and conflict but stress the value of unity and mutual support. The organizer needs to educate those workers who are unfamiliar with collective bargaining or are personally opposed to unions about the true function of unions and the bargaining process by providing workers with copies of union contracts and discussing specific provisions of these agreements, for example.

Union organizers are visible not only to their co-workers but to management representatives. As such, they may be the targets of ostracism, petty harassment, or even overt intimidation. Organizers with experiences as political or community activists understand the nature of confrontation in power relationships. Those whose family members are union members similarly understand the threat that an organizing drive can pose to a nonunion employer and the various forms of anti-union response. Organizers who are neither radicalized, politicized, nor union oriented may simply have experienced a raising and a dashing of promises and expectations (DiBicarri, 1985). The recognition of individual powerlessness to bring about real changes in salaries and working conditions and the embracing of the principles of unionism may deepen an organizer's commitment to fight for the rights of employees even under adverse conditions. In bargaining units in the public sector or in voluntary agencies in which the support for unions is strong or when unions exercise significant political influence, this risk taking will not be present. Frequently, organizers and officers of existing social service unions may be considered by management as prime candidates for administrative and supervisory positions because of the leadership they exert in the workplace.

OPPOSITION TO UNIONS

Since the 1970s, opposition to unions has increased dramatically. Labor–management consultants specializing in union busting have been employed to run anti-union election campaigns. When these campaigns have been conducted in some social service agencies, management strategies have involved frequent written and verbal communications with workers, usually through their immediate supervisors, explaining why they would be better off voting against the union. Unions may be portrayed as interlopers that would disrupt cordial relationships and impose external demands unrelated to the workers' needs. Unions also have been cast as dues-hungry organizations that are responsible for unnecessary strikes and accused of promoting rigidity and formality in staff relationships and working conditions. One agency director suggested that a 15-minute rest period under a union contract could require possible disciplinary action if a minute more or less was taken. Workers may be told that after unionization, their benefits will no longer be assured and will need to be renegotiated "from scratch" ("Community Mental Health Organizing," 1977).

Some employers also have initiated or retracted changes in salaries and employment conditions. If the carrot is offered, an unexpected salary increase may be promised or even delivered. If the stick is applied, previous commitments to wage increases and improved benefits may be withdrawn.

Management may also invoke legal obstacles that can delay the determination of the bargaining unit, the conduct of the election, or the certification of the union. For example, following a vote for union representation, one agency filed charges against the union, claiming that a union organizer had harassed and intimidated workers into voting for the union. At the formal hearing, the agency contended that the organizer, by virtue of his position as a psychiatrist with extensive credentials, qualifications, and high status, subtly intimidated his co-workers. The charge was dismissed, but union certification and the onset of bargaining were delayed by more than three months ("Community Mental Health Organizing," 1977).

Union organizers responded to the opposition of managers in a variety of ways. In one case, the organizing committee drafted an open letter to the administration, signed by nearly all the workers, announcing strong support for union representation and a readiness to face any agency tactic; the letter halted the anti-union campaign. In another instance, when a manager began to discuss the negative aspects of unionization at a staff meeting, an organizer demanded equal time and proposed that they debate the issues; the employer denied the request but suffered a serious loss of credibility ("Community Mental Health Organizing," 1977).

Among the staff, organizers can demonstrate how collective bargaining leads to economic improvements by comparing wages and benefits in unionized and nonunionized social service agencies. Similarly, they can characterize a grievance procedure that provides for representation and arbitration by a union steward as empowering to workers. Countering the negative stereotypes of unions, organizers can introduce the staff to historical materials that describe how unions have been the primary defenders of working people in their struggle for dignity and justice.

In the industrialized states, where bargaining units are large, unions and associations may compete for representation. In such an organizing drive, the state employer may not actively campaign against the union. For most workers, the choice will not be between union and nonunion representation but between which union will provide the better representation. This competition among unions is seen as wasteful and, under the AFL-CIO's newly established mechanism for solving intraunion conflicts, is less likely to occur in the future (AFL-CIO, 1985).

COLLECTIVE BARGAINING

After the majority of the employees vote for union representation or when the employer agrees to union recognition, then collective bargaining begins. For the workers, the first steps entail the election of officers and a negotiating committee that should be representative of the job classifications in the bargaining unit. In preparing the contract proposals, the committee usually meets with the members to solicit ideas and suggestions. The same process is followed by unions in renegotiating their contracts. In the case of renegotiation, the union normally submits a letter requesting that the contract be reopened 60 or 70 days before the termination of the agreement. The types of grievances and workplace problems that arose under the existing labor agreement are an important rationale for preparing new proposals. In larger units, information about priorities in bargaining issues can be gathered from membership surveys. The representative of the international union may also provide specific contractual language from other union contracts.

During this early phase, the management also makes plans. A management negotiating committee and legal counsel are designated, and negotiating positions are developed. The first negotiation session generally provides the opportunity for the members of each team to meet and jointly establish ground rules for bargaining. Ground rules typically involve the time, place, and frequency of meetings; the payment of employees for the time spent in negotiations; and the process of exchanging and agreeing to contract proposals.

The climate in bargaining is usually shaped by the events that preceded the election or by the experience of the existing labor–management relationship. If the social service employer resists accepting the union's legitimacy and rejects accommodation, then "hardball" bargaining will occur. Union proposals will be summarily rejected, and concession proposals will be made. In response, the unions may lobby agency board members or public policymakers, seek support from neighborhood groups or power blocs in the community, file charges of unfair labor practices, or engage in picketing or strike activity.

During negotiations with a community mental health agency in which this author was a participant, the union filed a complaint of unfair labor practices, charging the employer with refusing to implement agreed-on wage adjustments and with delays in bargaining. At the negotiating table, the employer also proposed sharp reductions in the number of holidays and vacation, sick, and personal-leave days. The hearings were conducted more than a year after the initial election, and the state employment relations commission found the employer guilty of failure to bargain. Shortly thereafter, the first collective bargaining agreement was reached.

Even when a labor–management relationship has been in place for a while, major conflicts may remain unresolved. For example, for 10 years, the union in a community health and social service agency had repeatedly proposed third-party grievance arbitration. The employer consistently rejected the union proposal, claiming that arbitration would undermine the authority of the board. The union contended that a grievance appeal process without arbitration could not be fair or objective. No agreement could be reached in mediation, and the employer terminated the agreement. The employees went out on strike, with grievance arbitration being the major issue in the dispute ("Chass Strikers," 1987).

Although the strike may be a harsh and undesirable consequence of the failure to reach an agreement, it is fundamental to the bargaining process. In strike situations, the parties involved can agree, individually or mutually, on arrangements to provide emergency services for clients. The strike and the management lockout are the most direct means of breaking through an impasse and compelling the other party to agree to terms. Their potential use forces the parties to reassess their positions, seek new means of compromise, and exhaust every avenue available to reach agreement.

When an accommodation between the social service employer and the union is reached, bargaining takes on a different face. Problems are discussed, and important information may be shared. Initial proposals are followed by mutual exploration and the sorting out of priorities by the respective parties. Once they resolve the minor issues, the parties may table the more difficult subjects. Package proposals may be made, and the parameters of an acceptable settlement to both sides emerge. A tentative agreement can be reached within a reasonable time. The tentative agreement is then brought before the union membership and employer policy-making body for final ratification.

In bargaining in the public sector, where complex issues are addressed, the skill and experience of the respective bargaining teams can help resolve difficult contract issues. When a third party, such as a state legislature, approves budgetary appropriations that affect wage negotiations, the union has to engage in lobbying and political activity to complement the bargaining process.

THE LABOR AGREEMENT

The collective bargaining agreement encompasses a broad range of economic and noneconomic provisions. Unions consider job security and protection to be the central features of the labor agreement. The grievance process and representation by a steward defend the employees' rights. The system allows the steward time off to investigate and process grievances, including the right of employees to have a representative present during a disciplinary action. The grievance procedure specifies time limits for grievances to be heard at different levels of the management and union organizations beginning with the worker, steward, and supervisor. Grievance procedures normally terminate with binding arbitration, and 95 percent of U.S. labor agreements include that provision (Balliet, 1981).

Union security and union shop provisions institutionalizing the union are also important components of the labor agreement. The union will propose that all employees in the bargaining unit join the union or pay a service fee. The union's rationale for negotiating such a requirement is that the union is legally obligated to represent all employees in a given bargaining unit. Without such a provision, employees choosing not to pay union dues or the service fee would still receive the same representation as do union members. In right-to-work states, in which provisions for union security are prohibited, union members are likely to resent "freeloaders."

The union also will propose that seniority rights be linked to job security and the allocation of jobs in the agreement. Under such provisions, layoffs occur strictly by seniority as long as employees with seniority can perform the available work. Transfer rights guarantee that such employees are given preference for comparable jobs over new employees or employees with less seniority. Promotions are based on seniority among workers with similar qualifications who meet the necessary requirements for particular jobs.

Job security also is protected under such contracts by leaves-of-absence provisions for health, education, and military purposes and increasingly for paternity as well as maternity leaves. These provisions provide for the reinstatement of employees after such leaves. Personnel files receive more attention in the labor agreement as well. Thus, a contract provision might limit the content and use of personnel files by guaranteeing the confidentiality of the files, requiring that employees be notified of material to be included, assuring the rights of employees to disagree with or file grievance claims about the contents, and restricting the use of disciplinary records and counseling memoranda to a specific period. The labor agreement might also include policy statements prohibiting sexual harassment, affirming nondiscrimination, restricting polygraph and drug testing, permitting supplemental employment, promoting health and safety, and limiting the contracting out of services.

Economic provisions of the agreement would include hours of work (length of the workweek, compensatory time, and overtime); paid time off (for holidays, sick leave, vacations, and personal and funeral leaves); insurance benefits (hospitalization, disability, life insurance, dental care, and retirement); and salaries. Besides specifying across-the-board increases, cost-of-living allowances, and annual step increments, the agreement could designate how education and experience will be treated among job classifications in a salary system. In the public sector, pay equity has become an important subject of salary negotiations. Studies comparing dissimilar jobs but using the same evaluation factors, such as skill, effort, and responsibility, have concluded that jobs that are held predominantly by women are paid less than are male-dominated jobs of comparable value ("Pay Equity Wrap Up," 1987). In San Jose, the first major collective bargaining agreement addressing pay equity provided for the upgrading of wage rates for clerical workers, librarians, and other traditional female jobs (Masten, 1982). In social work job classifications, these discriminatory wage disparities similarly exist, and unions representing social service workers are advocating for pay equity in the courts and state legislatures as well as at the bargaining table.

Social service unions also use the collective bargaining agreement to address professional and policy issues. Benefits related to professional interests include tuition reimbursement, sabbatical and educational leaves, time off to attend conferences and the reimbursement of the cost of doing so, the payment of professional dues and subscriptions, and flexible hours of work. When the union proposes some joint decision making in policy areas, however, the employer usually opposes such efforts strongly, claiming that standards of service and the conduct of the employer's operations are reserved management rights. The following account of the experience of one social service union's attempt to bargain on policy issues is illustrative.

In 1965, following the longest strike of public employees in New York City, SSEU's demands related to the size of caseloads and a joint caseload committee were accepted by a fact finding panel (Kendellen, 1969). In the next negotiations, the union presented demands for the revision of recipients' budgets in accordance with the Consumer Price Index, automatic clothing allowances, the right of recipients to fair hearings, and the provision of residential care. The city rejected the union's proposals, and another strike occurred. The city maintained its position that services to clients were outside the scope of bargaining and solely within the jurisdiction of the city.

An unpublished survey by the Center for Urban Studies, Wayne State University, of 69 social service, education, and fundraising voluntary agencies found that in 1985, union and management representatives held strongly opposing views on the appropriateness of policy issues as subjects for bargaining. In the areas of workload, job duties, employee evaluations, representation on agency committees, staff development, and agency policies and proposals, 79 percent of the union officers but only 28 percent of the management representatives considered these subjects to be appropriate for bargaining. Most of the collective bargaining agreements analyzed in the study included provisions related to job duties and employee evaluations. Workload provisions were found in one-third of the agreements and policy and program issues in only 10 percent.

The opposition of management to an expanded scope of bargaining may explain why some view bargaining by social workers to be less developed than bargaining by teachers (Shaffer, 1979). Teachers' workloads, including preparation periods and relief from extracurricular activities, are accepted as proper subjects for bargaining. The size of classes, once considered a policy issue, is accepted as a working condition. The consultation rights of teachers provide for a variety of labor-management committees. In social service labor agreements, the actual size of caseloads is often not specified; instead, workloads are subject to "reasonable" standards. If the standards are deemed unreasonable, they can be challenged through the grievance process. In many agreements, joint labor–management committees are established for the specific purpose of evaluating the caseloads of staff members. If social workers experience continued pressure for greater accountability and productivity, then their unions will make stronger demands in the areas of policy and workloads.

ADMINISTRATION OF THE AGREEMENT

In 1986, the New York City Chapter of NASW hosted a conference on social workers as professionals and union members. Representatives of AFSCME, SSEU, District 1199, and United Federation of Teachers discussed a variety of issues facing their unions under their respective labor agreements ("Crossing the Picket Line," 1986). Contractual disputes focused on productivity requirements linked to a rating system, the contracting out of services, overlapping job titles in lieu of social work titles, educational differentials in pay, massive changes in shifts, involuntary job assignments, and health hazards associated with video display terminals. Some of the disputes were processed as grievances; other disputes were being discussed at labor–management meetings and in ad hoc joint committees. Working conditions, such as productivity quotas, however, would legally require negotiations and mutual agreement by the parties.

The experience in administering the collective bargaining agreement is as important as the actual contract negotiations. What kinds of problems and disputes arise under the agreement? Which contractual provisions are subject to varying interpretations? Are provisions of the agreement applied consistently and uniformly? How are disputes settled? The answers to these questions will likely indicate how important and relevant the labor agreement is on a day-to-day basis.

Grievance settlements, especially arbitration awards, elaborate on the meaning and intent of the agreement. For instance, arbitration decisions in five discharge cases in one local union defined more explicit guidelines for disciplining for just cause. These discharges were predicated on the employees' unsatisfactory job performance, verbal abuse of co-workers, and failure to report to work (Tambor, 1986). In each case, the discharge was ruled as being without just cause and the grievant was reinstated with back pay. In their awards, the arbitrators cited the employers' failure to follow progressive discipline, their disregard of due-process procedures, and their inability to use the employees' evaluations as evidence of poor performance.

In a family service agency, this author was involved in a dispute in contract negotiations regarding merit increases. The employer argued that merit increases could be applied fairly and objectively on the basis of specific standards of performance. The union rejected that claim, criticizing the system for promoting divisions among the staff and a speedup of work. A joint committee, composed of representatives of labor and management, subsequently formed and shifted its attention to a broader and more substantive concern with improving the quality of work life and labor–management relations in the agency.

Reductions in funding in another agency brought the union and employer together in a special conference, in which this author participated, about possible layoffs. During these discussions, the union agreed to waive the layoff provision, and both parties—the line staff and the administration—accepted a short-term reduction in salaries.

As the parties apply and interpret the labor agreement with regard to grievances and issues of the workplace, the agreement becomes a living, changing document. The collective bargaining process continues while the agreement is being administered.

TRAINING AND RESEARCH IN LABOR RELATIONS

Social work research has paid scant attention to the impact of collective bargaining on social agencies. This gap in research is in marked contrast to the field of education, in which the experience of collective bargaining has been more intensely studied (Perry & Weldman, 1970). Moreover, much of the analysis of social work unionization has been focused narrowly. Questions of values related to strike activities and potential conflicts between unionization and professionalization have been prominent issues (Alexander, 1980; Rehr, 1960), but the unionization process, the scope of the labor agreement, the administration of the contract, collective bargaining, and the resolution of impasses are less likely to be studied. This lack of labor relations training and the narrow view of collective bargaining have contributed to the ambivalent attitudes of social work administrators toward unions, particularly in nonprofit agencies. Responding to the 1985 survey by the Center for Urban Studies, Wayne State University, of the impact of collective bargaining on the nonprofit agency, one social work executive concluded that unions are out of place in professional organizations and fuel mistrust, suspicion, and an adversarial relationship. Another agency executive suggested that workshops for labor and management representatives should be provided to address some of the following questions: Can the union model of the 1930s and 1940s be useful in the nonprofit agency? How can professional performance be recognized and rewarded in collective bargaining? Should performance or years of service be the measure of one's worth? Can unionism address equity?

For social workers who are union members, the experience with labor relations can be different from that of agency administrators. Social service workers who assume leadership positions as union stewards or local union officers are likely to undergo training in grievance processing and collective bargaining within the labor organization or through labor education programs in universities. In cooperation with universities and governmental agencies, unions also conduct special workshops in arbitration, labor history, labor law, health and safety, quality of work life, leadership skills, and political action for the general membership. Social work trade unionists tend to adopt a broader view of collective bargaining and, in this author's experience, do not perceive professionalization and unionization to be incompatible. However, despite their experience in collective bargaining, these social workers seem unprepared to deal with the conflict and power dimension of the bargaining process.

In the past few years, the profession has developed a greater interest in collective bargaining. After the 1979 NASW Delegate Assembly resolved to study the relationship between NASW and labor organizations representing social workers and to identify ways to prepare social workers for collective bargaining, NASW began to offer more and more workshops on collective bargaining. Furthermore, after sponsoring an all-day conference on social workers as professionals and unionists in 1986, the NASW

New York City Chapter established a permanent committee on trade unions and social workers. The committee's preliminary plans include a survey of union-NASW members in the New York City area.

Although only 10 social work graduate programs have been identified as offering significant content on unionization, collective bargaining, and the labor movement (Shaffer & Ahearn, 1983), many more such programs must be developed if social workers are to be prepared for their roles in labor and management. The continuing expansion of industrial social work and the growing involvement of social workers in joint labor–management health programs may further underscore the importance of introducing greater labor relations content into the social work curricula.

In the area of research and practice, the experience of collective bargaining in social agencies needs to be more extensively reported, shared, and analyzed. Collective bargaining agreements in social service agencies need to be surveyed systematically. The impact of specific provisions related to workloads and policy outcomes could be evaluated from the perspectives of management and unions. A greater understanding of the labor–management relationship itself also might be beneficial to the participants in collective bargaining. What determines whether a labor–management relationship is constructive or problematic? How do the union's goals affect the labor–management relationship? Are bad labor–management relations likely to be associated with impasse bargaining? In the 1985 survey by the Center for Urban Studies, Wayne State University, one social agency executive reported that when the agency presented information and the agency's rationale for its decisions to the union, rather than adopting a stonewalling attitude, labor–management relations improved considerably. What are the costs to management of adopting an authoritarian management style versus a participatory management style? In the first model, management may make some accommodation with the union but vigilantly protects its prerogatives by narrowing the scope of bargaining to mandatory subjects as defined under the law. In the second model, management accepts the union, permits a broad scope of bargaining, and welcomes the union's involvement in organizational policies.

The collective bargaining experience of other professionals— teachers, nurses, and faculty members of universities—also should be compared. Additionally, certain questions should be asked. How are professional issues addressed in bargaining by teachers? How are proposals that link performance with pay viewed by nurses and teachers? Can the academic model of governance, which provides for the faculty's control of curriculum, scheduling, and the evaluation of performance, be applied to bargaining in social work?

Many social service unions and social agencies use joint committees, similar to quality-of-work-life programs, to address mutual concerns, including morale, turnover, policy development, and staff development. These experiences, although rarely chronicled, provide crucial information about the problem-solving process.

As Slavin (1978) noted, the life space of the social service organization includes three systems—trustees, clients, and staff. When the staff members are represented by a union, they actively participate in negotiating their working conditions. For the administrator whose task is to relate to the unionized staff while coordinating the activities of the consumers of service and the board of trustees, specific knowledge of collective bargaining may be essential. The administrator must be prepared not only for actual contract negotiations but for organizational changes in planning, communication, and decision making that arise from the collective bargaining relationship.

REFERENCES

Adams, L. (1987). Union membership of wage and salary employees in 1986. *Current Wage Development, 39,* 3–8.

AFL-CIO Committee on the Evolution of Work. (1985). *The changing situation of workers and their unions.* Washington, DC: Author.

Alexander, L. B. (1980). Professionalization and unionization: Compatible after all? *Social Work, 25,* 476–482.

Arches, J. (1985). Don't burn, organize: A structural analysis of burnout in the human services. *Catalyst, 5,* 15–21.

Balliet, L. (1981). *Survey of labor relations.* Washington, DC: Bureau of National Affairs.

Chass strikers seek arbitration, pension, parity. (1987, September). *Michigan AFSCME News,* pp. 1, 3.

Community mental health organizing. (1977). *New American Movement Discussion Bulletin.* Detroit, MI: New American Movement.

Crossing the picket line: Do we or don't we? (1986, May). Panel discussion held at a conference sponsored by the New York City Chapter, National Association of Social Workers, Hunter College, New York City.

DiBicarri, E. (1985). Organizing in the Massachusetts purchase of service systems. *Catalyst, 5,* 45–50.

Fabricant, M. (1985). The industrialization of social work practice. *Social Work, 30*, 389–395.

Fisher, J. (1980). *The response of social work to the Depression.* Cambridge, MA: Schenkman.

Galper, J. (1980). *Social work practice: A radical perspective.* Englewood Cliffs, NJ: Prentice-Hall.

It pays to belong to a union. (1987, May–June). *Collective Bargaining Reporter, 39*, p. 3.

Kendellen, G. (1969). The social service employees union: A study of rival unionism in the public sector. Unpublished master's thesis, Cornell University, Ithaca, NY.

Lefkowitz, J. (1972). Unionism in the human services industries. *Albany Law Review, 36*, 603–631.

Levine, G. (1975). *Collective bargaining for social workers in voluntary agencies.* Toronto, Ont., Canada: Association of Professional Social Workers.

Making the union work in states without bargaining laws. (1987, July 13). *AFSCME Leader*, pp. 1–3.

Masten, G. (1982, September 15). Comparative worth can end inequities. *USA Today*, p. 8A.

Medoff, J., & Freeman, R. (1984). *What do unions do?* New York: Basic Books.

National Association of Social Workers. (1971). *Standards for social work personnel practices.* Washington, DC: Author.

Patry, B. (1978). Taylorism comes to the social services. *Monthly Review, 30*, 30–37.

Pay equity wrap up. (1987, August 24). *AFSCME Leader*, p. 1.

Perry, C., & Weldman, W. (1970). *The impact of negotiations in public education.* Worthington, OH: Charles A. Jones.

Ratner, L. (1985). Understanding and moving beyond social workers' resistance to unionization. *Catalyst, 5*, 79–87.

Rehr, H. (1960). Problems for a profession in a strike situation. *Social Work, 5*, 22–28.

Shaffer, G. (1979). Labor relations and the unionization of professional social workers. *Journal of Education for Social Work, 15*, 80–86.

Shaffer, G., & Ahearn, K. (1983). Preparation of social workers for unionization and collective bargaining practice. *Arete, 8*, 53–56.

Shaffer, G., & Ahearn, K. (1981). Unionization of professional social workers: Practice and training development and implications. Paper submitted to the NASW Professional Symposium, 1981.

Sherman, W., & Wenocur, S. (1983). Empowering public welfare workers through mutual support. *Social Work, 28,* 375–380.

Slavin, S. (1978). *Social administration: The management of the social services.* New York: Haworth.

Stieber, J. (1973). *Public employee unionism: Structure growth, policy.* Washington, DC: The Brookings Institution.

Tambor, M. (1973). Unions and voluntary agencies. *Social Work, 18,* 41–47.

Tambor, M. (1979). The social worker as worker. *Administration in Social Work, 3,* 289–300.

Tambor, M. (1986, January). The application of just cause in the workplace. Paper presented at a conference of Local 1640, AFSCME, Detroit, MI.

Tudiver, N. (1982). Business ideology and management in social work: The limits of cost control. *Catalyst, 4,* 25–48.

Wagner, D., & Cohen, M. (1978). Social workers, class, and professionalism. *Catalyst, 1,* 25–53.

Weitzman, J. (1975). *The scope of bargaining in public employment.* New York: Praeger.

7

The Place of Social Group Work in Organizations

Joel Walker

MUCH OF THE RECENT CONCERN for improving the effectiveness and efficiency of American organizations has been stimulated by examinations of Japanese-type management and its success in the marketplace. One major component of both Japanese management theories and Theory Z approaches that have been adapted to the needs of American businesses is increased attention to interactions among employees. Another component is the emphasis on group processes in organizations, such as employee participation groups (Bonner, 1981); quality circles (Ingle & Ingle, 1983; Marks, 1986); teamwork in public agencies (Feinstein & Brown, 1982); and even group psychotherapy (Aschner, 1985). As a result, the professions of psychiatry and psychology are rediscovering traditional task group techniques and devising new group and quasi-group strategies for such organizational interventions (Reed & Di Salvo, 1985).

A review of the literature on management and social group work reveals a number of potential areas of organizational life in which the method and skills of social group work may converge with the needs of managers for effectiveness (Goodman, Rawlin, & Argote, 1986; McGrath, 1984; Payne & Cooper, 1981; Peters & Waterman, 1982). In this chapter, the author examines the rational link between the knowledge, skills, and abilities of social group workers and the concerns and needs of managers in organizations—a link that has heretofore received only modest attention. The author also discusses the conditions that make such a link desirable, the types of groups that are evolving from the convergence of the two interest systems, and the projected benefits of these groups.

ORGANIZATIONAL GROUP DYNAMICS

Because of the complex nature of today's organizations, understanding how groups work is important to effectiveness (Meyer, 1979). Lawrence and Filer (1965) postulated that every complex organization is, by definition, made up of multiple small work groups comprising seven to nine persons in interaction. These work groups are formed on several bases, including shared values, culture, or goals or common technology.

Work groups are formed to satisfy numerous sociopsychological needs of the individuals involved, including recognition, prestige, safety, the achievement of tasks, satisfaction, and self-actualization. Other bases for the formation of such groups—the members' values, personal needs, sexual preferences, age, religion, and motivational levels—may accelerate differentiation if they are confined to task-oriented groups or retard differentiation if they cut across the groups (Goodman, Rawlin, & Argote, 1986).

Groups in organizations tend to develop persistent patterns of behavior in their relations with each other. A complex set of givens, such as organizational arrangements, conditions under which tasks are performed, leadership styles, and social and economic environments, produce certain requirements for activity, interaction, and sentiment in any organization. Hackman and Walton (1986) described how an organization makes the transition from a small face-to-face group to a more complex multigroup organization through policies that are aimed at aligning individual, small-group, and organizational interests.

What these theorists seem to be saying is that however the subgroups are differentiated formally is the basis for social organization by virtue of the attendant blockages to interaction. Furthermore, there is a requisite structure of relationships among tasks that is inseparable from the type of technology and specialization involved, the geography of the territory in which the tasks are performed, and the time it takes to perform the tasks. Nevertheless, within these limitations, alternative structures still may be possible and functional (Lawrence & Filer, 1965).

Organizational Concerns

Complex organizations typically confront a number of major work-group, intraorganizational, and interorganizational problems that are susceptible to group interventions. Two major issues are (1) the struggle to increase productivity and effectiveness and (2) the need to reduce conflict (Weiner, 1982). Although conflict may be intradepartmental, it is usually interdepartmental, involving such problems as the clash of ideas and values or disputes over who has legitimate authority. Other problems include the lack of purpose and direction in building work groups or conflicts among team members (Strauss & Sayles, 1980), the need to increase participation in work groups to increase production, and the insufficient coordination and supervision of task groups and other mechanisms that link parts of an organization.

Decision making is a consistent issue, according to Guzzo (1986). Further issues/problems are communication, the need to increase the motivation and initiative of individuals and work groups, the creation and management of innovations and changes, the orientation of employees to the goals and styles of an organization, and the development of leadership at all levels of an organization.

The solution of the problems that reduce an organization's effectiveness is high on the agenda of contemporary managers. Aschner (1985) stated that so many aspects of daily living affect employees' performance of their jobs that organizations and unions have come to realize that attention to the needs of employees in the workplace is both cost effective and humane. Ouchi (1981), Peters and Waterman (1982), and Price (1968) outlined the overall benefits to organizations and the probability of higher levels and quality of output from an organization's focus on the needs and motivation of employees. Japanese management techniques and their American variations are the practical results of these concepts.

Many organizations—both private and public—have responded to this new management perspective by instituting work groups whose aim is the better achievement of goals. California Northrop in southern California; General Electric Corporation in Cleveland; Hoffman-LaRoche and Banker's Trust in New York City; General Foods in Westchester County, New York; and the New York City Human Resources Administration are but a few of the organizations that have established comprehensive group programs.

Theory Z Organizations

The first priority in a Z-type organization is productivity (Ouchi, 1981; Peters & Waterman, 1982). Most theorists believe that increased productivity is the major impetus for the development of Theory Z organizational styles. The concomitant human relations activities are intended to foster high productivity. The central features of the Theory Z approach include *management by wandering around,* coined by Peters and Waterman to refer to the planned visibility of managers and their communication with employees; egalitarianism and the democratic participation of employees in the organization; and the development of the interpersonal skills necessary for effective decision making by the group. Other important features are the increased loyalty of employees through their fair and humane treatment, public recognition of achievement through symbols and awards; the increased motivation of employees through the group process; and quality circles (formal employee–management problem-solving groups). In addition, Theory Z organization focuses on both the work and home life of employees in the quest for productivity. Flexible work schedules, EAPs, alcohol and drug counseling, stress management, financial counseling, day care, and health and medical care all contribute to the enhanced satisfaction and productivity of employees.

ROLE OF SOCIAL GROUP WORK

What organizations see as their concerns and needs (Peters & Waterman, 1982) in relation to the achievement of tasks and increased effectiveness is directly linked to the directions, structural processes, and skills of group work (Klein, 1961; Shulman, 1968; Toseland & Rivas, 1984; Zander, 1982). The instruments of group work are designed to create a climate for problem solving and an opportunity for individuals and organizations to work on tasks, challenges, and personal situations in pooled thinking with others.

Background

Social group work emerged in the early twentieth century as a system of knowledge aimed at enhancing the quality of life of individuals in groups by encouraging their personal development and by helping them to participate fully in the democratic society, especially when institutional obstacles to their full access to opportunity existed (Coyle, 1930, 1947; Follett, 1942). Group workers were enablers, advocates, teachers, organizers, and helpers. Most of all, however, they were facilitators—facilitators of a process that helped collectives of different individuals "work" effectively together to accomplish desired goals. Since its inception, group work, through research, has integrated significant social science elements of communication, role and psychological theory, and cognitive and behavioral theory into its social provision and task-centered knowledge systems and theories of the social psychology of influence (Garvin & Glasser, 1974). Its growth has been marked by the development of social group work as a methodology that has the ability to clarify assumptions about the reality of groups and to examine their functioning properties. As Cartwright and Zander (1960) have stated, by the late 1930s, the practical and theoretical importance of groups had been documented empirically (p. 19); there was evidence that the established dynamics could be applied to a variety of life situations: family life, work groups, classroom committees, and other experiences. Lewin (1951) further established that the different influences in the processes of group dynamics could be measured and evaluated.

These developments in social group work came at a "time when administrators and organization theorists were beginning to emphasize the importance of groups and of human relations in administration" (Cartwright & Zander, 1960, p. 19). They set the stage for social group work in organizations through the early contributions of Follett (1942) on dynamic administration and Reynolds's (1951) relationships with labor unions. Most of the earlier social work programs in organizations were membership assistance programs that were sponsored by unions and concentrated on helping individuals with various levels of adjustment problems that required some form of counseling.

Broader Focus

That earlier focus on the individual worker has broadened over the years to include groups in organizations that deal with a variety of challenges to daily living, including quality circles, groups on day care, parenting, alcohol and drug counseling, money management, and stress management (Aschner, 1985). Masi (1981) estimated that there are now thousands of group programs in organizations. Many of these programs are management sponsored and classified as organizational development services, rather than social group work services (Keys & Walker, 1985).

A significant development recently has been the establishment of occupational social work programs and curricula for practice in schools of social work. Primary among these programs are the Center for Industrial Social Welfare, Columbia University, and programs at Hunter College, New York City, the University of Southern California, and the University of California at Los Angeles. In addition, many organizations, such as General Foods Corporation, have assigned a coterie of staff to coordinate group programs in the workplace (Keys & Walker, 1985).

VALUE OF SOCIAL GROUP WORK

Social group work provides occasion for members of the group to share ideas and derive a common wisdom—to get answers, respond to questions, and learn about others and the differential constraints they face (Zander, 1982). The processes of social group work develop conditions that foster communication and creative thinking among participants and allow members to work on problems and complete tasks in a cooperative rather than a competitive climate. Both these conditions are essential for the effective management of tasks. Shaw (1981) found that when group members view the tasks as cooperative, a larger percentage of their actions receive positive organizational responses. Luft (1985) reported that when the interdependence of participants is fostered, members begin to work more effectively to gain information on how to get common work done. Hokenstad and Rigby (1977) indicated that when this cooperative process is nourished, participation is rewarded and increases, contributions are encouraged, and criticism and judgments are debated. They noted that group leaders can be facilitators of this process.

Group work is important to individuals and organizations because the complex nature of this rapidly changing society affects the quality of the life experiences of workers and the production goals of organizations. Furthermore, workers and organizations share the common concerns of integration of minorities and women into the workforce, automation, expansion and contraction of the labor force, relocation, retooling, low morale, job security, gratification from work, and worker–management relationships. Enhancing the capacity of groups of individuals to work together and increasing the organization's ability to be more productive are goals shared by organizations and social group workers (Price, 1968).

GROUP WORK SKILLS

What social workers do systematically is to help individuals talk to each other, understand different positions, accept a negotiated perspective, understand expanded views, reach a consensus, work together on collaborative tasks, make decisions, and develop mutually confirming processes through interaction with others. The skills needed for working with groups of individuals in organizations may include (1) defining the requirements and limits of tasks and the situations in which activities are performed, (2) challenging obstacles to cooperative work and collective efforts, (3) determining the common aspects of tasks and situations that are useful to both the organization and group members in attaining goals, (4) facilitating mutual-aid processes, (5) mediating conflicts and reducing stress, and (6) helping the organization to learn from its experiences, through evaluation and feedback to improve its ability to identify and solve problems (Friedlander & Schott, 1981). Communication and problem-solving skills, subsumed under these larger facilitation processes, include focused listening, transactional and redirectional skills, the management of feelings, the identification of communication signals, and issue-recognition skills. Other skills, such as providing working data, clarifying and interpreting organizational and group constraints, offering alternatives, universalizing or particularizing problems, and negotiating obstacles to cooperative efforts, are inherent elements of this process (Schwartz & Zalba, 1971; Shulman, 1968).

A conceptual framework for this new group work approach to organizations emphasizes group work's knowledge base of human behavior in task groups, communication theory, the motivation of groups, skills in problem solving and resolving conflicts, and self-actualization processes for group members. In this approach, the group worker's knowledge, values, and skills would be linked to such organizational concerns as innovation, productivity, and monitoring of the achievement of tasks and the motivation, morale, recognition, and general well-being of employees.

Using the concepts of several group work and organizational theorists, the possible points at which connections can be made between the knowledge base of social group work and the needs and concerns of organizations can be depicted (Table 1). If intersecting lines were drawn between the organizational tasks and concerns and the group work skills, they would meet on mutually congenial levels to create the effect of a spider web.

Table 1.
The Link between Group Work Skills
and Organizational Concerns[a]

Group Work Skills[b]	Organizational Tasks, Needs, and Concerns[c]
Developing the problem as a common issue	Fostering the efficient advancement of work groups and increasing the members' motivation
Obtaining a statement of the organization's goals	Integrating the group's norms and the organization's norms
Defining the limits and requirements of a situation	Increasing the productivity, safety, and health of groups monitoring in quality circles and the effective acceptance of supervision
Facilitating participation	Enhancing the satisfaction of employees and recognizing their performance
Toning down strong positions	Solving the problems of the work groups
Enhancing underemphasized positions	Solving the problems of the work groups
Providing working data	Providing feedback and evaluation
Developing a democratic climate	Solving the problems of the work groups and increasing the members' motivation
Mediating and resolving conflicts	Reducing and resolving conflicts and managing reactions to stress
Developing a climate of negotiation and cooperation	Effecting communication and solving the problems of the work groups
Helping to bring about shared decisions	Increasing the cohesiveness of the work groups
Helping the group accept mutual decisions	Integrating groups' norms and the organization's goals
Negotiating feelings	Providing feedback and evaluation and enhancing the satisfaction of employees
Providing evaluation and feedback	

[a] Congruence measures are possible on multiple levels at several interactional points.
[b] Based on the work of Klein (1961), Shulman (1968), Tosland and Rivas (1984), and Zander (1982).
[c] Based on the work of Ouchi (1982), Peters and Waterman (1982), and Strauss and Sayles (1980).

Application of Skills through Practice Modes

The organizational practice modes through which social group work skills are being applied to increase the effectiveness and efficiency of organizations are as follows:

Quality-of-Work-Life Groups

The purposes of these groups vary in organizations, but, in general, the groups attempt to create a better quality of life and work environment for employees. The groups are usually voluntary participation groups that work together on collaborative concerns. Concerns may include creating trust between the organization and its employees, improving decision making, increasing morale, making work more effective, resolving employees' problems, improving safety and health in the work environment, and recognizing the performance of employees (Wallace & Szilaqyi, 1982, p. 416). The groups also may act as a complement to collective bargaining; the Rushton experiment (Goodman, Rawlin, & Argote, 1986, p. 21) and the Human Resources Administration project in New York City (*Quality of Work Life*, 1985) are recent examples.

Quality Circles

Quality circles are a form of employee participation taken from Japanese management. The premise on which they are based is that the involvement of employees in various areas of the organization increases the motivation of individuals and the performance of work groups. Working in small groups, it is believed, improves communication and makes possible the more humanized and effective production of work. The groups, it is thought, increase the employees' morale in that they meet the survival and social needs of employees and provide a greater opportunity for self-actualization (Ingles & Ingles, 1983, pp. 49–56).

Maintenance of Employees and the Prevention of Illness

Many EAPs operate in organizations that use group work skills related to the prevention of illness, the management of stress, and the solution of family and personal problems that affect the performance of employees, such as alcoholism, drug abuse, child care, and recreation. Many companies, including Banker's Trust, IBM, General Foods Corporation, and Hoffman-LaRoche, have such programs that are significant for effective and efficient production (Aschner, 1985; Trost, 1987).

Orientation to and Socialization in the Organization

The integration of employees conceptually into the goals and norms of the organization through the provision of information, education, and training and helping them understand the requirements and constraints under which the organization functions can be fostered by systematic small-group processes. Often, the organization's relationships with the public are reflected by the attitudes of its employees. General Motors Corporation has based a massive advertising campaign on how employees present the corporation, and CitiBank considers its community relations role to be critical to its effectiveness in the market (Paul & Foulkes, 1987; Trost, 1987).

Reorganization, Layoffs, and Automation

In a fluid and complex economic system, organizations often must make difficult decisions that will affect the job security of a large number of employees. The process is often exacerbated by rumors, both negative and positive, and by inaccurate information that is disseminated, which hampers the employees' performance and ability to produce and lowers their morale. Social group workers can provide accurate information, control negative rumors, and help employees reorient themselves to the situation in small groups. Russell (1985) reported that many of these issues became the domain of social work intervention when the General Electric plant in Cleveland had to lay off employees in 1984. The need for skilled facilitators to help employees work through their grief at the loss or relocation of their jobs, reorient themselves, analyze and reinterpret their skills, or retrain clearly fit the group work method.

Committees, Task Forces, and Advisory Groups

Committees, task forces, and advisory groups serve many purposes in organizations. Such groups may have a short- or long-term purpose or may begin as short-term single-purpose groups and evolve into long-term multipurpose groups that have an impact on employees and programs. According to Guzzo (1986), important decisions are made in these aggregates within the complex framework of organizations; thus, group guidance of these structures can be significant to an organization's effectiveness (*The Human Resources Administration and You*, 1985).

Client Advocacy Groups

Client/consumer advocacy groups are related to the needs recognized by employees who provide direct services and who then participate in decision making related to the design of programs and procedures for delivering services. Many of the groups work on the assumption that those who are closest to the provision of services often have insights that others who are placed more distantly in the organization do not have (*see* chapter 9; Paul & Foulkes, 1987; Wegenast, 1983, pp. 57–61).

Preretirement Groups

The development of corporate responsibility for employees' health, pensions, and retirement has led to the establishment of systematic preretirement groups by many companies, including IBM and Mobil Oil Corporation (Paul & Foulkes, 1987). Ozawa (1985) pointed out that such groups are economically expedient for organizations and make sense in terms of increased productivity and social planning.

COLLABORATION

American management is becoming increasingly oriented to people, and the use of groups on a variety of levels is an inherent part of the structure of many organizations. To this perspective, social group workers bring a systematic methodology of skills, observation, analysis, influence, negotiation, and evaluation that can be critical to the attainment of goals. This methodology is buttressed by the developing curricula of schools of social work. It can be applied by social workers as practitioners, organizational developers, labor relations personnel, and management consultants in a variety of organizational arrangements. It seems rational that organizations should seek these resources from the social work community and that group workers should market these skills to contemporary organizations. The increasingly complex economic, social, and technical factors that influence today's workplace affect productivity, the quality of work life, and individual performance and self-actualization. Therefore, the goals both of management and of social group work will be enhanced through task-system collaboration. Although inevitable strains in values, control, and cultures should be taken into account (Kurzman, 1987), these strains seem negligible when one considers the larger potential for collaboration that can be achieved.

REFERENCES

Aschner, C. (1985, October). A study of group work in industry. Paper presented at the Sixth Symposium of the Association for the Advancement of Group Work, New Brunswick, NJ.

Bonner, J. S. (1981). Applying Japanese management strategies to educational management. *Michigan School Board Journal, 68.*

Cartwright, D., & Zander, A. (1960). *Group dynamics.* New York: Harper & Row.

Coyle, G. L. (1930). *Social process in organized groups.* New York: Richard R. Smith.

Coyle, G. L. (1947). *Group experience and democratic values.* New York: Woman's Press.

Feinstein, B., & Brown, E. (1982). *The new partnership: Human services in business and industry.* Cambridge, MA: Schenkman.

Follett, M. P. (1942). *Dynamic administration.* New York: Harper & Bros.

Friedlander, F., & Schott, B. (1981). The use of task groups and task forces in organizational change. In R. Payne & G. Cooper (Eds.), *Groups at work* (pp. 191–210). New York: Wiley.

Garvin, C., & Glasser, P. (1974). Social group work: The preventive and rehabilitative approach. In M. Sundel, P. Glasser, R. Sarri, & R. Vinter (Eds.), *Individual change through small groups* (pp. 39–41). New York: Free Press.

Goodman, P., Rawlin, E., & Argote, L. (1986). Current thinking about groups: Setting the stage for new ideas. In P. Goodman & Associates (Eds.), *Designing effective work groups* (pp. 1–31). San Francisco: Jossey-Bass.

Guzzo, R. A. (1986). Group decision making and group effectiveness in organizations. In P. S. Goodman & Associates (Eds.), *Designing effective work groups* (pp. 34–39). San Francisco: Jossey-Bass.

Hackman, J. R., & Walton, R. (1986). Groups under contrasting management strategies. In P. S. Goodman & Associates (Eds.), *Designing effective work groups* (pp. 189–195). San Francisco: Jossey-Bass.

Hokenstad, M., & Rigby, B. (1977). *Participation in teaching and learning.* New York: International Association of Schools of Social Work.

The human resources administration and you. (1985). New York: Oversight Committee, New York City Human Resources Administration.

Ingle, S., & Ingle, N. (1983). *Quality circles in service industries.* Englewood Cliffs, NJ: Prentice-Hall.

Keys, P., & Walker, J. (1985, October). Practice models for a new group work approach to organizational systems. Paper presented at the Sixth Symposium of the Association for the Advancement of Group Work, New Brunswick, NJ.

Klein, J. (1961). *Working with groups*. London: Hutchison University.

Kurzman, P. (1987, Spring). Perspective on ethical issues in industrial social work. *Update* (Hunter College, New York), p. 11.

Lawrence, P., & Filer, J. (1965). Concepts in organizational change. In. J. L. Bailey, R. L. Katz, C. Orth, III, J. E. Clark, L. B. Barnes, & M. N. Turner (Eds.), *Organizational behavior and administration* (pp. 153–155). Homewood, IL: Dorsey.

Lewin, K. (1951). *Field theory in social work*. New York: Harper & Row.

Luft, J. (1985). *Group processes*. San Francisco: Mayfield.

McGrath, J. (1984). *Groups: Interaction and performance*. Englewood Cliffs, NJ: Prentice-Hall.

Marks, M. (1986). The question of quality circles. *Psychology Today, 20,* 42–47.

Masi, D. (1981). *Human services in industry*. Lexington, MA: Lexington Books.

Meyer, C. (1979). Introduction. In C. Meyer (Ed.), *Making organizations work for people* (pp. 3–5). Washington, DC: National Association of Social Workers.

Ouchi, W. G. (1981). *Theory Z: How American business can meet the Japanese challenge*. Reading, MA: Addison-Wesley.

Ozawa, M. (1985). Economics of occupational social work. *Social Work, 30,* 442–445.

Paul, R., & Foulkes, F. (1987, November 29). Containing retiree health care expenses. *New York Times,* sec. 3, p. 2.

Payne, R., & Cooper, G. (Eds.). (1981). *Groups at work*. New York: Wiley.

Peters, T. J., & Waterman, R. H., Jr. (1982). *In search of excellence: Lessons from America's best-run companies*. New York: Warner Books.

Price, J. C. (1968). *Organizational effectiveness*. Homewood, IL: Richard D. Irwin.

Quality of work life. (1985). New York: New York City Human Resources Administration.

Reed, R., & Di Salvo, C. (1985, October). Negotiating the corporate workplace. Paper presented at the New York Workshop Conference, Rye, NY.

Reynolds, B. (1951). *Social work and social living.* New York: Citadel.

Russell, J. (1985, October). Social services and retrenchment. Paper presented at the Sixth Symposium of the Association for the Advancement of Group Work, New Brunswick, NJ.

Schwartz, W., & Zalba, S. (Eds.). (1971). *The practice of group work.* New York: Columbia University Press.

Shaw, M. E. (1981). *Group dynamics: The psychology of group behavior.* New York: McGraw-Hill.

Shulman, L. (1968). *Social group work.* New York: Council on Social Work Education.

Strauss, G., & Sayles, L. R. (1980). *Personnel: The human problems of management* (4th ed.): Englewood Cliffs, NJ: Prentice-Hall.

Toseland, R., & Rivas, R. F. (1984). *An introduction to group work practice.* New York: Macmillan.

Trost, C. (1987, November 30). Best employers for women and parents. *Wall Street Journal,* p. 1.

Wallace, M., & Szilaqyi, A. D. (1982). *Managing behavior in organizations, U.S.A.* Glenview, IL: Scott, Foresman.

Wegenast, D. (1983). *The application of group leadership skills to case management in child protective service.* Unpublished doctoral dissertation, City University of New York.

Weiner, M. E. (1982). *Human services management: Analysis and applications.* Homewood, IL: Dorsey.

Zander, A. (1982). *Making groups effective.* San Francisco: Jossey-Bass.

8

Tools and Systems for Modern Managers

Leon H. Ginsberg

MODERN MANAGEMENT HAS LED to the better understanding of such standard items as time-management systems, internal communications, staff development programs, and a variety of other practical aids for the effective running of an organization. Some of the tools that seem most important in today's managerial context are explored in this chapter. That context, of course, is one that is evolving but that is different from the social work management of an earlier time, as some of the more theoretical discussions in chapters in this book suggest. There is an increased emphasis in the social work literature on conserving and using resources effectively, as well as managing in times of declining resources (Hasenfeld, 1984; Knighton & Heidelman, 1984). One theoretician (Stoesz, 1986) traces the transition of social welfare into a corporate enterprise that is little different, except for the subject matter, from a corporate enterprise that is dedicated to service or the production of goods. The ideas presented in this chapter are drawn from the management literature and the author's practical experiences.

TIME MANAGEMENT SYSTEMS

One preoccupation of modern management theorists is the importance of time to an organization. Nothing is more costly and, therefore, more valuable than the time of the management of a corporation or, in the case of this book, of a social agency.

116

A variety of time-management systems are commercially available to help managers use their time more effectively. The simplest is the calendar that allows managers to create weekly, monthly, and yearly plans to ensure that tasks are completed and that activities are spread out sufficiently for adequate lead time and preparation. Sophisticated calendars specify planning objectives, time frames, and other devices that are designed to help managers make better use of their time.

Some systems probably are more helpful than others. Their utility depends on the type of organization and its objectives and on the personal characteristics and needs of the managers. Perhaps the most important principle is to avoid spending so much time using a system that one becomes lost in the details of charts, outlines, and other devices, and fails to achieve the real managerial objectives of the organization. The author knows of one manager who was so intent on keeping accurate records of his work that he used three stopwatches in his office—one for managerial activities, another for the development of information, and a third for his personal activities. Ultimately, the manager used none of the clocks because the system was too complex. Some managers do well with calendars on which they make brief notes; others prefer more elaborate systems. The main purpose of any system, however, is to facilitate the completion of tasks and to use one's time to the maximum advantage. Indeed, that is the objective of good management—to achieve, to the maximum extent possible, the objectives of the organization with the fewest resources possible. Some time-management experts suggest that the manager plan not only the work activities but also personal activities. Organizing all one's time with a single system appears to be a means of helping managers perform more effectively.

One resource that social work agencies may overlook is the manager's time. Most management systems and improvement efforts are designed to reduce the manager's obligations for some functions so he or she may devote more time and energy to other functions. Of course, this does not mean that the manager should hurry through supervisory meetings, planning efforts, or communication with the board of directors or other authority groups. Some of these efforts take an extensive amount of time and others take less. The principle is that the manager should devote no more time than is necessary to any function.

Executive Communications

Probably the greatest savings in time can result from being more effective in organizational communications because so much of a manager's time is spent in communication. Many managers find it efficient and effective to communicate with staff, other agencies, and even clients in writing. Through written communications, both the sender and the receiver can maintain a record of what was communicated, which can provide a clear basis for subsequent conversations or conferences. Written communications usually force all the parties in a situation to be concrete and brief about a matter under discussion.

Effective written communications can be time consuming or rapid, depending on the mechanics used to put the ideas and information on paper. Many managers use inexpensive means of communicating in writing, such as word processors, typewriters, or written structured memorandums to get their information to others. For longer, more formal documents, managers often dictate onto tapes or other devices, and their communications are transcribed later by members of the support staff. Written communication can be expensive if the manager dictates to a secretary who makes a verbatim copy of the comments in shorthand, because this form of dictation takes the time of both the manager and the secretary; it also can be costly if the manager writes lengthy memorandums in longhand.

Almost any form of written communication, however, is less costly than the face-to-face meetings used by many managers to reach decisions, give instructions, or otherwise carry out their responsibilities. A meeting takes the time of two or more people, often requires extensive oral communication before the ideas being discussed are clear to all the participants, and may lead to significant misunderstanding. The culture of management in some organizations leads people to believe that written communications are abrupt and impersonal while meetings, conversations, and oral communications are more humane and friendly. Of course, managers' communications should be neither friendly nor unfriendly; rather, they should be precise and efficient, which means they should use as little of the staff's time as possible.

None of this discussion, however, contradicts modern management's emphasis on the visibility of managers and the need for managers to achieve some of their objectives by personally visiting and viewing the agency's operations—"management by wandering around" (Peters & Waterman, 1982; Peters & Austin, 1985). Such activities as holding general staff meetings so all employees can ask questions and become aware of new developments in the organization, as well as making personal visits to work sites, are important symbolically and are a means of keeping the manager informed of the realities of the organization.

It is necessary to provide appropriate training, consultation, and equipment to develop a communications system for an agency. Some large organizations that sell dictating and transcribing equipment may provide, without additional cost, training in how to make the best use of that equipment in managing the agency. Small agencies that cannot afford equipment or personnel for communications may find it beneficial to pay a word processing or materials production service that lends equipment or provides dictating services through ordinary telephones. A few hours a week of such services are often enough to streamline communications in the agency.

Communication through Meetings

Meetings often are essential for the effective management of human service programs. However, they should be called only when they are really necessary—when the purpose and the agenda are clear—and should be only as long as they need to be (Townsend, 1984). For example, a meeting may be used to bring together all the people who must be involved in decision making and the meeting should proceed to make that decision, or a meeting may be called to share information about a client, an issue, or a program. Any written materials on the subject should be distributed in advance so that people can be prepared to ask questions or make judgments about the issue. Sometimes meetings are needed to inspire people to change their attitudes or to move forward in achieving the agency's mission; these purposes often make the time expended worthwhile.

Two other rules about meetings are important. The first rule is to avoid confusing the purpose of the meeting. If the goal is to inspire, then it should not appear that the purpose of the meeting is to reach a decision. Likewise, if the goal is to inform the participants of a decision that already has been made, it should not be implied that decisions will be made in the meeting.

The second rule is that the cost of all the components of a meeting should be determined in advance, including the total transportation costs, the rental of the meeting room, meals and refreshments, support services, and the preparation of documents. The cost of the salaries, wages, fringe benefits, and time spent in getting to the meeting of those participants who are employed by the agency should be calculated as well. Many managers are shocked to discover that a simple one-hour meeting with a handful of key people may really cost several hundreds or thousands of dollars. Thus, managers need to evaluate whether a meeting was worth the expenditure and whether they might have found other, less expensive ways to achieve the same objectives. It is advisable to calculate the costs of a meeting before it is scheduled so one can determine whether the meeting is worth holding. Many routine, recurring meetings that have little or no agenda might be eliminated if managers think about their real costs.

OFFICES

Because social agencies, by and large, are supported either by taxes or by voluntary contributions and tend to serve disadvantaged people, luxurious offices often are viewed as inappropriate. Some social work managers, however, especially those who direct large public agencies, think that people who allocate hundreds of millions and even billions of dollars in resources should have facilities that are comparable to those of corporate personnel who control comparable budgets. On the one hand, offices that are lavish invariably raise questions about why the agency is not spending more money on its services and its clients and, consequently, less on its offices. On the other hand, many social agency offices often are too austere and unattractive for effective working conditions. What should a social work office look like? This question is important because the physical setting of one's work has an impact on one's performance.

Social workers need adequate offices just as much as do other professionals. Therefore, their offices should be sufficiently large, well heated and air conditioned, well lighted, and generally comfortable enough for anyone who is likely to visit.

Offices should be maintained adequately. The paint should be fresh and the paneling, if any, should be clean. Windows should be washed and appropriately maintained, and desks, chairs, tables, and other office furniture should be orderly and attractive. Effective managers tend to make sure that their decorations are attractive and appropriate. Excessive wall coverings, such as posters, personal photos, and the like, can be distracting. Therefore, it often is wise to make use of the services of an office furnishings company or a professional interior decorator. One will not necessarily spend more money decorating an office with professional help than by oneself, and the results may be significantly better with professional consultation. At times, the quality of the work done by the organization; the reaction of the board staff, and clients;

and the ability of the organization to receive funds may be closely connected to the appearance of the agency's offices. The rule, then, is to establish offices that enhance the agency's ability to achieve its objectives without lavish furnishings that are more closely associated with the personal needs and desires of the agency manager.

LUNCHES AND COFFEE BREAKS

In some organizations, lunches and coffee breaks are abused by employees, who spend too much time away from their responsibilities for social purposes. For example, weekly covered dish lunches that exceed the allotted lunch time may interfere with the work of the organization. Making a weekly ritual out of an event that should be reserved for holidays and special occasions, such as birthdays, weddings, or births, is an error that requires monitoring and correction.

In other agencies, lunches and coffee breaks are used by managers to communicate with their staffs. For instance, some agencies hold brief meetings several times a week during coffee breaks to apprise all staff members of new developments in programs and trends in the field. These periodic informal meetings are a useful vehicle for bringing employees up-to-date. It should be noted, however, that agency policies and public laws require specified rest periods for some employees throughout the workday. Therefore, many agencies make these meetings voluntary when they are scheduled during lunch or break times or organize them at times other than the required rest periods.

Some managers of voluntary agencies find it productive to hold lunch meetings with their boards of directors or officers of the boards, who have free time only at lunch. Other managers consider lunch meetings to be an opportunity to earn the good will of a funding organization or an agency whose cooperation is needed. These lunch meetings also may be convenient to establish relationships with managers of other agencies or to hold discussions with staff members of the same agency who find it useful to meet in a different setting. It should be pointed out, however, that some highly competent managers rarely accept or set up lunch invitations because they do not think such meetings are effective.

CONSULTANTS

Theorists of modern organizational management often suggest that it is useful to employ consultants to help the managers and their staffs reach their objectives (Kelly, 1987). Implementing a new plan is costly and disruptive. Hiring a consultant can save the agency a significant sum of money if the consultant knows what the manager wants to know. It can be costly and wasteful of the organization's resources if the manager is not clear why the consultant is needed by the organization. Some principles of the effective use of consultants include the following:

■ Be as specific as possible about the problem to be addressed. That is, if a consultant seems to be needed to attend to personnel issues, the task should be defined specifically and concretely (such as "the development of a revised compensation system for support staff and professional social workers"). It might be tempting to hire a consultant to raise the employees' "morale" or to "improve the budget," but these are not the real issues. Therefore, unless the task is defined carefully, the organization is likely to hire the wrong consultant or the right consultant who is inadequately prepared to help solve the organization's problems.

■ Demand specifics from the consultant. If the consultant is going to help develop a new system for personnel, information storage, or fundraising, be sure the consultant has prepared a written proposal before he or she visits the agency. Most consultants or consultant groups can provide an organization with written examples of plans for projects in a specific area that they devised for other organizations. If a consultant does not have such written materials, it may be worthwhile to find another consultant because without such examples of previous work, the manager cannot determine whether the consultant can do the job. Similarly, after the consultant visits the organization, he or she should submit a written report and specific, concrete recommendations to be followed. Both types of reports should be reviewed before the contract is signed.

■ Obtain references from other organizations that have engaged the services of the consultant and request their reactions to the consultant before the contract is signed. It is not as important to know whether the organizations liked the consultant as it is to ascertain what the consultant achieved for the organization and how the consultant's recommendations are being used.

■ Make the contract with the consultant specific and concrete. Consultation services are usually expensive. If they are not clearly defined, the organization and the consultant may have a bitter difference of opinion about what services are covered; for instance, a manager may not realize that a consultant's bill may cover expenses as well as compensation for services.

■ Find out if the national organizations to which the agency belongs offer consultation services. Some voluntary associations provide equal or better services for less money than do private consultants. The American Public Welfare Association, Child Welfare League of America, and some religious organizations, for example, provide consultation services. Such services often are offered at a low cost to organizations that are affiliated with them.

PERSONAL RELATIONSHIPS

A common problem in organizations, including social welfare organizations, is the development of personal relationships among the staff. These personal relationships are particularly difficult when they involve a romance between a manager and a staff member. Although they are common, such relationships may be harmful to the organization because they color the organization's efforts and, from time to time, become the governing factor in how an organization operates. When decisions begin to depend on these personal relationships, rather than the organization's needs, the personal contacts have gone too far. Of course, it is possible for a superior and subordinate who are infatuated with one another to work effectively and intensely on an organizational project to the benefit of the organization. However, if that relationship sours, the effort—indeed the whole organization—may fall apart. Although many happy permanent relationships—even marriages—have developed between organizational colleagues, they are still better avoided than pursued.

Office romances have the same shortcomings as does nepotism. That is, they constitute situations in which managers make decisions based not on the organization's needs and objectives but on the needs of relatives, in the case of nepotism, or lovers, in the case of office romances. Office romances can be addressed by the manager through direct counseling with the people who are involved; with reassignments and transfers of one or preferably both the people involved; or, in extreme cases, by termination of the employment of one or both of those involved. Such measures will dampen the enthusiasm of employees for one another.

Of course, the one-sided romantic pursuit of one employee by another often can constitute sexual harassment, which is forbidden under federal law and requires action by the manager to eliminate it. Sexual harassment may include comments of a sexual nature, the use of humor with sexual overtones, physically touching another employee, or persisting in inviting another employee to socialize. Such actions can be dealt with directly through some of the means suggested for responding to office romances, as well as more direct measures including suspension and termination. The manager who overlooks sexual harassment once it has been reported faces the possibility, along with the perpetrator, of being legally culpable for it.

Of course, there is virtue in some personal contact between managers and employees in an organization. Workers need to know the human side of the manager and need to understand that he or she is not concerned only about work and about obtaining the maximum amount of effort from each worker. Yet, it is not always advantageous for employees to know everything about their managers. The manager who has an alcohol problem, for example, does not benefit from bringing that problem to the attention of employees. This is not to suggest that managers need to exude an air of mystery. It does mean that they should maintain some distance from those who serve under them.

Managers who hold receptions or parties in their homes or other places outside the office communicate to employees that they care about them as people and want to please them. Whether the parties take place during holiday seasons or other times, employees generally feel positively toward such gestures. The test that managers may use to determine what to do, how to do it, and how often to do it is similar to the test that many social workers apply when they decide which steps to take in their professional work with clients. That is, they determine whether the action is being done for the client's benefit and pleasure or for theirs. If it is for the client's benefit, it often is acceptable. If it is for the social workers' pleasure, then they are using clients for their purposes rather than for the clients'.

AWARDS

Many organizations use awards of various kinds to boost the morale of employees and to motivate them. Modern management theory suggests several principles for providing this type of incentive. First, one must determine precisely what the award will achieve for the organization and how its ability to achieve those ends might be maximized. For example, an award for achievement given to only one or two people may simply further honor those who have been honored in other ways, and hence may offend the rest of the employees and do nothing to increase the motivation of the person who is receiving the award. The second principle, then, is that awards should be achievable by many employees. Some organizations give cash bonuses to all employees who meet some specified, easily attainable standard of performance, such as coming to work on time.

The third principle is that awards should have an economic value, rather than be solely symbolic. Employees tend to ignore or at least fail to be motivated by plaques, badges, lapel pins, or certificates. These types of awards may be beneficial for symbolic reasons at the time they are given, but they may never be used again. The ideal award improves the functioning of the organization by helping the recipient to do his or her job better, but it also has some tangible benefit for the employee. One good example is the award given by a state department of mental health to its employee of the year: a parking place close to the office building—closer than that of the director. If that award were given monthly and 12 different top employees were given such parking spaces each year, the cost would be minimal, the value of the reward would be significant, and the functioning of the organization would be likely to improve. Small salary increases, bonuses, new office equipment, a better office, or better furnishings are all awards that might make a difference.

PRESENTATIONS

Depending on their purpose and the audience, effective presentations by managers about their products, capabilities, and proposals for new services often require carefully designed audiovisual material, well-rehearsed oral commentaries, and brevity. Ill-prepared, inarticulate presentations of reports in which the main facts are obscured or unclear or in which the written materials are illegible often render an excellent idea unacceptable.

Some of the principles of effective presentations should be obvious but often are overlooked. For example, social workers frequently present proposals for a program, an idea, or a change to an older or more powerful audience, such as a board of directors, a legislative committee, or a funding and allocation group for a united fundraising organization. With this type of audience, certain fundamental principles should be obvious. For example, printed materials should be brief, have wide margins, and be set in large type, because people aged 40 and over often have difficulty reading small print. Given the choice between straining their eyes or admitting they cannot see the printed words, many older participants will simply ignore the materials that are presented.

In addition, members of boards, legislative committees, and funding groups often are exposed to dozens of presentations and ideas every month. They may be readily bored by a presentation that sounds like the last 10 presentations they heard. Therefore, effective presenters often try to do something different with written materials, with oral comments, and audiovisual media, such as videotapes, slides, and films. Furthermore, some presentations often benefit from the inclusion of testimony by clients or other direct participants in service programs to augment the proposals of the professionals.

How one looks when making presentations often also makes a difference. Therefore, it is worthwhile for presenters to follow the clothing norms of the group to whom they are speaking. Molloy's (1975a, 1975b, 1988) books on successful dressing for men and women executives are based on some research and seem to have validity for influencing groups of people. Molloy persuasively argues that many managerial pursuits have failed because of inappropriate dress or succeeded because of the careful selection of clothing. Although his books are focused more on corporate settings than on social agencies, social work managers may find it beneficial to become familiar with his research and the suggestions based on it. Because of the close connection between social work and people in the corporate and business community, especially through agency boards, Molloy's writings may have particular relevance for social work managers.

EDUCATION, TRAINING, AND STAFF DEVELOPMENT

Staff development and training are important considerations for any manager. Although such efforts have traditionally been part of the agenda in social work agencies, they have been adopted by industries and businesses as well. Thus, training units, training centers, and formal college courses and institutes are now central parts of the management of most large corporations, including General Motors, McDonald's, Electronic Data Systems (part of General Motors), and IBM. It is generally recognized that because secondary and higher education do not specifically prepare new employees for the kinds of work their employers require, education and training are essential to the organization's mission.

Educators often distinguish between educational programs and training programs. *Training,* by dictionary definition and in practice, is undertaken to help make a human or an animal proficient in a specific skill or activity. In social work, staff members may be trained to use new forms, computer intake systems, or automated equipment. *Educational programs* are undertaken to facilitate the understanding of problems and programs, as well as the performance of skills. Educational programs are designed to help workers decide how to approach and evaluate a problem and which skills are most appropriate to use in a specific situation. By definition, education extends beyond the acquisition of specific skills to the development of the person in several dimensions, especially the intellectual.

Educational programs usually are broad and general and are designed to help people deal with a variety of unpredictable future circumstances, including tasks and problems that are not known at the time the education is provided. Well-educated professionals know the importance of staying current in their fields and how to find out about new developments and the means to cope with them. Social workers, whether they have a baccalaureate, master's, or doctoral degree, will, in a few years, find themselves confronting practice issues and problems that their instructors and the literature of the time did not contemplate. However, well-educated professionals are able to adjust to new problems and new circumstances.

Schools of social work are more concerned about the larger issues and the long-range future, whereas potential employers are interested in employees who can immediately and efficiently assume agency responsibilities. This difference in focus may create tensions between the two groups. The answer for employers is to provide training for new employees that will be a practical supplement to their education. Even the military follows this model; military academies provide the broad, career-long preparation that the armed services follow with some form of technical training that is necessary before new officers can assume their professional duties.

The distinction between education and training offers several clues for managers who want to work with their staff members to help them perform effectively. The first clue is to avoid duplicating the efforts of institutions of professional education. Social agencies and other employers usually are not as good at preparing people professionally as are colleges and universities. What they do best is to provide specific training in the tasks that employees must perform to help organizations reach their goals. Therefore, the second clue is to focus a training program specifically on the agency's tasks. Showing workers how to complete application forms, how to maintain records on clients, how to use the agency's computer system, and how to implement the agency's policies are among the appropriate subjects for a training program.

Practical Training Versus Theoretical Training

Educators and trainers alike have discovered that most learners, no matter what the task, do best when the training provided is more practical than theoretical. Thus, the third clue is to provide practical training. For example, a training program on making home visits to clients is most effective when the learners actually make home visits with a mentor who is a long-term employee of the agency. Additionally, an hour's hands-on experience in using a computer system—perhaps entering information with a dummy program for a dummy case—is likely to have a greater impact than would a day's lecture on computer systems. Although this advice sounds simple and obvious, the reality is more complex.

All that has been said about training thus far leads to the fourth clue for managers: the organization must have specific learning outcomes in mind before it embarks on a training program. When it does, it can tell its training staff or those with whom it contracts for training services what it expects its employees to know once their training is completed. Furthermore, the organization should determine, through tests and other evaluative procedures, whether the objectives have been achieved. It cannot do so, however, if the objectives are vague, such as to make the trainees "better" social workers or "more effective" employees. Not only are such terms ambiguous, there are situations in social work in which one person's definition of "better" might be the same as someone else's definition of "worse." Therefore, it is far better to specify goals in terms of outcomes; for example, to increase the number of food stamp applications taken per worker per day from six to 10, or to develop discharge plans that meet the requirements for third-party payments in one-fifth the time that it now takes.

In sum, managers need to know what they want their training programs to be. When they prepare these programs, their focus ought to be on training, rather than on the broader, more philosophical, education. They must specify the outcomes in concrete, behavioral terms—in terms of what the employees will be able to do once the training is completed.

Internal or Contracted Programs?

Managers often are faced with the choice of having an internal training staff or contracting with educational institutions or private firms to provide education and training to employees. As in other cases when this choice is required, such as determining whether to use an accounting firm or to hire one's own accountants or whether to hire software programmers for the computer system or to contract with a software firm, managerial circumstances should be the deciding factor. In large organizations in which there is a constant demand for training because of the high turnover or expansion of staff, having an internal training staff makes sense. Generally, the costs are lower and it is convenient to have employees on hand who are thoroughly oriented to the organization's structure and purposes. In small organizations or those whose need for training is only intermittent, contracted services often are more economical, even though the cost per hour of training may be greater than in a program that has its own employees, because the organization pays only for the number of hours it requires instead of for extensive unused staff time or for unnecessary training. Better prepared training consultants can do more in a few hours than can less-well-trained internal staff. As is the case with many other kinds of professional services, contracting is sometimes the least expensive way to obtain help.

In practice, however, large agencies frequently use a combination of full-time internal staff and contracted services. Many times, the training staff does some basic work for new employees and carries out continuous training programs for employees who need routine preparation for their work. When the agency needs training in some new method or policy or help in solving a newly identified problem, the training staff contracts with experts to provide that specialized assistance to employees.

Because contractors may attempt to persuade managers to purchase training services they do not need, it is especially important for managers to specify the outcomes they wish to obtain. Many training contractors attempt to sell as many extra services as they can to their customers so they can make greater profits. For example, training contractors may attempt to persuade an agency executive or training staff that employees would benefit from "sensitivity training" or other programs that do not have specific outcomes and that may not fit the needs of the agency. As is the case with so many products or services, one should buy only what one needs—no more and no less.

EDUCATIONAL TRAVEL

One of the items that auditors and others who evaluate agencies scrutinize most often is the amount of money that agencies spend on travel to professional meetings, training conferences, and other away-from-the-agency activities. For reasons that are not always clear, many auditors assume that travel is primarily recreational and that agencies are spending funds on travel that could better be spent in other ways.

The fact is that many training conferences, visits to counterpart agencies, and other activities that involve being away from the agency are inexpensive ways to learn a great deal in a short time. Sending a few staff members to a regional or national conference on a particular subject, such as new ways to deal with homeless clients or victims of abuse, or investigating methods for using technology for planning services, may be cheaper than hiring consultants to train employees in these areas. When an agency's employees participate in large meetings with specialists, the agency, in effect, is sharing the cost of that training with all the other agencies that have sent employees.

The value to the agency of staff members' attendance at conferences is also enhanced by the formal and informal discussions of the conference with colleagues after the attendees return. Some agencies provide for structured, required sessions at which those who attend conferences make presentations on what they learned. In other cases, selected staff members spend time with the conference participant learning some of what he or she learned. But even outside the formal systems, the results of conferences usually are shared with colleagues over lunch, at breaks, or at other times in the course of the daily routine.

Although the costs of meals and lodging are high, the greatest cost is the time of the staff member who is in the training session. That staff person's salary is likely to be much greater than the registration fees, travel, meals, and lodgings that are associated with any group training activity outside the agency. Generally, the manager must ask, Is the training important for the functions of the agency and, if so, what is the least expensive way of obtaining it? Sending people to a conference may be the most efficient and least costly means, but only if the objectives of the conference fit the agency's needs. Some managers may consider training conferences to be fringe benefits for employees. Of course, the purpose of such trips is not to have a good time but to learn some new skill or method, to establish contacts with colleagues, and the like. Sometimes a staff member is sent to an out-of-town meeting to help him or her develop contacts that might make relocation possible, especially if the employee is dissatisfied with the agency or the agency is dissatisfied with the employee.

Generally, all travel to educational meetings and professional conferences should be for a specific purpose, and that purpose must be carefully evaluated by the manager. If the meeting fits the purpose at a reasonable cost, then the educational conference or travel for training is a legitimate expenditure.

MANAGERIAL RESPONSIBILITIES

Management, in many ways, comprises many small activities that, together, constitute a coherent whole. The application of management skills to social work practice requires a sound, conceptual approach to the subject, along with fundamental knowledge of some of the tools managers use in achieving their organizational objectives (Peters, 1987; Waterman, 1987).

Managers operate at many different levels in a typical organization. Chief executive officers, middle managers, supervisors—people in various capacities with varying responsibilities—all manage, but they have different managerial tasks and use differing management tools.

Although a variety of activities are defined as management functions, it is not suggested that all of them are necessary preoccupations of the agency's top management. In fact, effective chief executives in larger agencies delegate most ongoing duties to personnel at other levels of management so they are free to carry on some of the more important responsibilities of building the program and helping its relations with board members, governmental bodies, and the broader public (Brawley, 1983).

However, it is axiomatic in management that the person at the top is responsible for all that occurs in the organization. Therefore, even those responsibilities in large organizations that are specialized, technical, and delegated to other managers remain part of the domain of the chief executive, who must know about and find the means to monitor them. In social work's pervasive small agencies, the manager often directly administers activities.

REFERENCES

Brawly, E. A. (1983). *Mass media and the human services.* Beverly Hills, CA: Sage.

Hansenfeld, Y. (1984). The changing context of human services administration. *Social Work, 29,* 522–529.

Kelly, R. F. (1987, March). How to choose a consultant. *Inc.,* pp. 95–96.

Knighton, A., & Heidelman, N. (1984). Managing human services organizations with limited resources. *Social Work, 29,* 531–535.

Molloy, J. T. (1975a). *Dress for success.* New York: Warner Books.

Molloy, J. T. (1975b). *The woman's dress for success book.* New York: Warner Books.

Molloy, J. T. (1988). *New dress for success.* New York: Warner Books.

O'Toole, J. O. (1987). *Vanguard management.* New York: Berkley.

Peters, T. J. (1987). *Thriving on chaos: Handbook for a management revolution.* New York: Alfred A. Knopf.

Peters, T. J., & Austin, N. (1985). *In praise of excellence.* New York: Random House.

Peters, T. J., & Waterman, R. H., Jr. (1982). *In search of excellence: Lessons from America's best-run companies.* New York: Warner Books.

Stoesz, D. (1986). Corporate welfare: The third stage of welfare in the United States. *Social Work, 31,* 245–256.

Townsend, R. (1984). *Further up the organization.* New York: Alfred A. Knopf.

Waterman, R. H. (1987). *The renewal factor: How the best get and keep the competitive edge.* New York: Bantam Books.

9

New Management in Action: A Case Study

Paul R. Keys

PUBLIC HUMAN SERVICE ORGANIZATIONS often are viewed as so large, rigid, politically controlled, and diverse that management through people-centered techniques is impractical, if not impossible. Yet, as in any field, a few agencies stand out as examples of excellence. These agencies seem to avoid the usual administrative traps and to turn everyday problems into unique opportunities. In this chapter, a large, urban-county comprehensive human service agency—the Broward County (Florida) Department of Human Services (DHS)—is analyzed. This agency not only was committed to these principles and techniques, but received local political support and increased the effectiveness of its programs by using them. The examples and conclusions drawn from this extensive case analysis may serve as a primer on administrative techniques, especially for executives of public agencies at the city and county levels.

BROWARD COUNTY

Broward County, Florida, is the urban county immediately north of Dade County–Miami. Its major cities include the well-known Fort Lauderdale, Hollywood, Pompano Beach, and Deerfield Beach, as well as the lesser known Dania, Davie, Hallandale, Margate, and Oakland Park. In all, there are more than 15 incorporated cities in the county.

Broward County is a major tourism-trading area, port, and metropolitan area. Since the early 1970s, the county has been one of the fastest-growing areas in the country. From 1976 to 1979, the period of this analysis, the county's population went from approximately 800,000 to over one million. As with the majority of urban counties in Florida, the rapid growth in population created the need for rapid expansion of public services. Moreover, the expansion quickly moved the county into new governmental structures to accommodate the changing needs of the population.

STRUCTURE OF HUMAN SERVICES

Broward County is governed by a seven-member nonpartisan Board of County Commissioners, elected at large, but representing specific legislative districts in the county. The county administrator, appointed by the board, serves as the chief executive. The chairperson of the board, elected by members of the board, is the chief elected official of the county. The commission auditor, equivalent to a legislative "inspector-general," reports directly to the county board. The sheriff is elected independently, and there are other statutory county officers. Department heads, called "directors," are hired by the county administrator, with the consent of the county board. Although they report to the county administrator, they serve at the pleasure of the county administrator and the board in "unclassified" positions.

The county underwent a major governmental reorganization in the late 1970s. As part of the reorganization, DHS was created from a diverse collection of independent county agencies that had reported directly to the county board. After the reorganization, DHS comprised 12 divisions: (1) Social and Health Services; (2) Alcoholism and Drug Abuse; (3) Animal Control; (4) Emergency Medical Services; (5) Youth Services; (6) Veterans' Affairs; (7) Law Enforcement Planning; (8) Pretrial Services; (9) Probation and Parole; (10) Community Development (administering housing-related and community development block-grant activities); (11) Human Relations Commission (with a five-member, volunteer board); and (12) Consumer Affairs. The county stockade, the county correctional facility for adjudicated male offenders of "minor" crimes, was also part of the department. The sheriff operated the county jail for pretrial and short-term detention. By historical accident, the sheriff also operated the long-term detention facility for females.

Another outcome of the reorganization was that preference was given, by ordinance, to hiring a professional social worker as the director of DHS. In the late 1970s, the only graduate school of social work in South Florida was Barry College (now Barry University); hence, the professional social work presence in the area was weak, and many departmental employees were trained in other human services disciplines. The new department was set up to coordinate the various countywide human service functions, with the goal of ensuring the effective delivery of services. This was not just a cost-cutting move, because the county leaders genuinely were interested in providing the highest quality services at the lowest cost.

Major human service programs in Florida, such as AFDC, food stamps, Medicaid, child welfare, family services, and health and mental health services, are administered by a state agency—Florida Health and Rehabilitative Services (HRS)—which has district offices. In metropolitan areas, HRS districts roughly correspond to the county's boundaries. Public hospital services are provided by hospital districts. State mental health funds and plans are administered by county mental health boards using state funds.

County services are primarily funded by and address problems that are specific to Broward County, which, like all counties in Florida, is responsible for services to indigent persons who are ineligible for the state-sponsored services. Because the counties could receive contracts from the state to provide specific services, a county human service department, with a favorable board, could have adequate funds and innovative programs. Thus, any county in Florida could have a flexible and innovative array of services, depending on the local political situation. This was the case in Broward County, which had a history of the complex county-supported services just described. The earlier political conservatism of the county was an advantage in that the county commission provided local funds directly to local services. These local services could be flexible because few state or federal rules governed their application. Changes could be made rapidly, based on the needs of the county. Only a majority of the Board of County Commissioners had to be convinced for a program to be revised or a new service to be implemented. And, once a service was created, it could continue unchanged as long as there was a demonstrated need, or it could be revised quickly if the needs changed.

Each city in the county had a human services office, comprising 1 to 10 staff members. These offices were funded by the respective cities and were not affiliated with the county. They concentrated on the provision of specific city services, such as senior citizens centers, information and referral, and some counseling. In addition, the county had a number of private agencies that provided the typical array of services

of such agencies. The new director of the reorganized DHS, an MSW
social worker, was hired in March 1976.

APPLICATION OF NEW MANAGEMENT CONCEPTS

Theory Z Management

Theory Z management includes the concepts of Alston (1986), Ouchi
(1981), Peters and Austin (1985), and Peters and Waterman (1982), as
well as such Scandinavian management principles as worker democracy
and work teams and various aspects of communications theory. A
primary component of the theory is the development of intrinsic motivation so that employees largely manage themselves (Peters & Waterman,
1982, p. 72) and can exercise a high degree of "self-actualization" (p. 80).
The employees' assumption of personal responsibility for assigned tasks
increases their effectiveness and reduces their need for close supervision.
These ideas are just beginning to be mentioned in the public administration literature (Starling, 1986) and are not yet part of the mainstream
of public service management.

Theory Z was the basis of the managerial style that the new DHS
director brought to the department. These principles are outlined as
follows.

Action Orientation

Called a "bias for action" by Peters and Waterman (1982), this concept
was exemplified by the department's predilection to initiate programs,
rather than respond to its environment. This proactive approach is similar
to the idea of the administrator as advocate (Perlmutter, 1985; Perlmutter
& Slavin, 1980; Richan, 1981) and Berg's (1980) idea of the "proactive"
manager. It has sometimes been discussed as a specific managerial tactic (Buskirk, 1976, p. 92), but seems to be a novel idea in social work,
where the term "administrator" is synonomous with "bureaucrat"
(Neugeboren, 1985, p. 91).

The department was generally the first to propose solutions to the
county's problems within its purview, taking them to the county board.
It sought out the viewpoints of its "publics" or constituency, put them
into recommendations for action to the board, and worked to implement the recommendations once they were passed. Few actions were
disapproved by the county board. One reason for the board's acceptance

of the department's proposals was that the department tended to hold discussions with individual board members and constituents and did not take the proposals to the board unless there was a strong likelihood of their passage.

Group Process

The use of group decision-making techniques is a major feature of all the modern management approaches. The department used the principles of group process to solve problems and develop programs. The techniques were simple and applied consistently. The steps in the process were as follows:

Step 1. Either the department director called a meeting of those most directly involved and outlined a problem or need or the staff proposed and idea for discussion and support.

Step 2. Joint goals and objectives were discussed and agreed on by the staff who were involved and the department director. Then a team of staff members was assigned to develop the proposals and was given the necessary resources to do so. A team leader was selected, usually by team members, and subcommittees were created by the team, as needed. A memorandum from the department director formally recognized the team and spelled out its authority to the rest of the department. For staff members below the rank of divisional director, the department director held earlier discussions with their supervisors, although the ideas had usually been transmitted through the supervisors and divisional directors.

Step 3. The staff and the department director discussed the progress, obstacles, future direction, and future needs of the team in weekly meetings.

Step 4. A plan or proposal for a program was agreed on by all concerned and was accepted by the department director, perhaps with minor modifications.

Step 5. Constituencies (interested citizens, community groups, and allied agencies) were built and educated about the merits of the proposal. Details were agreed on by the constituencies, who informally consented to support the new programs.

Step 6. Informal discussions were held with the county administrator and individual county legislators for support, feedback, and direction.

Step 7. If informal discussions with the county board indicated support for a proposal, even with modifications, the proposal was placed on the agenda of the county commission so it could be voted on.

Constituents and staff were notified and appeared at the board meeting, supporting documents were presented, and the new direction was argued before the county board after a consensus was reached. This consensus building often included contacts with individual legislators by the program's constituents, orchestrated by the department director and the development group.

Step 8. The sponsoring division implemented the program after it was approved, but other personnel and budgetary modifications were often required to finalize staffing patterns for the new program.

Step 9. Press releases were prepared to announce the benefits of the new program to the public and to legitimate the program politically.

The process worked less than perfectly on some occasions. Most often, failures were due to a division's resistance to an idea that was proposed by the department. An example of a proposal that met with resistance is given in the section on *Problems/Resistance.*

Organic Structure

A second major new management approach used by the department was organic organization when the divisional leadership was capable of adapting to it. This structure went hand in hand with employee-initiated change. In using this approach, the department director assumed that the expertise for implementing a proposed change was to be found at the level of personnel who were proposing the change. The director also presented problems to divisions so they could come up with a proposed solution. In time, the flexible, organic structure enabled units to adapt and to solve problems quickly, often without the department director's intervention. It should be pointed out, however, that the department director, through retirements, reorganization, and resignations, was able to appoint new directors for the majority of the divisions. The new appointments were filled by persons who were committed to this new style of management.

The concept of organic structure was pioneered by Burns and Stalker (1961), Lawrence and Lorsch (1967), and Mintzberg (1979). Organic principles are associated with complex, rapidly changing organizational environments; long-range planning; flexible and changing organizational structures; peer supervision; decentralized decision making (at the level at which there is expertise); fewer rules; jobs with a broad scope; horizontal and vertical communication channels; and loyalty to the work group or team.

Because the department was new, the environment was changing constantly. Thus, the rigid application of mechanistic principles soon would have caused dissatisfaction among the constituents. New, often ad-hoc, structures were created regularly, in the form of various task forces and committees, to develop new programs, to explore new opportunities, or to resolve old problems. Typically, long-range viewpoints were adopted in approaching issues (*see, for example,* the team solution to the placement of clients who required emergency services described under *Client Advocacy/Case Management* beginning on page 156).

Also, through long-range planning and the anticipation of problems and potential solutions, the department, rather than the politicians, usually identified and established priorities for dealing with human service problems and issues. Because the department was able to define the direction of proposed solutions, it did not fall into the trap of allowing itself to be blamed by political leaders for nearly insoluble problems.

Using organic principles, the department used the same techniques to solve and prevent future problems. Decisions were not programmed (Simon, 1970) and, at times, were based on "hunches." The department's structure was flexible; in addition to task forces and ad-hoc committees, there were many temporary planning, implementation, and problem-solving groups. The department director supported any division that showed it had a need to change its structure for increased effectiveness by presenting recommendations for such changes to the county commission. Personnel were often exchanged among divisions, and new structures and positions were created to solve a particular problem. For the most part, these reorganizations were developed by the employees themselves.

The department never got around to developing a rules or operations manual, although such a manual was discussed on a number of occasions. Instead, departmental memorandums on specific subjects were developed and distributed. Most often, these memorandums concluded a decision on a changed direction. They were more of a codification and summary of many previous discussions and oral agreements than a unilateral direction to staff by the department director. Hence, little explanation of them usually was required, although they were available for "historical" purposes and as a record of prior agreements. The bottom-up style of management was a reflection of the department's decentralized structure and decision-making style.

The scope of jobs in the department was broad, with many employees taking the initiative for suggesting an improvement and then being charged to oversee that improvement without reference to their specific job descriptions. Job descriptions were often changed, on the basis of employee drafts, after a new direction was approved by the county board and implemented. It is obvious that given the various employee task forces and committees, the authority for problem solving and the initiation of policy rested at the level of the most qualified person, whether he or she was the department director or a staff member in a particular division. Sometimes a line staff person requested a meeting to propose a new idea; at other times, the department director called together a team of persons who had the expertise needed at the moment.

Communications generally consisted of advice, counsel, and information, either at weekly meetings of the divisional staff or in regular meetings of the project teams. Communication might run vertically, in the case of departmental-division discussions, but it might just as likely run first horizontally among divisional persons and only later be presented to the department for discussion, approval, or ratification. An illustration of the latter type of communication occurred after a weekend escape by prisoners from the stockade. The divisional director was immediately on the scene, coordinating the county's efforts and studying ways to prevent similar escapes in the future. On Monday, he presented a full report to the department director, with suggestions for a press statement and a proposal for an increased physical security plan for the facility. In the report, he also recommended additional training and selection procedures for guards and the name of a recognized correctional consultant who could refine and implement the plan. The plans were not new; they were developed by the Criminal Justice Planning Division but had been blocked by the sheriff's consistent political opposition to plans for correctional facilities that were not under his control.

The plan was discussed intensely and gained strong support from the constituents who were members of the department-created advisory group, the Offender Programs Advisory Committee (OPAC). The plan was presented to the county board, in the form of a supplementary budget request, as the "solution" to similar future episodes. This action forestalled the politicians from blaming the department for "inaction." It focused the issue as follows: How much more money does the department need to prevent like incidents in the future? Using this crisis as an "opportunity technique" (Koestler, 1963) the department was able to incorporate into the same package many correctional plans that had been set aside because of the lack of funds. After much press coverage recommending that the stockade be turned over to the sheriff (the sheriff had supporters in the local media), the county board made the politically difficult decision to continue the department's jurisdiction over the facility and to approve, from reserves, funds requested for security and other changes. The issue never arose again, and the department, with OPAC, proceeded with its other plans for correctional social services (forensic services) and other correctional programs.

Although the new style of management created loyalty to the department, the primary beneficiary of the staff's loyalty was the division or smaller unit (the group or work team), which is consistent with organic principles. In their assignments to committees and task forces, team members established relationships that enabled them to be effective in later projects.

The management style, although seemingly chaotic and ad hoc, actually focused on specific, but often unwritten, goals and objectives. The primary focus was on results, often through the principles of Management by Objectives (MBO). A mixture of subjective performance measures, such as hunches and the "feel" of a project (Peters & Austin, 1985; Peters & Waterman, 1982), and objective measures, such as quarterly MBO meetings, written reports on new projects, and monthly reports of ongoing activities that were read religiously by the director, were used in making decisions. This style is consistent not only with Lawrence and Lorsch's (1967) and Mintzberg's (1979) objective and subjective performance criteria for organic organizations (McCormick & Ilgen, 1985) but with Peters and Waterman's (1982) "simultaneous loose-tight" properties. These principles are further summarized in chapter 1.

Lean and Mean Structure

The structure of the department was always "lean." For the first few years, the only staff members in the director's office were the director and a secretary. Later, the office consisted of the director, an executive secretary, and four administrative assistants (one of whom was a graduate student in social work who was in a nine-month block placement from Barry College).

Administrative assistants, by design, had no decision-making powers. They were responsible for reviewing all incoming written materials in their assigned areas (organizational and staff development, community relations, coordination of the work of divisional employee representatives, fiscal and budgetary matters, program development, and grant writing) to ensure that they were consistent with the director's principles and policies. If the materials were routine, the assistants signed them for the director. If they were major or controversial, the assistants presented them to the director, often with recommendations attached. The assistants also were charged with management by wandering around—a concept delineated by Peters and Waterman (1982). For example, the staff development assistant and the director's main assistant were charged with bringing problems to the director's attention that they discovered in their own "wandering," on the theory that employees might tell them what they would be reluctant to tell the director. These problems would be acted on, when appropriate, and the assistant would notify the originator of the changes that were brought about by his or her suggestions or complaints.

Calls from the public, clients, allied agencies, community leaders, and divisional directors were handled by the director, who, often to the amazement of callers, answered his own telephone. Thus, the structure was designed to keep the director in close touch with all events in the department. Assistants gathered information and handled recurring and routine matters, which freed the director to "wander around" and deal directly with constituents, new program areas, the county administrator and county board, community leaders, the state, and allied agencies (both the administrators and the members of boards and committees).

The administrative assistants were selected carefully for their consistency with the director's style and aims, highly trained in county and departmental expectations, and given wide latitude within their areas of responsibility. Often they were assigned to monitor specific teams or task forces between weekly meetings with the director in case immediate questions arose or a specific decision or support was needed. The director was usually in the field, but, through county communications and a voice pager, was always available to the staff.

This organizational style is also congruent with the *Pareto principle* of time management (Alston, 1986), which states that 20 percent of the actions in any job or activity are responsible for 80 percent of the results. As applied to management, this principle means that 80 percent of the activities (the majority of the time spent in a job) are responsible for only 20 percent of the director's effectiveness or results. The director simply designed the office to allow him to concentrate on those 20 percent of the activities that were essential to the effectiveness of his position, delegating the 80 percent that were not. Monitoring or early warning systems were developed that enabled him to spot emerging problems in the less-essential activities.

Depending on the size of the division, the department usually had no more than three levels of supervision between line workers and the department director (Figure 1). A large division might be composed of line workers, supervisors, a program director, a deputy divisional director, and the divisional director (three levels). A small division would be composed of line workers, supervised by the divisional director (one level), with perhaps an administrative assistant to the director. A medium-size division might be composed of line workers, supervisors, and the divisional director (two levels). This structure facilitated flexibility and quick communications at all levels.

A deliberate decision was made not to create the position of deputy director. Therefore, the administrative assistants handled only specific tasks and had no supervisory duties in the divisions. The assistants were trained not to attempt to speak for the director or to use the director's name in the divisions without specific, written authorization from the director. The goal was to avoid a common circumstance in large organizations in which eager assistants give directions and issue orders to line staff "in the director's name" without the director's knowledge. Subordinates may assume that the order is an official one from their legitimate superior and carry out instructions that may be at cross purposes to those of the director or the manager of their division. Such actions by assistants are likely to cause serious conflicts, one of which is decreased morale among line managers.

A second reason for the lean staff was that the director wanted to remain in contact with the day-to-day operations of the department. The administrative assistants freed the director from routine administrative duties so he might devote more time to creative management, field visits, political and interagency relations, and innovative programming. His close communication with divisional directors also was a check against the administrative assistants' potential abuse of authority.

Contingency Management

Contingency theory, often called situational or path-goal theory (Blake & Mouton, 1964; House, 1971; House, Filley, & Kerr, 1971; Korman, 1976; McCormick & Ilgen, 1985), assumes that there is no one best way to supervise and that models of administrative behavior are not found by studying the personal characteristics or leadership styles of successful managers. Rather, it presumes that effective managerial leadership in a given situation is contingent on a variety of factors that reside

Figure 1.
Human Service Department after the Reorganization

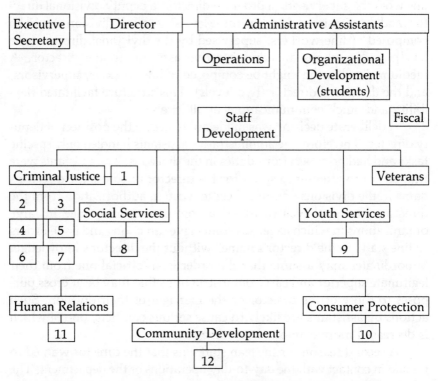

1 = Offender Programs Advisory
    Committee
2 = County Stockade
3 = Release on Recognizance Program
4 = Victim-Witness Liaison Program
5 = Citizen's Dispute Service
6 = Pretrial Services Program
7 = Probation and Parole Office
8 = Elderly and Handicapped
    Transportation Program
9 = Runaway Youth Facility
10 = Consumer Protection Board
11 = Human Relations Commission
12 = Community Development
    Advisory Committee

in the manager, the specific employee, and the particular managerial situation (Strauss & Sayles, 1980). In using this theory, a manager will adapt the technique to the situation. Hence, the same manager may utilize an authoritarian (structured) approach with some employees (such as recalcitrant employees or units), a supportive, laissez faire approach with others (highly motivated and effective professionals, for example), and a consultative-counseling approach with others (for instance, motivated but new and inexperienced employees). This was a guiding theory in the department.

The primary example of contingency management was the way in which the director related to each division as a separate entity requiring a specialized approach. Divisional directors were selected who were compatible with the innovative and flexible value orientation of the department. However, they varied in their congruence with the values of the department. The directors of the divisions of Youth Services, Criminal Justice, and Human Relations, who were most in agreement with the values, were given wide latitude to innovate and implement new programs. But in the Social Service Division (SSD), despite a few new staff members who met the criteria, the top leaders were locked into a rigid structure. Hence, some of the bottom-up principles were applied, selectively, to specific people and situations and a more controlling form of management was applied to the division as a whole. Eventually, the divisional managers were changed to reflect the departmental style. The Community Development Division (CDD) and the stockade were primarily Theory X-style organizations (Ouchi, 1981) and were supervised closely, although supervision of the stockade eventually was given to a newly reorganized division and a director whose views were consistent with the department's style.

Because the aim of the department was to balance the mix of structure and support according to the environment of each division, the department director might drastically change his management style in meetings with persons from different divisions. He would be supportive and encouraging and less directive with the innovative and flexible divisional directors, more directive with those whose divisions had a mix of employee capabilities, and most directive with inflexible divisions. In general, the more professional and proactive divisional managers, as described in chapter 1, required less direct supervision (structure) and more support, in the form of consultation, approval of their direction, and the removal of roadblocks to their already formulated plans.

Trust in Employees'/Staff Development

Another operating principle was trust in the abilities of employees and a related commitment to employee development. Recruiting criteria placed much more emphasis on the skills, potential, commitment, innovativeness, initiative, and problem-solving ability that the department needed and would require in the future than on years of experience. As a result, DHS hired many "inexperienced" people. These new staff members were given positions that were consistent with their potential and the needs of the department, with the expectation that they would be innovative and make their own decisions, after appropriate orientation and consultation. Staff development, therefore, was made a high priority.

Supervision was a consultative device in that employees were expected to think through problems and bring solutions to supervisory sessions. Initiative was rewarded in the form of an "almost made it" award (a personal letter praising an effort) to those who had attempted a major innovation.

Those who were most vocal and persistent in pursuing some improvement in the department were put in charge of resolving it. They were led through the steps in problem solving and the identification of opportunitites and were supported for their efforts. The department director acted as a consultant, removing obstacles that were presented in the weekly feedback meetings. When a problem needed formal intervention to be resolved, it was placed on the departmental agenda; that is, the director went to the Finance Division, the county administrator, the county board, or other appropriate agencies to remove the barrier.

Formal staff development activities included the following:

■ On a rotation basis, divisional directors were invited to attend the county administrator's weekly meeting of department directors. This device enabled them to gain a better understanding of the changes in the department, political considerations, and the county administrator's and department director's views of the county operation. Moreover, it provided them with visibility at the highest levels of the county administration. (They were the only divisional directors in the county to take part in these meetings.)

■ For every major new initiative, the lead staff person, or team leader, was invited to present his or her program to the county administrator and often to help convince the county board to approve the new program. These actions stimulated the team leader to think more broadly about the effect of the proposal on the county and gave him or her additional exposure to the perspectives of top-level policymakers.

■ An administrative assistant in the director's office was placed in charge of departmentwide staff development. Volunteer staff-development coordinators were selected in each division. The departmental and divisional committees developed an ongoing series of educational sessions that were conducted by volunteers, local college professors, businesspersons, clients, and others.

■ Attendance at local, regional, and national conferences was encouraged. Specific budgetary items were allotted for conferences and staff development. When funds were not available (or ran out), the employees were given time off for attendance. Attendees were often scheduled to report back to a staff meeting on how principles discussed at a conference were applicable to a division or to the department.

The result of these staff-development processes was that the department served as a training ground for county employees who often were sought after and promoted to other positions in the county and state. Although the turnover was not above average, the majority of persons who left the department went on to better positions.

Although this policy may seem contrary to good personnel practices, it was a benefit to the department in many intangible ways. First, many employees were upgraded in the department itself. Second, many of those who left assumed higher county or state posts from which they could assist the department. Finally, the department enjoyed an excellent reputation as a well-managed and effective organization, and this reputation was an important political factor in dealing with the county board.

Management by Wandering Around

The management by wandering around principle also was used extensively. Early in his tenure, the department director discussed his wish to visit divisions on a drop-in basis. The purpose would be to talk with directors, staff, and clients to gain a better understanding of the effects of the department's programs.

The divisional directors were asked to suggest ways that the drop-in visits might be carried out, on a regular basis, with a minimum of inconvenience to them and their operations. A compromise was reached; the divisional directors agreed that the visits could be unannounced but proposed that no division would be visited more than once a month. Management by wandering around did not include regularly scheduled visits to divisional staff meetings.

Management by wandering around visits were usually brief and enabled the director to get a feel of the organization. The director would chat briefly with the divisional directors, employees, and clients and would scan bulletin boards to see how central office communications to employees were being handled. At times, the employees would offer

off-the-cuff suggestions for improvements, or their manner and ensuing discussion might indicate the existence of problems.

A frequent device was the inclusion of two-way discussions with
the department director in a division's staff meeting. The meetings were
conducted by the division director, however. After the divisional director
introduced the department director, the department director would open
up the floor to any items that the divisional employees wanted to bring
up, saying that this was a routine meeting and that he was not there to
make any on-the-spot decisions. He emphasized that he was there to listen
to anything they had to say about the department and he would follow
up, in the event that action was required (follow-ups usually were made
through their divisional director, with a specific announcement that they
were in response to the comments or queries at an earlier meeting). In
the beginning, this statement usually produced a few moments of silence,
but then one person would invariably open the discussion with items
that were uppermost in the minds of the staff members, and a discussion ensued. These meetings eventually became much more of a dialogue
once it was realized that the department director would follow up on
the staff's complaints and suggestions.

Another form of management by wandering around consisted of
regular visits with community leaders throughout the county—persons
with an interest in the human services, such as city leaders, advisory
board members, local activists, and clients. By design, the meetings took
place in these persons' homes, offices, or similar sites (playgrounds, community centers, a friend's house, or restaurants). These visits were
invaluable as a public relations device and in assessing the pulse of the
department and public attitudes toward it. Moreover, excellent suggestions for improvements often came from these visits. Criticisms could
be discussed informally and often were resolved. The director avoided
undercutting the staff, however, through on-the-spot decisions; rather,
he said that he understood the issue, would confer with the staff, and
then would get back to the person or ask the divisional director to do
so. Reports of these meetings were given to the divisional directors with
comments or suggestions for improvement. When further contact was
indicated, the appropriate divisional director would follow up and
write monthly reports on the item to the director. A major result of
these management by wandering around techniques was the building
of a large reservoir of goodwill and support for the department's policies,
programs, and budget among many community leaders in all parts of
the county.

Open Communication

Open communication (Strauss & Sayles, 1980) was another principle followed by the department. Because most of the initiatives were developed in a bottom-up fashion, many distortions in communication were prevented by using this principle. In addition to the team structure and management by wandering around, two other devices were used by the department to further communication:

1. An internal program of suggestion boxes placed in appropriate locations in each division. The staff members were encouraged to submit minor suggestions through this system such as to paint the parking lot or to explain the impact of new changes that were decided at the county board's last meeting. (Major proposals were handled through the steps described previously.) The director, later an administrative assistant, monitored this box and developed appropriate responses to the suggestions that were made.

2. A system of employee representatives in each division. Representatives were chosen in an election by the employees (the county employees were not unionized) or they volunteered and were accepted by the divisional employees. These representatives served as a conduit for resolving the problems of employees in a division. They first approached either a supervisor or the divisional director, and their last recourse was the department director. Usually, problems of unfair promotions or the lack of promotions, conflicts with supervisors, unfair treatment, or retribution by a supervisor or an administrator surfaced in this way, although problems with a new departmental directive or regulation of the county commission also could arise. These problems were analyzed by the department director, and appropriate action was taken. Occasionally, the department director proposed changes in the regulations on the basis of this input or reviewed and changed the staffing, purchasing, scheduling, supervisory, or personnel practices. The employee who raised the issue was always notified (through the employee representative) about the action that was taken in response to his or her query or suggestion.

In addition, the county had a three-step grievance system that applied to all the departments. Problems were to be brought first to the supervisor, then to the deputy divisional director or the divisional director, and, finally, to the department director. The department director had three to five working days to answer the complaint and to take action after reviewing the grievance, discussing the resolution of the problem with the division, and agreeing to or directing a solution. The employee was notified on an official grievance form (with the director's response handwritten on the form). If the grievance was not resolved after these steps, the employee could take the complaint to the county administrator or the county commission. A similar process was followed for affirmative action grievances.

Citizen Participation

The literature focuses on the recalcitrance of the bureaucracy in accepting the input of citizens (Litwak, Shiroi, Zimmerman, & Bernstein, 1983) or the need to organize linkage mechanisms to gain the attention of a reluctant bureaucracy (Burke, 1983). Few focus on the role of citizen participation in developing a mutually desirable relationship of citizens and the bureaucracy. Vandervelde (1983) summarized the benefits of citizen input as involvement, influence, and power. Heller's (1971) study of business executives noted the following benefits: the improvement of the technical quality of decisions, greater satisfaction, freer communication, the training of subordinates, and the facilitation of change.

In the author's view, the new management of public agencies must include appropriate contributions by citizens, even though the rules on citizen participation in federal programs have been relaxed. Citizen input is a management tool as well as a participatory device. It has several advantages for the manager of a public agency:

■ It is a forum for communication with various constituencies who may help or hurt the program. It is generally better to talk with potential foes than to ignore them. At the least, this device allows the manager to hear information that he or she may not be told by the staff.

■ It is a constituency-building device. Committees, advisory groups, public forums, coalitions, and the like are all good means of communicating and building support for programs and for the budget of a public agency. The manager may select those local leaders or others who are able to intercede with legislators, governing boards, and other advisory bodies. Often, supporters of specific legislators may be chosen, which allows the manager to make an invaluable political inroad into the informal political process in the legislators' districts.

■ The needs of and changes in a program may be communicated to the general public and to legislators.

■ The community's perceptions of the agency can be formally or informally brought to the manager's attention so the manager does not ignore minor problems that later mushroom into full-blown crises.

■ In Broward County, citizen participation was used in a number of ways, two of which follow.

OPAC

OPAC—composed of persons who had an interest in better correctional programs, including citizens, employees of the program, judges, volunteers, and staff members of private agencies—was a strong counterbalance to the power of the sheriff. Its members were able to interpret and present the results of the staff correctional task forces to the media, legislators, and others without political risk to the appointed staff. The chair was an innovative elected official with strong connections to supporters of the human services on the county board.

The result of this process was agreement among the principals on a new direction for criminal justice services in the county. Practically, this meant political support for initiating many of the new correctional programs. Of special note was the Citizens Dispute Service (CDS), a low-cost alternative (free to clients) to the county courts. CDS eventually proved so effective that it was turned over to the county court system for administration.

The department formed citizens advisory committees, task forces, and committees to assure that all aspects of a new program were considered during the planning process. For example, volunteers and retired judges were invited to help define issues and responses for the developing CDS. Community leaders, mandated by federal regulations to participate in the Community Development program, were consulted, individually and collectively, to a much greater degree than was required on matters of planning and construction in their communities.

Satisfaction of Citizens

Community satisfaction with the department was facilitated by the director's visits to community leaders. These visits brought the department closer to the community in that the leaders knew who to go to when they were dissatisfied and thought that their input was used (they were told when changes were made in response to their suggestions). The leaders responded by giving increased political support to the department, because most of the feedback that the members of the county board and the county administrator received was positive and reflected broad support for the goals and the leadership of the department. Furthermore, the citizens' groups also were more satisfied with the department's services and programs because, in essence, they helped design them.

Because of the citizens' committees and the director's visits with community leaders, the goals of the department were relatively well understood for such a large and diverse organization. Opposition, owing to misperceptions of the department's goals, was minimized by the high level of direct contact with the community.

The departmental staff, especially the divisional directors, were brought into direct contact with the citizens' groups and community leaders. The result was that they gained a greater understanding of the community's needs and fears (in the case of correctional programs) and hence were able to provide better programs and services.

Implementing Change

This aspect of the citizen-participation process was the most useful to the department. The work of citizens' committees and other advisory groups allowed policies to emerge when the department director, for political reasons, could not advocate or oppose them publicly (in the case of political appointments). The following is one example:

A sit-in by blind students at a branch of the local community college was organized to publicize the transportation problems of handicapped students in general. When the students blocked the county's bus routes, at least one county administrative person suggested that the police be called. Rather, the county administrator sent the department director to the scene to meet with the demonstrators. Talks took place on the spot and later adjourned to a building at the college, where a committee was formed to discuss needed changes in transportation.

The department director scheduled regular meetings with the committee to devise recommendations for meeting the students' needs. A cooperative working relationship developed. In future meetings, the department presented state and federal reports analyzing strategies for transportation of the handicapped that were sucessful in other communities and invited transportation officials of the county to speak.

The student leaders decided that a combination of more ramps for the county buses and specialized door-to-door transportation was a good approach for Broward County. The difficulty was that the plan required additional expenditures for transportation vans. The strategy that was adopted was for the department to make researched, technical recommendations to the board that were supported by a coalition of handicapped groups. As a result, eight county vans were purchased, and a substantial portion of their riders were handicapped students.

The proposal to allow the County's Human Relations Division (HRD) to impose fines (it only had negotiation and investigatory powers for discrimination problems) called for the adoption of a similar strategy. Although the department director was in favor of this idea, the county administrator and a number of county commissioners were opposed to it. Therefore, the following strategy was used:

Leaders of various community groups formed a coalition to press for a changed ordinance to give the HRD increased powers. Given the county's opposition, the director could not take a public stand in favor of the changes. Instead, he held weekly luncheon meetings with coalition leaders at which strategies were discussed and compared. The "leanings" of the members of the county commission also were discussed, and the coalition then contacted supporters in the county board's legislative districts to get them to talk in favor of the ordinance to the legislators. The department's staff and coalition leaders provided constant feedback to each other on the proposed changes and on the ebb and flow of support. The result was the county board's vote for the change in the ordinance—a vote that was predicted accurately several weeks in advance.

Champions of Service

The idea of champions of service (Peters & Austin, 1985; Peters & Waterman, 1982) was embodied in the many divisional staff members with proposals for new services who were placed in charge of the development and implementation of the innovation, normally as leaders of teams or task forces. Such persons were recognized formally as the originators of the ideas and were given the time and authority to develop them. Weekly consultations nurtured the ideas; when the proposals were ready for implementation, the department director presented them to the county board. The champions often were rewarded with promotions to positions in the new service programs they had devised (the pretrial programs, CDS, Client Advocacy Program [CAP], Criminal Justice Division, Victim-Witness Liaison program, and others).

INNOVATIONS

Using the new management approaches, DHS received a substantial amount of national and local recognition for its efforts. In 1977, the

National Association of Counties gave the department seven awards for innovative programs in the county: CDS, the Victim-Witness Liaison program, CAP, the social services program at the stockade, the runaway youth facility, the Elderly and Handicapped Transportation Service, and pretrial services. In addition, the local newspaper published a series of full-page human-interest stories about the county's youth services and comprehensive plan for youth services, highlighting the future needs of youths in the county.

Moreover, the department enjoyed an excellent reputation among most political leaders, which often was visible at the time of budgetary appropriations. It also had a good working relationship with city, state, and voluntary human service agencies on most issues and participated in a monthly human service leadership forum for the resolution of problems held by the Community Services Council. Cooperative state relationships and contracts were developed to meet the needs of the county's and state's youth services and residential treatment facilities. Other measures were consistent with Patti's (1987) definition of the effectiveness of services, such as changes in the department's client system, the quality of services, and consumers' assessments of the quality of services.

As was mentioned earlier, the new structure of the department facilitated many innovations by the employees of the various divisions. The director and staff, using the new management principles, developed numerous programs, some of which are discussed in the following sections.

Correctional Services

One of the first proposals, from the Pretrial Division, was to establish CDS. This proposal consisted of a plan to train volunteers to act as nonbinding arbitrators for the "minor disputes" that were clogging the county court system, implementation of the program on a limited basis while further volunteers were being trained, and ultimately the establishment of a countywide CDS. A second proposal from the same division was to establish a program, to be conducted by the Pretrial Division in conjunction with the Probation and Parole Division, of pretrial release (after background study and classification) for specific classes of offenders.

Another proposal from the Pretrial Division was to study the feasibility of instituting a social services unit in the county stockade to classify offenders in the facility and to provide individual counseling,

family counseling, job-readiness assistance for soon-to-be-released offenders, help in establishing eligibility for AFDC and other benefits for
the families of offenders, and general prerelease services to reduce
recidivism. The stockade was administered traditionally and had few
well-trained guards. Thus, resistance to the proposal was anticipated
because it had come from outside the prison-oriented stockade system.

The final proposal from this division was to incorporate the new,
primarily volunteer, Victim-Witness Liaison program into the county
government. This program provided many services, including rape
counseling, the transportation of victims and witnesses to court, and their
orientation to court procedures.

After a series of discussions of the feasibility and acceptance of these
proposals in the county, the division and the department director agreed
that the division would form task forces of employees to develop an implementation plan for each proposal. The number and composition of
the committees, timetables, and other details were left to the divisional
director. Regular weekly times for the submission of progress reports
to the department director were set; these reports were to include attention to ways of addressing the political issues inherent in each proposal.
The sheriff, widely regarded as the most powerful political figure in the
county, viewed all correctional proposals as his personal domain and
was, therefore, opposed to the new proposals and, by extension, to their
originators. It later became apparent that even the term "correctional
services" could not be used in connection with the proposed programs,
because the term would be a red flag to the sheriff that would intensify
his opposition.

Once the implementation plans were completed, OPAC was created
in an attempt to resolve the apparent dilemma. Composed of persons
who were interested in the new programs, including volunteers and
citizens, OPAC was chaired by a progressive county judge who believed
in the proposals for their humaneness for specific persons in the correctional system, as well as their potential for reducing the ever-expanding
backlog of court cases. OPAC not only proved to be an effective lob-
byist with the largely favorable county commission, but went on, with
the assistance of the planning unit of the federal Law Enforcement
Assistance Administration, to endorse a plan for the restructuring of the
entire commission-controlled system of correctional services.

All the new programs were eventually approved by the county commission, and federal funds were provided for staffing. A later OPAC
plan called for the reorganization of the commission-controlled

correctional services into one new division, the rationale being that more attention could be given to filling gaps and better integrating the county's services with this new organizational structure. The new division was named the Criminal Justice Division, to avoid calling the sheriff's attention to its creation. Although the proposal was developed and supported by staff of the pretrial and other divisions, it was presented publicly to the commission by OPAC and was passed quickly, with little discussion, by a sympathetic acting chairperson, who had been briefed (as had other favorable legislators) on the potential opposition by the sheriff.

Client Advocacy/Case Management

CAP

SSD designed a new service to meet the needs of emotionally disturbed and indigent clients who were not eligible for any type of assistance. (The division had a general assistance budget, governed by county-developed procedures for determining eligibility.) These clients included adolescents and others who needed placement in residential facilities, older persons who required placement in nursing homes or other facilities, and clients who needed emergency services in the form of one month's rent or a mortgage payment to avoid eviction or foreclosure. Many of these clients were in such dire need that relatives or city agencies called members of the county commission directly with urgent appeals for assistance.

Timely services then became a political issue with elected officials. For example, at 5:30 P.M. on a Friday, after the county offices were closed, a director of one of the city offices (not affiliated with the county) called a member of the county commission to obtain emergency placement for an emotionally disturbed, acting-out adolescent. This commissioner, a strong advocate of services, vowed to the department director to stay in her office until the adolescent was placed. A series of hurried telephone calls to SSD staff at home effected a reasonable placement.

The director thought that a new approach to all persons with this type of need was called for so that future crises could be prevented. Rather than issue a directive, the director called a meeting of SSD administrators and supervisors to discuss a comprehensive plan. SSD staff were asked to form a task force to study the issues quickly and to propose a comprehensive package to be taken to the county board, because they were the experts who were closest to the issues. A supervisor who had been vocal in calling for action on a number of social services issues was chosen to head the task force.

The SSD staff had become accustomed to a rigid management style and found the idea of being asked to recommend solutions to be novel and potentially threatening. Therefore, the director held weekly meetings with the task force for feedback and support. He also gave written authorization for the task force to use the time and resources that were necessary to reach a solution to the issue, including permission to reschedule the work time of team members for meetings and to conduct a comprehensive review of all procedures related to this type of client. The result was the following proposal for CAP, which essentially involved the setting up of a case management structure in the division (Weil and Karls, 1985). The client advocacy team would consist of one CAP worker for each of the three county district offices. There would be an overall CAP team leader (one of the three team members), and each worker would be on call after hours, via a pocket pager, to handle crises. The CAP workers would set up procedures with other staff of the division for the referral of at-risk cases to CAP workers before a crisis actually occurred. The director asked the team members to present their final report and recommendations for the program to the county administrator.

When the new program was implemented, CAP workers were authorized to use whatever means were necessary to solve a client's problem comprehensively. CAP workers often interceded with the local housing authority for emergency housing placements, took clients to state offices to speed up the determination of eligibility, found jobs for clients or worked with the employment service to help find such jobs, assessed patients for nursing home placement, and directly contacted nursing home administrators. A key point was that, in their official capacity, CAP workers expertly represented the clients in other human services systems. If problems arose, they were authorized to call the department director, who called or wrote the directors of other agencies in behalf of the client. Eventually, special referral forms were devised, the CAP team was expanded, and CAP workers were upgraded, so they were given higher pay and discretionary titles within the county system. These changes were made in recognition of the workers' professionalism and independence.

It should be noted that all the changes were the result of proposals by the employees who were directly involved. The department director usually ran interference for the divisional staff with the personnel department, staffs of county agencies, and the county commission. After the CAP concept became institutionalized, the CAP staff continually recommended changes to make the program more effective. Later, they recommended increasing the county's general assistance and nursing home budgets, giving supporting documentation from their caseload. A 120-percent increase was appropriated for these services in the midst of the county's new zero-based budgeting process. The director never again received a call for a crisis placement.

Consumer Affairs Division

Another example of employee-initiated programs occurred in the Consumer Affairs Division, which was responsible for offering advice and education to and interceding with businesses to handle complaints from consumers. Before its reorganization, the division could only negotiate—not impose sanctions. When additional federal funds for employment and training became available, the staff of the division proposed an expanded outreach and consumer protection function to the department. This proposal was for new staff for neighborhood-based consumer education forums and, in some cases, regular visits to home-bound elderly people. Processes similar to those used for the development of the correctional program and CAP were used to implement these new programs. A divisional planning group was charged with submitting recommendations to the department director, followed by a joint setting of goals and objectives for the new program with the department director. The means and the structure were the idea of the staff members who were most directly involved and who had brought the proposal forward. As a result, a Consumer Protection Board (CPB) was created.

CPB was instrumental in obtaining support to revise the county's consumer affairs ordinance to include large daily fines for offending businesses. In addition, it performed an invaluable political function when the reorganized Consumer Affairs Division sought a new director. Given the attractive salary for the position, a number of local politicians sought appointment to the job. Normally, the department director would recommend a candidate to the county administrator. Given the political overtones, it was anticipated that strong pressure would be brought on the department to hire a politically connected person for the job, which called for a strong professional with expertise in consumer affairs. By turning the selection process over to CPB to present a list of three names to the county administrator, the department director was shielded from political pressures in the appointment process, and a proved professional manager and consumer advocate was selected as the new director of consumer affairs. The volunteer CPB, composed of county leaders who were favorable to the purposes of the department, was in a better position to resist outside political pressures.

Youth Services

The film *Where the Boys Are* and the media's coverage of the Fort Lauderdale beach scene have lured youths from all parts of the country. Hence, the city and the county periodically are inundated with teenagers and preteenagers who have run away from home. To deal with the problem, the Youth Services Division (YSD) created a 24-hour runaway youth house. Lodging, counseling, and reunions with parents in other parts of the country were the focus of this facility. Before the youth house was opened, a YSD staff committee drafted a plan to educate and involve the surrounding neighborhood so that the resistance to such a facility would be minimized. Staff members went door to door, interviewing neighbors, explaining the purpose and describing the residents of this soon-to-be-opened facility, listening to the neighbors' views, and inviting them to receptions and an open house to meet the youths. Some of the neighbors were invited to join the advisory board. As a result, the resistance to the facility was negligible, and neighbors often volunteered to help with specific activities.

YSD also operated a Youth Services Outreach Team that consisted of on-call workers. People could telephone the division with a complaint, such as excessive noise, auto racing, or roving groups of youths. The workers would be dispatched to these areas of disturbance before the police were called or instead of the police.

Not all the YSD initiatives required additional funds. For example, YSD, together with the department director, devised a plan that incorporated written agreements by the county, state, and school board that defined the components of the countywide response to the problems of youths, including the needs, tasks, activities, and goals. A separate section of the plan enlisted the aid of nonprofit organizations. A major provision set priorities for preventative and educational services to school dropouts.

Transportation

Human Services Bus Task Force

The generation of ideas for increased effectiveness was encouraged at all levels. For example, the direct services staff thought that the large population of elderly people who lived in condominiums could be helped more readily by a roving bus, staffed by divisional workers, who could provide outreach services on the spot and, if necessary, take an elderly person to and from a particular service. This idea also was suggested by a member of the county board. The director called together the direct services staff of all the divisions to devise a plan. He decided to involve this level of staff, without supervisors, because the matter had been discussed extensively by the line staff.

The director created the Human Services Bus Task Force, although the county administrator's office gave it only lukewarm support. The task force was departmentwide and reported to the department director through an administrative assistant. The first proposal was to redesign a used county bus (the bus system was county operated). All steps in the problem-solving process were followed. One subcommittee negotiated for a bus from the county's Transportation Division, and another subcommittee was charged with finding a low-cost air-conditioning unit, because a new unit would cost more than the $2,000 allocated for the entire budget of the project.

The problem of the noise and fumes emanating from an old less-than-perfect bus idling in parking lots (air conditioning is essential in the south Florida heat) proved harder to resolve. The entire project was put on hold for a number of weeks because the only choice seemed to be to overhaul the bus or to purchase a bus that was in better condition. Perhaps the most important aspect of this team effort was that it continued long after the department director left and finally succeeded in getting the county board to appropriate funds for a new vehicle designed to the team's specifications.

Social Services Transportation Program

A second example of an innovative transportation program, which later became a separate division, was the transportation program established within SSD. This scheduled door-to-door service transported elderly and handicapped persons (who were referred by directors of various agencies in the county) to shopping and various types of services throughout the county. Approximately 66 specially equipped vans were in operation by the late 1970s, and more were added from various funding sources at regular intervals. The program constantly experimented with new forms of scheduling to serve more people with the same number of vans. One such experiment was the use of radio-controlled vans and computerized scheduling.

Rescheduling a County Bus Route

The SSD staff found that many clients in the southern part of the county were continually late for their appointments at the health clinic. Although these clients lived only a few miles away, one bus connection was so erratic that it was difficult to determine how long it would take to get to the clinic. The staff approached this problem in a novel way, because budgetary constraints precluded the assignment of vans to these clients.

A team studied the problem and came up with the idea of changing the route and schedule of this county bus. Its members laid the groundwork for this request to the county administrator by suggesting that the bus route be extended. When the county's transportation officials objected to the lack of a bus turnaround and a new bus stop, the team convinced the owner of the shopping center in which the health clinic was located to redesign and repaint the parking lot to provide a turnaround and bus stop. Despite the county administrator's initial favorable reaction, this change was never implemented. Later, the health clinic was moved to a more accessible location.

Zero-based Budgeting

Broward County was one of the first counties to use zero-based budgeting. Departmental task forces assisted in the transition from line-item to zero-based budgeting so that it was completed on schedule. This transition is an example of how efficiency and cost-accountability functions also may work better with the people-centered new management techniques. Because they were familiar with the services, the line staff were better able to establish priorities for programs than were the budget analysts. In many public agencies, such decisions are made from the top down, with little input from the staff of the programs, which leads to resistance from and the lowered morale of the staff. In the department, however, the process was well understood, and the line staff and the department director simply used the new and complicated process as an opportunity to explain and promote their services.

Public Relations Team

In addition to the staff-initiated programs, department-devised projects called on personnel from every division to solve a common problem or to act on a common opportunity. The need for a positive and proactive public relations plan for the entire department is one example. The department director called together a team of persons from various divisions whom he observed had expertise in public relations and community relations to find a systematic way to communicate departmental activities more professionally. An employee in HRD, who had public relations training, was chosen to head the team.

Personnel in the divisions volunteered to channel news to the team leader, who arranged for media coverage. The team also planned exhibits in shopping centers to highlight the work of the departmental units and to distribute information on services to potential clients. Efforts to obtain the human services bus, however, took precedence over these public relations projects and generated a number of human-interest stories; nevertheless, the newly hired divisional directors proved adept at publicizing their own programs without the team's assistance.

PROBLEMS/RESISTANCE

Community Development Division (CDD)

The organic process worked less than perfectly on some occasions, owing to resistance by some divisions. An attempt to restructure CDD, to bring a minority person into an administrative position, and to shift the focus of the division from a "bricks-and-mortar" approach to a social-purposes approach is an example.

CDD administered the federally funded Community Development Block-Grant program, which, among other things, provided funds for the renovation and construction of housing and, in general, the restoration of neighborhoods. The federal guidelines contained a stringent requirement for community participation. The citizens' advisory committees were unanimous in their preference for using the funds for such social purposes as the creation of neighborhood playgrounds and community centers and the expansion of day care facilities.

The citizens' advisory committees and minority leaders also were vocal in opposing the failure of the division's leadership to appoint a minority person to any administrative position. At this time, a member of the county board wanted to attach additional federal employment funds to the division, to be used for environmental and beautification efforts in the county. The time seemed appropriate for a reorganization to accomplish all these aims.

The group processes discussed earlier were initiated but met with strong resistance in the division. The divisional director was asked to prepare a plan that would include the creation of a new management position and administrative unit to handle countywide environmental/beautification programs, the promotion of a minority supervisor to head the new unit, the addition of 700 positions to the new unit, using federal employment and training funds, and the design of procedures to review the community-development planning processes, including the appointment of the mandatory community advisory committees and the incorporation of more social purposes into the community development plan.

The divisional director repeatedly sent plans that did not include these goals to the department director and appealed to the county administrator to overrule the department's initative. The department director finally had to demand a specific plan from the divisional director to monitor the division's planning processes more closely. Despite this resistance, the division was reorganized to incorporate the desired changes, which decreased the community's pressure for the resignation of the divisional director, who was considered unresponsive to the community. The new unit was able to interact easily with the vocal advisory committees. However, the department director still had to monitor the operation of the new unit closely for several months to ensure that the arrangement was working as intended.

HRD

HRD engaged in two major projects. One was never completed, and the other was implemented after a great deal of political debate. The first innovation had to do with including the gay and lesbian population in the definition of a protected class, so it would come under the division's protection. Negotiations with gay rights activists were ongoing and without rancor but did not produce such a change in the HRD ordinance. A second initiative was to change the division's ordinance to include monetary sanctions against violators of the county's affirmative action ordinance, which covered public accommodations, housing, employment, and so forth. After intensive lobbying by civil rights groups, allied agencies, and the directors of the city offices that were not affiliated with the county, the ordinance was, by a close vote, changed to allow public hearings and fines for violators. These lobbying activities were coordinated by the department, although other groups took the public lead in pressing for the change.

APPLICATIONS OF PRINCIPLES

Many employees of public human service agencies throughout the country, although afraid to say so publicly, privately criticize organizational policies in which top administrators do not communicate with line staff, who daily face a multitude of front-line problems and have numerous recommendations that are not listened to. Such input from employees appears to be undesired, overlooked, or received negatively as "gripes." Secret reorganization plans, with all the attendant disastrous effects on morale and productivity, are, as most public employees will verify, the rule. Furthermore, relations with the mass media are handled defensively, which ensures that the staff, the organization, and clients are continually subject to self-serving political attacks. Often, the input of citizens is viewed as a "threat," rather than as a legitimate source of ideas for programs and support by a constituency that, if handled properly, can be a source of strength. DHS avoided many of these ills by the application of the new management principles discussed.

Many of the programs pioneered by DHS in the late 1970s are still being debated or are just being implemented in counties across the country. Many major urban areas still have weak human relations commissions, pretrial services, and dispute-resolution services. Programs to assist victims of crimes are still rare, as are forensic services in county jails, the case management of social and mental health services, and mobile human service units.

As was evident in this case study of the DHS, public agencies need not be rigid, bureaucratic, and autocratic organizations to be efficient and effective. Even with stringent regulations and political constraints, such agencies may creatively solve the problems with which they are charged. Using the new management principles outlined here, such agencies may provide essential services to clients in an innovative manner while maintaining a fluid structure that enhances their employees' satisfaction, development, and creativity.

REFERENCES

Alston, J. (1986). *The American samurai: Blending American and Japanese managerial practices.* New York: Walter de Gruyter.

Berg, W. E. (1980). Evolution of leadership style in social agencies: A theoretical analysis. *Social Casework, 61,* 22–28.

Blake, R. R., & Mouton, J. S. (1964). *The managerial grid.* Houston, TX: Gulf.

Burke, E. M. (1983). Citizen participation: Characteristics and strategies. In R. M. Kramer & H. Specht (Eds.), *Readings in community organization practice* (3rd ed., pp. 105–126). Englewood Cliffs, NJ: Prentice-Hall.

Burns, T., & Stalker, G. M. (1961). *The management of innovation.* London: Tavistock.

Buskirk, R. H. (1976). *Handbook of managerial tactics.* Boston: Cahners Books.

Heller, F. A. (1971). *Managerial decision-making.* London: Tavistock.

House, R. J. (1971). A path-goal theory of leader effectiveness. *Administrative Science Quarterly, 15,* 180–206.

House, R. J., Filley, A. C., & Kerr, S. (1971). Relation of leader consideration and initiating structure to R and D subordinates' satisfaction. *Administrative Science Quarterly, 15,* 19–30.

Koestler, F. (1963). Crisis, opportunity or both? In F. A. Koestler (Ed.), *Dealing with controversy.* New York: National Public Relations Council of Health & Welfare Services.

Korman, A. K. (1976). Considering initiating structure, and organizational criteria: A review. *Personnel Psychology, 29,* 349–361.

Lawrence, P. R., & Lorsch, J. W. (1967). *Organization and environment.* New York: Irwin.

Litwak, E., Shiroi, E., Zimmerman, L., & Bernstein, J. (1983). Community participation in bureaucratic organizations: Principles and strategies. In R. M. Kramer & H. Specht (Eds.), *Readings in community organization practice* (3rd ed., pp. 70–91). Englewood Cliffs, NJ: Prentice-Hall.

McCormick, E. J., & Ilgen, D. R. (1985). *Industrial psychology.* Englewood Cliffs, NJ: Prentice-Hall.

Mintzberg, H. (1979). *The structuring of organizations: A synthesis of the research.* Englewood Cliffs, NJ: Prentice-Hall.

Neugeboren, B. (1985). *Organization, policy, and practice in the human services.* New York: Longman.

Ouchi, W. G. (1981). *Theory Z: How American business can meet the Japanese challenge.* Reading, MA: Addison-Wesley.

Patti, R. (1987). Managing for service effectiveness in social welfare organizations. *Social Work, 32,* 377–381.

Perlmutter, F. D. (1985). Human services at risk. Lexington, MA: D. C. Heath.

Perlmutter, F. D., & Slavin, S. (1980). *Leadership in social administration.* Philadelphia: Temple University Press.

Peters, T. & Austin, N. (1985). *A passion for excellence: The leadership difference.* New York: Random House.

Peters, T. J., & Waterman, R. H., Jr. (1982). *In search of excellence: Lessons from America's best-run companies.* New York: Harper & Row.

Richan, W. C. (1981). *Social service politics in the United States and Britain.* Philadelphia: Temple University Press.

Simon, H. (1970). Traditional decision-making method. In H. A. Schatz (Ed.), *Social welfare administration: A resource book* (pp. 190–193). New York: Council on Social Work Education.

Starling, G. (1986). *Managing the public sector.* Chicago: Dorsey.

Strauss, G., & Sayles, L. R. (1980). *Personnel: The human problems of management* (4th ed.). Englewood Cliffs, NJ: Prentice-Hall.

Vandervelde, M. (1983). The semantics of participation. In R. M. Kramer & H. Specht (Eds.), *Reading in community organization practice* (pp. 95–104). Englewood Cliffs, NJ: Prentice-Hall.

Weil, M., Karls, J. M., & Associates. (1985). *Case management in human service practice.* San Francisco: Jossey-Bass.

10
▲

Administering Alternative
Social Programs

Felice Davidson Perlmutter

IN THESE TIMES of increasing political conservatism and turbulence, social work executives are challenged continuously by the necessity of maintaining the integrity of their programs, while facing the realities of economic decline and fiscal cutbacks. The literature on social administration is replete with these concerns (Perlmutter, 1984; Slavin, 1980; Wilson, 1980).

In the 1980s, there has been a proliferation of various types of new social agencies, organized to serve new or existing needs in more flexible and appropriate ways. Although special attention must be paid to the role of all the people involved, including the organizers, board members, staff, and consumers, the concern here is with the executives who are administering these programs. Generic technical skills that are necessary for administration are important in any organization, but this discussion will highlight the unique and overarching requisites that are inherent in alternative organizations that require special leadership skills.

A definition and description of alternative social programs is presented in this chapter and is clarified through case illustrations. Additionally, the implications of these programs for administration are discussed. Attention to this topic is of critical importance, because the mortality rate of alternative agencies is disproportionately high; not only is there a risk that an agency may not survive, but what is of equal importance is the risk of losing the unique attributes of the alternative organization and becoming a traditional bureaucracy just to survive.

ATTRIBUTES OF ALTERNATIVE PROGRAMS

The social work profession should welcome alternative social programs, because, historically, most social agencies in the voluntary, nonpublic sector resembled these programs, particularly in their early stages of development. The existence of a variety of unsolved social problems served as the stimulus for the creation of voluntary social agencies when the treatment of, or response to, these problems appeared both pressing and possible. Furthermore, the founders, with the élan of a social movement, took the situation into their own hands to rectify the inequities in the larger society (Perlmutter, 1969).

Although the early social agencies in the voluntary sector and the new alternative agencies are similar, Grossman and Morgenbesser (1980) pointed out that the early voluntary agencies have themselves become sufficiently bureaucratized and static so that new agencies are now required to meet new needs. These new agencies differ from the traditional ones on many dimensions, the seven most important of which are as follows:

1. The new programs are deeply committed to social change. They are concerned not only with changing the larger external system, but with altering internal procedures and structures to assure a democratic and egalitarian operation (Schwartz, Gottesman, & Perlmutter, 1988). The provision of service is necessary but not sufficient.

2. Directly related to the first dimension is the focus on governance and policymaking. Alternative organizations often are reluctant to acknowledge the reality and legitimacy of authority and power as being instrumental for the achievement of the organization's goals because the values of equality and collegial participation are the overriding ones.

3. The new programs are designed to meet the needs of special populations that are not being served by existing agencies in the voluntary or public sectors. Usually, these groups have a characteristic that is not acceptable to, or accepted by, the larger society, thus making explicit a set of values that can be viewed as "precarious," in contrast to the "secure" values that underpin the traditional programs (Clark, 1956).

4. The services themselves often are exploratory or innovative and are not available in the existing repertoire of the traditional agencies.

5. The personnel in these organizations are either deeply committed from an ideological perspective or are closely identified with or even part of the group at risk. They include a broad range of people, from volunteers to paraprofessionals to professionals.

6. The size of these organizations is a critical variable. Smallness is valued because it permits face-to-face interactions among the various participants and more individualized attention to the needs of consumers (Kantor & Zurcher, 1973).

7. Alternative organizations usually are in a marginal position economically, because the resources available to the traditional health and welfare agencies, both from public and private funds, are not available to them. Thus, Parsons and Hodne (1982) pointed out that in the design and development of an alternative agency, the resource base must be as vital an aspect of the planning as is the mission.

These seven variables that characterize alternative programs will now be examined in greater detail within the context of two alternative organizations. (Note that the terms "programs," "agencies," and "organizations" will be used interchangeably.)

Two alternative agencies serve as the basis for the case illustrations in this discussion. One is a direct service agency that provides services to a consumer group; the second is an indirect service agency that raises funds for alternative direct services agencies. Both are located in Philadelphia.

The Elizabeth Blackwell Health Center for Women is a nonprofit woman-controlled facility originally organized in 1974 to provide abortion services to women in reaction to negative experiences in commercially run abortion programs. Over the years, Blackwell has broadened its repertoire of services. In addition to the original abortion program, it now includes pregnancy testing, routine gynecological services, a birthing center with full prenatal care, nutritional counseling, menopause workshops, an insemination program, and, most recently, testing for AIDS. The center is guided by the following three principles:

1. Health care is a right; the profit motive in health care can negatively affect equality of care;

2. The needs of the consumer should be the utmost consideration in organizing . . . health care . . . . Consumers should be active participants in their personal health care and participate in the decision-making activities of the health care system;

3. Health care should . . . emphasize maintenance of health and prevention of disease . . . and take into account physical, mental, social and environmental conditions. ("Statement of Principles," 1975, p. 1)

The facility is run according to two major assumptions that are explicated by feminist administrative theory (Ferguson, 1984): a nonhierarchical, participatory structure is essential and the mission of the organization must focus on structural change, not merely on the provision of services.

The *Bread and Roses Community Fund* was founded in 1977 as a public foundation that provides financial support to organizations that are working for fundamental social change in the greater Philadelphia area. Special priority is given to small community-based groups that have limited access to traditional funding sources because they are considered too small, too new, or too controversial.

The internal organization of the fund has been carefully designed to reflect its philosophy; it is thus unique as a fund that practices what it preaches vis-á-vis alternative agencies.

UNDERSTANDING ALTERNATIVE ORGANIZATIONS

The seven attributes are discussed using the following case illustrations.

Social Change

The commitment to external social change usually is the stimulus for the founding of an alternative organization, because there is a pressing problem that must be solved and little attention is being paid to it in the society at large. Although external problems have been the stimulus for the creation of all social agencies in the voluntary sector, a distinctive difference must be highlighted. That is, in contrast to most social agencies, alternative agencies are not content just to address a particular problem; they feel compelled to *push for change* in the larger society.

Blackwell was started with a mandate to offer abortion services to women that would respect the consumer as a person who not only needed to understand the process but who would be entitled to participate in the decision making that was needed in each case. Blackwell's philosophy is explicit regarding entitlement to care; health maintenance and the prevention of disease; and its nonprofit status, designed to provide care to women of all income levels, ages, racial and ethnic backgrounds, and life-styles, including lesbians as well as heterosexuals.

Blackwell works to influence the extensive sophisticated and traditional medical system in Philadelphia. It has provided a broad array of nontraditional services that not only provide options for women but demonstrate the efficacy of alternative care. For example, not only was Blackwell a pioneer in the use of midwives, but it provides an out-of-hospital birth center. Although it is primarily a service delivery agency, it views its advocacy role as central to its existence; thus, its board of directors and staff members are actively involved in the political process at the state and local levels. The active anti-abortion positions at both the federal and the state levels will undoubtedly require Blackwell's greater commitment to this external thrust, while it simultaneously struggles to meet the ongoing demands for service.

Bread and Roses is particularly interesting in regard to the external social change function. Not only does it fund organizations that are committed to social change, it is an activist group in that it plays a watchdog role and supports and encourages advocacy. The fund is particularly active in publicizing the problems in the community and the activities of the various organizations it supports. Several examples of the activities of its grantee organizations illustrate this thrust:

■ The Kensington Joint Action Council organized a coalition of 33 North Philadelphia organizations in this low-income area to challenge the lending policy of a major Philadelphia bank that did not meet the requirements of federal law under the Community Reinvestment Act of 1977. The coalition won a $50 million, 3-year settlement.

■ The Disabled in Action, a group composed of people with various degrees of disability, has successfully brought to public attention the need for public transportation for people in wheelchairs and with other special needs.

■ The Philadelphia Lesbian and Gay Task Force has released a study that documents the discrimination, harassment, and violence that gays and lesbians have experienced in the community and has recommended various responses, including legislation and police training.

■ The Action Alliance of Senior Citizens of Greater Philadelphia has played a major role in the struggle to maintain special programs and discounts for senior citizens, including discounts from the Philadelphia Gas Company and a special transit program provided by the state.

Thus, the role played by Bread and Roses in social change is perhaps best understood by examining the organizations it elects to support. All are dealing with complex problems and reflect precarious social values in this society.

Internal Governance

Internal change is addressed through a concern with governance and participatory democracy; alternative organizations are suspicious of hierarchy and authoritarian decision making. This is a critical dimension that requires the most sophisticated arrangement, because the method of dealing with decision making often determines an organization's capacity to survive. Two dangers exist. On the one hand, the system may be unable to delegate authority to any subgroup and may founder in the struggle to achieve a consensus; on the other hand, the participatory ideals may be sacrificed for the goal of survival. Both Blackwell and Bread and Roses have developed interesting, complex, and effective strategies for dealing with this central issue.

Blackwell has made a continuous and self-conscious effort to assure a participatory, nonhierarchical structure that will effectively meet the organization's requirements while acknowledging the reality and legitimacy of authority and power as a functional imperative for accomplishing its goals. Its carefully planned system of checks and balances is designed to allow decisions to be made, when necessary, while ensuring participation, when possible.

First, the Board of Directors has special attributes. It is elected by consumers and is composed of individuals, primarily women, with special expertise or commitment to Blackwell's goals, who are representative, in terms of race, age, experience, and life-style, of the women to be served. Furthermore, one-third of the board is composed of elected staff members, and all board committees must include staff representatives ("Bylaws," 1976).

Second, every staff member is encouraged to participate in decision making, and mechanisms are continuously being created to help all levels of staff respond to issues that affect the organization. Thus, the administrative staff works to frame the questions, so all staff members can focus on an issue, consider options, voice opinions, and arrive at an agreement on the direction to be taken. New staff often have to "unlearn" attitudes of powerlessness that they bring with them from past experiences in traditional work environments and are reminded of the mechanisms provided for their direct involvement in decision making.

Third, in contrast to personnel procedures in traditional agencies, all staff members, except for the executive director, are hired and fired by a staff committee whose membership is rotated among all staff on a quarterly basis. This committee also sets the salary levels, within a range set by the board. Only the executive director is hired by the board, as is the usual procedure, but it should be noted that, even in this regard, the staff participates actively, because one-third of the board members are staff. Although Blackwell addresses the problem of participatory governance in numerous ways, at all levels, and on all issues, the ways cited here serve to illustrate the checks and balances in the organization.

Bread and Roses is equally sophisticated in dealing with its internal governance procedures that are designed to avoid elitism. It is an organization of approximately 500 members, consisting of three constituencies: (1) donors, (2) volunteers, and (3) representatives of grantee organizations. At its annual membership meeting, two boards are elected, each with a clear mandate.

The Board of Directors is responsible for all policy and procedural decisions except for those dealing with funding. The board must be composed of a minimum of 18 members, with representation as follows: four members must represent groups funded within the past year; nine are elected at large; two are donor members; two are from the Community Funding Board; and one is a staff representative, usually the executive director.

The Community Funding Board deals with all aspects of funding, including applications, allocations, grant-making policies, and procedural decisions. It must have a minimum of 12 members, all of whom are committed to and actively involved in social change activities.

Guidelines have been developed that assure that diverse interests are represented on both boards. Thus, one-half of each board must be women; one-third must be people of color; and one representative must be gay and one must be lesbian on each board.

Because Bread and Roses is a granting agency, similar to United Way, it has unique concerns. One priority is to assure a broad donor pool so that a variety of interests can be served. Any person who contributes $50 or more can serve on the board—a critical stipulation, because more than 50 percent of the donors are wealthy. In this way, Bread and Roses has dealt with the problem of the control of policy by a small cadre of wealthy donors.

A sophisticated mechanism also has been developed that recognizes the special needs and conflicts of the wealthy donors who are struggling with their ideological commitments. Two types of services are available to donors. The first is a "Women and Money" group, which is self-led and self-directed; Bread and Roses serves an administrative function only in that it sends out the mailings. The group develops its own agenda, which serves both a self-help and an educational function. Bread and Roses is directly engaged in the second service—the sponsorship of two donor conferences each year. Workshops are presented, usually in the following three areas: (1) personal (for example, money and friends and money and family); (2) technical (for instance, how to manage wealth); and (3) political (such as which candidates are dealing with important social issues).

Special Populations

Blackwell and Bread and Roses serve special populations with unique needs. Blackwell was organized because the traditional obstetrical and gynecological services of the medical establishment were not meeting the special needs of women—not only the reproductive needs of the young, but the special needs of women of all ages who are at different stages in their lives. It seeks to serve women of all economic levels who might otherwise be deprived of services.

Bread and Roses defines its target populations as local advocacy organizations that, as described earlier, are too small, too new, or too controversial to receive traditional funding. Local advocacy organizations are active in human and civil rights, peace and disarmament, workers' rights, and environmental concerns, among several other issues.

New Services

Services to these special populations usually are not readily available in other settings. At Blackwell, the original concern with abortion services has been broadened to include a vast array of obstetrical and gynecological services. Two will be mentioned here because they are unique or controversial.

The first is an out-of-hospital birth center, staffed by certified nurse-midwives, that provides a unique alternative childbearing option. The second is a controversial artificial insemination program for fertile women, such as unmarried heterosexual women or lesbians, for whom pregnancy is socially unacceptable.

Bread and Roses does not itself provide services; however, it makes possible a broad array of services advocated for or provided by the numerous groups it funds. It must be noted that Bread and Roses is always seeking new groups to fund. It sees its function as providing seed money for organizations to help them get started, especially because groups usually need a history of accomplishment before they can seek funding from more conventional sources. Two different groups that were helped with seed money were an organization called "Peace Tools," which consisted of high school students seeking to use the arts as an alternative to drugs and gangs, and a new project introduced to a professional health society that focused on the consequences of nuclear activity as a health concern.

Personnel

Personnel also are dealt with in a manner that differs from traditional settings. Blackwell's approach to personnel can be of heuristic value in other settings. The principles of staff participation in governance have been described earlier, as has the intent that staff be representative of the women to be served by the agency. This attention is illustrated by Blackwell's approach to salary. Because the organization is committed to a philosophy of equity, it limits the dramatic disparity usually encountered in professional settings. This was easier to achieve in the early years when the staff was relatively homogeneous. As the services became more diversified and more complex, so, too, did the staff.

Currently, the staff consists of physicians, social workers, health educators, nurse practitioners, options counselors, health care assistants, and clerical staff. Not only do the staff members have different levels of training, but many staff members have been with Blackwell for years, while others are new. This complexity generated tensions, and decisions had to be made regarding salary that would meet the needs of the staff while remaining committed to Blackwell's ideology.

The board and staff gave careful consideration to this issue and developed a mechanism for dealing with it in 1982. (Until that time, the only increases were across-the-board when there was money available or no increases when resources were lacking.) A formula was implemented, as follows: a staff member receives a flat increase on the anniversary date of her employment, the amount ($300 to $500) based on the number of years she has been employed at Blackwell, and the board grants an annual cost-of-living increase, which, in odd years, is a percentage of the individual's salary and in even years is a percentage of the median salary. In this way the disparity issue has been addressed, at least in part. This solution has been accepted over the years, and the issue is no longer one of active concern.

At the outset, there was little differentiation among the staff and jobs were even rotated. As the agency has grown and developed, however, it has been necessary to delineate staff roles more precisely. For example, some staff members began to play supervisory roles with students, volunteers, and other staff members. Although this change has introduced some hierarchical structure into the agency, the staff members relate to each other as peers because of the careful and deliberate protection of participatory and collegial mechanisms. Thus, regardless of level, all staff members have access to information and decision making and are eligible for board membership. Furthermore, the staff committee retains the responsibility for hiring and firing staff members.

Staff participation in decision making is not a process without cost, because it is difficult for staff members to move beyond their particular interests and knowledge of the organization and they often do not have a broader, or long-range, organizational vision of Blackwell. Therefore, ongoing discussions and staff development are a necessity, more critically so than for most agencies. But the benefit of maintaining the commitment to participatory democracy and governance is the overriding concern. The issue of personnel is less instructive vis-á-vis Bread and Roses, because there are only three staff members, each with a separate portfolio (an executive director, a fund raiser, and a grants associate).

Size of an Agency

Smallness of size is an important characteristic of alternative organizations. It permits the implementation of the central principle of participatory democracy.

Despite its increasing size and complexity, Blackwell protects the capacity of its participants to have face-to-face interactions. The agency has grown dramatically in 11 years. Its annual budget has increased from $220,000 to $800,000; services have increased from 5,000 to more than 10,000 visits; and, what is most important, the personnel have increased from 8 to 35 full- and part-time staff members and from 12 to 40 volunteers and students. In addition, the board has increased from 15 to 21 members.

Blackwell may be at the point of making critical decisions regarding its future growth and development, for it is clear that continued expansion would have serious consequences for its ideological commitments. The carefully designed mechanisms for full staff participation, which depends on face-to-face contact, could be lost, to the detriment of the unusual design of this organization.

Although smallness of size is not a necessary attribute for the organizations that Bread and Roses fund, most of the groups are small because they have staked out a particular point of view and ideology. However, there is face-to-face contact between the organization and all the applicants for funding, and the grantees can remain directly involved through the governance mechanism. It should be noted that Bread and Roses operates with only three staff members and enhances its capacity through the effective involvement of a large cadre of volunteers.

Resource Base

Resources are limited in all human service systems, but the situation is more extreme for the alternative agencies. Although much attention has been paid to the fund-raising strategies of these agencies, the problem is complex, because it entails not only sophistication in fundraising and development work, but care to assure that the mission of the organization is not distorted by the need to raise money (either in the amount of time consumed for this activity or its influence on policy).

Blackwell's funding sources have remained fairly consistent over the years. Approximately 80 percent of its money is generated from fees for the services it offers, thus providing the agency with a dependable base. The remaining 20 percent is obtained from foundations and private donations. Blackwell's basic strategy is to stay unrestricted by its funding sources so it will be free to set policy in any direction that meets women's special health needs. (Only on one occasion, one year after it opened, did the agency obtain governmental funds for a cancer screening program with a minimal grant of $2,500.)

Bread and Roses seeks donors from as broad an economic base as possible. Consistent with its philosophy, it values the smallest contributor and makes eligible for its board anyone who donates more than $50. Although it has attempted to diversify its base of support, at least 70 percent of its funds come from individual donors. Because more than half its income comes from a small number of wealthy donors, with gifts ranging from $500 to $10,000, it is critical that decision making and governance remain with a broad base of contributors—not just with people of means.

Bread and Roses recently has joined with several other funds in Philadelphia that are seeking to be included in the payroll deduction programs of large corporations and businesses. In addition, it is part of the Donor Option Program, which allows contributors to United Way to designate agencies that are not members of United Way to which employee contributions may be allocated.

It is essential that Bread and Roses maximize the flexibility of its income strategy to protect the complex grant arrangement it maintains. Although in its early years all grantees received the same amount of funding, the current mechanism allows for three types of grants: donor advised, emergency and discretionary, and general fund distribution. Because donors can express their particular preferences and emergencies always arise in this vulnerable grantee population of agencies, the development of resources must be a creative and unorthodox process for this fund that serves unorthodox and nonmainstream agencies.

It is evident that both Blackwell and Bread and Roses have given much thought and planning to their financial strategies. Both recognize that fundraising is an essential element in the struggle of alternative agencies to stay alive.

IMPLICATIONS FOR ADMINISTRATION

The egalitarian nature of alternative organizations, as well as their other characteristics, suggests that leadership/administration in these organizations is a unique phenomenon that must be carefully explored and developed. It can be conceptualized only partly in terms suggested for social administration, as succinctly formulated by Slavin (1980), or in broader generic administrative terms. The following comments explore this problem with the intent of stimulating further debate and discussion.

In an earlier article (Perlmutter, 1983), this author discussed three types of constraints experienced by middle management and placed them in the following order: (1) professional, (2) organizational, and (3) personal. Although these variables remain relevant for the discussion of the administration of alternative programs, a reverse, more appropriate, order is suggested: (1) personal, (2) organizational, and (3) professional. Consequently, this section relates the needs of the agencies to these characteristics to sharpen their understanding as the basis for a better matching of executive leadership with program. This author believes that special individuals are needed for these positions and that although the usual leadership traits discussed in the management literature may or may not be necessary, they are certainly not sufficient.

Personal Characteristics

Personal characteristics have been deliberately placed first in this ordering to acknowledge and emphasize the fact that leadership in this system is unconventional and, to use a metaphor from the field of architecture, "form follows function." Characteristics that are discussed in this section include values and ideology, risk taking and flexibility, comfort with difference, and the capacity to tolerate an economically insecure situation. A charismatic leadership style also is considered.

Of greatest importance is the individual's personal ideology and value framework, because the change efforts of the agency are central to its existence. The emphasis of alternative organizations on social change in the larger system requires a person who shares this commitment on a personal level. However, it is not enough to be a social activist in the broader sense. It is essential that the administrator ideologically identify with the particular social problem that the alternative agency is addressing. The dual demands for leadership in a cause-oriented context are complicated enough when one works in a traditional setting, let alone a fringe one.

The second personal characteristic of importance is the interrelated capacity for risk taking and flexibility. The growth and development of alternative programs is unpredictable and dependent on a variety of factors. What is clear is that the environment of such programs is not stable. Not only must the leader be able to handle this instability, and perhaps even thrive on the challenge, but he or she must set the tone that helps all the personnel deal with this reality.

Third, the administrator of an alternative program must be comfortable with difference. This characteristic is particularly vital, because many different types of people are involved with the organization, as consumers, supporters, or board members. In fact, the capacity of the organization to attract different types of people is distinctly tied to its mission.

Finally, related to the risk-taking quality is the necessity, and the capacity, to tolerate periods of economic insecurity. Not only are these positions low paying, but the total economic base often is unstable and unpredictable.

These specific qualifications will undoubtedly limit the pool of potential candidates. Nevertheless, it is important that they be recognized at the outset to prevent the personal and organizational trauma that would result from naïveté.

The issue of charismatic leadership is not clear cut, as it may be in other settings. Although this author suggested in an earlier article (Perlmutter, 1969) that charismatic leadership is appropriate at various stages in a traditional agency's development, the alternative agency is a different entity. Charismatic leadership may be dysfunctional in the alternative agency because it may dissuade or discourage other participants from remaining actively involved. It is not that leadership is not appropriate, but the nature of the leadership requires careful consideration and assessment.

Organizational Characteristics

It is necessary to understand the unique nature of the alternative agency to assess the implications for leadership. Not only is the organization dealing with complex social problems, something it shares with other human service agencies, but it is an agency whose mandate is not acceptable to the broader system. The implication of this fact of life is that the executive must, first and foremost, serve an ongoing watchdog/advocacy function because the broader system requires constant education and persuasion. In other settings, an organization's mission often is forgotten or ignored, but in the alternative agency, it glows like a beacon to light the way for all its participants.

Related to the advocacy role is the urgent need for constant fundraising and development work. Again, although this work is a requisite of leadership in all organizations, it is on the front burner at all times in alternative agencies. The readiness and capacity to seek new audiences cannot be overstated (Brawley, 1984), and the more creative and initiating the search, the better.

Finally, the continuous search for and development of new organizational responses to meet the mission of the alternative agency cannot be overemphasized. The agency can never rest on its laurels. Thus, for example, Blackwell's continuous evolution of new programs and new services demonstrates its capacity to seek new modalities to meet the evolving needs of its target population.

Professional Characteristics

It is not accidental that professional characteristics are discussed last in this listing of requisites for effective leadership in alternative organizations. Although these characteristics may be desirable for the achievement of some organizational goals and standards, they are not required a priori.

However, it is important to examine the possible role and contribution of the social work administrator. It can be helpful to relate the trinity of social work values, skills, and knowledge to this analysis. In regard to values, social work's values are clearly compatible with the social change and advocacy orientations of alternative agencies, as well as with the value of participatory democracy and self-management (Adizes & Borgese, 1975), a sine qua non of alternative agencies. The social work administrator must not only accept and be committed to this value, but he or she must be nonauthoritarian and ready to work in a nonhierarchical setting.

Focusing on the value of self-management leads directly to a consideration of the knowledge base of social administration. Attention to the formation of policies and the process of governance is essential and is linked to a focus on working with boards and lay committees. Furthermore, an understanding of social policy and the relevant legislation is necessary, especially because much activity may be taking place in the courts and be linked to entitlements. And last, but not least in the knowledge category, is an understanding of the planning process.

Administrative skills can be an important contribution to leadership in the alternative agency. Interpersonal skills must include the ability to work one to one, with small groups, and with broader community groups within and outside the power structure. In addition, mediating skills can serve a vital function, because, in many situations, sophisticated techniques are required to resolve conflicts. This is not to suggest that conflict cannot serve a positive function; in fact, this is an area in which social work administrators need to develop more expertise.

The final area of administrative skill is staff development; that is, the recruitment, deployment, and training of all kinds of personnel, including volunteers, paraprofessionals, and professionals. The staff development activity in an alternative agency will have some unique emphases, related to the particular characteristics of this type of organization. Of prime importance is the recognition that the personnel that are most likely to be recruited, at all levels and for all positions, will be ideologically committed to the program. Furthermore, a large proportion of the personnel cohort will be volunteers, who seek meaningful participation and responsible decision making in this social movement of their choice (Sills, 1957).

In addition to recognizing the importance of a sophisticated staff development program to help the volunteers and nonprofessional staff members in their demanding work (Schwartz, 1984), the executive must be sensitive to a variety of issues that directly affect the staff, including process versus product, the rotation of jobs, staff turnover, and staff burnout. There are no ready-made solutions, but a delicate balance exists in these small organizations in which the priority for providing direct service may come into conflict with administrative requirements for survival (Hooyman, Fredriksen, & Perlmutter, 1988).

Alternative programs serve a critical function in our rapidly changing and complex society. They must not only be encouraged to develop, but must be protected and nurtured. Leadership in this sector is a complex phenomenon that merits further research. It is hoped that this analysis of the administration of alternative agencies will be of heuristic value for that process.

REFERENCES

Adizes, I., & Borgese, E. M. (1975). *Self-management: New dimensions in democracy.* Santa Barbara, CA: American Bibliographic Services-CLIO.

Blackwell Health Center for Women. (1975). *Statement of principles.* Philadelphia: Author.

Blackwell Health Center for Women. (1976). *Bylaws.* Unpublished manuscript.

Brawley, E. A. (1984). *Mass media and human services: Getting the message across.* Beverly Hills, CA: Sage.

Clark, B. R. (1956). Organizational adaptation and precarious values. *American Sociological Review, 21,* 327–336.

Ferguson, K. E. (1984). *The feminist case against bureaucracy.* Philadelphia: Temple University Press.

Grossman, B., & Morgenbesser, M. (1980). Alternative social service settings: Opportunities for social work education. *Journal of Humanics, 8,* 59–76.

Hooyman, N. R., Fredriksen, K. I., & Perlmutter, B. (1988). Shanti: An alternative response to the AIDS crisis. In F. D. Perlmutter (Ed.), *Alternative social agencies: Administrative strategies* (pp. 17–31). New York: Haworth.

Kantor, R., & Zurcher, L. (1973). Concluding statement: Evaluating alternatives and alternative valuing. *Journal of Applied Behavioral Science, 9,* 381–397.

Parsons, P., & Hodne, C. (1982). A collective experiment in women's health. *Science for the People, 14,* 9–13.

Perlmutter, F. D. (1969). A theoretical model of social agency development. *Social Casework, 50,* 467–473.

Perlmutter, F. D. (1983). Caught in-between: The middle management bind. *Administration in Social Work, 7,* 147–161.

Perlmutter, F. D. (1984). *Human services at risk: Administrative strategies for survival.* Lexington, MA: Lexington Books.

Schwartz, A., Gottesman, E. W., & Perlmutter, F. D. (1988). Blackwell: A case study in feminist administration. In F. D. Perlmutter (Ed.),

Alternative social agencies: Administrative strategies (pp. 5–15). New York: Haworth.

Schwartz, F. S. (1984). *Voluntarism and social work.* Lanham, MD: University Press of America.

Sills, D. L. (1957). *The volunteers.* Glencoe, IL: Free Press.

Slavin, S. S. (1980). A theoretical framework of social administration. In F. D. Perlmutter and S. S. Slavin (Eds.), *Leadership in social administration* (pp. 3–21). Philadelphia: Temple University Press.

Wilson, S. (1980). Values and technology: Foundations for practice. In F. D. Perlmutter & S. S. Slavin (Eds.), *Leadership in social administration* (pp. 105–122). Philadelphia: Temple University Press.

11

▲

Modern Management and the Nonprofit Sector

Russy D. Sumariwalla

ENVIRONMENTAL FORCES that are challenging the nonprofit sector—specifically the human service subsector—and the responses of some nonprofit organizations in using the "new" management thinking that has emanated primarily from the for-profit sector are described in this chapter. The first section broadly defines and describes the so-called nonprofit sector. The second section discusses some of the key issues and environmental trends that are affecting the sector and the contemporary management ideas that have been adopted by nonprofit agencies. The third section reviews how one nonprofit system—United Way— implemented some of these precepts. The concluding section presents some implications for transplanting modern management thinking into the nonprofit soil.

ABOUT THE SECTOR: A BIRD'S-EYE VIEW

One may postulate that some rudimentary form of voluntary organizations existed from the time that societies began organizing on this planet. Over the centuries, as governmental and commercial institutions became more formal and entrenched, so did the so-called third-sector institutions. The three-sector polity thus evolved in the United States and elsewhere over hundreds of years, but it was not specifically articulated or studied until the early twentieth century (Hall, 1987).

Because the focus here is on the *nonprofit sector*, it is important to be clear about what is meant by it. Thus, what follows is a definition and description of this sector at both the macro and the micro levels so that the discussion may be related to the study and practice of social work (for various theories of the nonprofit sector, *see* Hansmann, 1987; Holtman, 1983; James, 1987; Newhouse, 1970; Weisbrod, 1974).

Neither Government nor Business

On the map of American society, one of the least charted regions is variously known as the voluntary, the private nonprofit or simply the third sector. Third, that is, after the often overshadowing worlds of government and business . . . The third sector—made up of nongovernmental, nonprofit associations and organizations—remains barely explored in terms of its inner dynamics and motivations, and its social, economic and political relations to the rest of the world . . . .

Yet it is within this institutional domain that nearly all philanthropic input—giving and volunteering—is transformed into philanthropic output—goods and services for ultimate beneficiaries. (Commission on Private Philanthropy and Public Needs [Filer Commission], 1975, p. 31)

With these words, the Commission on Private Philanthropy and Public Needs—commonly called the Filer Commission, named after its chair, John H. Filer—introduced its report *Giving in America* (1975). One is hard put to find a more eloquent or more insightful description of and discussion about the nonprofit sector than the one contained in this report. Thirteen years after its publication, the report remains the most complete and definitive study of the voluntary nonprofit sector in the United States.

After an intensive review, the commission concluded that the third sector is most broadly defined in negative terms—by what it is not. The sector is not government and it is not business. Conceptually, this is probably the best brief description of this major segment of our society.

After noting the outside boundaries of the sector, the commission report shifted to a narrower domain—the world of philanthropy—"a domain made up of private groups and institutions that are deemed to serve the public interest rather than a primarily self-benefiting one" (Filer Commission, p. 32). The commission used the legal approach to include organizations that are "immune from income taxes and eligible to receive tax-deductible contributions from individuals and corporations" (p. 32). But even here, it noted that it was treading on "fluid and shifting" grounds. Its focus was on Section 501(c)(3) of the Internal Revenue Code (IRC). (*See* Table 1 for a categorical listing of Section 501(c) tax-exempt organizations.) To qualify for an exemption under this section, an organization must operate exclusively for one or more of these purposes: charitable, religious, scientific, literary, educational, testing for public safety, and prevention of cruelty to children or animals. However, as the commission discovered, even these boundaries, although narrower than those set by the nongovernment–nonprofit definition, are "immensely broad and vague." The commission asked, somewhat rhetorically, What is charitable? What is educational? What is religious?

The commission also resisted the temptation to establish a definition or principle by which nonprofit, nongovernmental organizations can be judged to be in the public interest and thus a proper concern of and channel for philanthropy. It wisely recognized that a certain flexibility is desirable, both philosophically and legally, in defining the public interest, noting:

> One of the main virtues of the private nonprofit sector lies in its very testing and extension of any definition of the public interest, so it would be counter-productive to try to establish boundaries in more than a general, expandable sense. (p. 33)

Moreover, recognizing that none of the existing names is universally admired, the commission made no attempt to attach a new, better name to the territory under examination. Thus, throughout its report, the commission opted to use the terms, "voluntary sector," "private nonprofit sector," "nonprofit sector," or "third sector," interchangeably; however, it excluded (except when otherwise specified) organizations that primarily serve the interest of their members.

The following is the proposed working definition of the sector at two levels—(1) the all-inclusive level and (2) a narrower level. The *nonbusiness–nongovernmental (NB–NG) sector* may be defined as

> the totality of all those organized entities whose basic organizing purpose is not to make profit for its members or owners, and, though operating within the general legal framework, whose acts or day-to-day operations do not possess the sanction or authority similar to those normally identified with duly elected or otherwise legally created governmental entities. (Sumariwalla, 1983, p. 7)

The reader will note that the term "nonbusiness" is preferred over the term "nonprofit" and that it was proposed by the Financial Accounting Standards Board as being more accurate (Anthony, 1978). The term

Table 1.

Internal Revenue Code, Section 501(c): Exempt Organizations,
as of December 31, 1987

Section of IRC	Description of Organization	Number of Entities
501(c)(1)	Corporations organized under Act of Congress	41
501(c)(2)	Title-holding corporation for exempt organizations	5,719
501(c)(3)	Religious, educational, charitable, scientific, literary, testing for public safety, or prevention of cruelty to children or animals organizations	400,160
501(c)(4)	Civic leagues, social welfare organizations, local associations of employees	130,170
501(c)(5)	Labor, agricultural, and horticultural organizations	69,782
501(c)(6)	Business leagues, chambers of commerce, real estate boards	56,989
501(c)(7)	Social and recreation clubs	56,379
501(c)(8)	Fraternal beneficiary societies and associations	87,999
501(c)(9)	Voluntary employees beneficiary associations	10,460
501(c)(10)	Domestic fraternal societies and associations	16,890
501(c)(11)	Teachers' retirement fund associations	9
501(c)(12)	Benevolent life insurance associations, mutual ditch and irrigation companies, mutual or cooperative telephone associations, and similar organizations	5,462
501(c)(13)	Cemetery companies	7,851
501(c)(14)	State-chartered credit unions, mutual reserve funds	6,615
501(c)(15)	Mutual insurance companies or associations	941
501(c)(16)	Cooperative organizations to finance crop operations	18
501(c)(17)	Supplemental unemployment benefit trusts	696
501(c)(18)	Employee-funded pension trusts	9
501(c)(19)	Post or organizations of past or present members of armed forces of U.S.	24,605

Table 1. (Continued)

Section of IRC	Description of Organization	Number of Entities
501(c)(20)	Group legal services plan organizations	203
501(c)(21)	Black-lung benefits trusts	21
501(c)(22)	Withdrawal liability payment fund	0
501(c)(23)	Veterans organization (organized before 1880)	0
501(c)(24)	Pension plan termination trust	0
501(c)(25)	Title holding corporation or trust	0
	Total	881,019

SOURCE: U.S. Department of the Treasury, IRS.

"nonprofit," although in common usage, has caused some misunderstanding because it implies that these organizations may not or do not make a profit—an excess of income over expenses. Not only do many of these organizations have excess income, they engage in related or unrelated activities to generate it. Alternatively, some have considered the term "not for profit" to be a more accurate description (United Way, 1974).

The NB–NG sector, as just defined, may be divided into two broad categories: public-interest entities (PIEs) and all other NB–NG entities. For the purposes of this chapter, the PIE subsector is defined as

the totality of all those organized entities whose basic organizing purpose is to promote or advance some public, social or group good—as contrasted with those organized primarily to benefit its membership—via one or more of the following: provision of direct assistance or personal services; advocacy; public education; propagation of ideas and information; distribution of financial and non-financial resources; and, voluntarism and volunteer work. (Sumariwalla, 1983, p. 7)

As is true of all classification endeavors, this division of the NB–NG sector creates a problem of classifying borderline or dual-purpose entities. Religious organizations are one major group that is susceptible to this problem. This author thinks that religious entities whose primary purpose is to provide for the spiritual development and guidance of its members should not be classified under the PIE subsector. However, auxiliaries or adjuncts of religious entities that are established specifically to provide health, welfare, education, and other human care services may be included in the PIE subsector. (See Figure 1 for alternative approaches to classifying the NB–NG sector and PIE subsector within the context of all organizations of society.)

Figure 1.
Alternative Approaches to Classification of Organizations

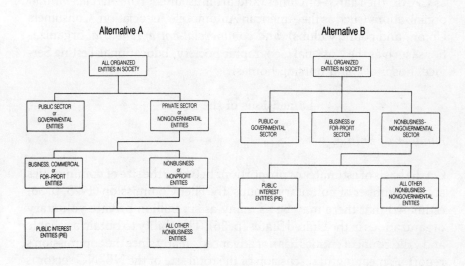

Alternative A

Alternative B

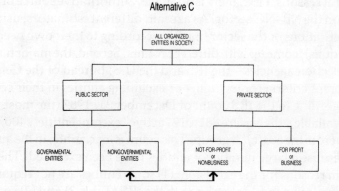

Alternative C

Hansmann (1987) proposed another approach to classifying this sector on the basis of the source of income and the manner in which these entities are controlled. His four-way categorization involves *donative-mutual* organizations (such as Common Cause, the National Audubon Society, and political clubs); *donative-entrepreneurial* organizations (such as CARE, the March of Dimes, and art museums); *commercial-mutual* organizations (such as the American Automobile Association, Consumers Union, and country clubs); and *commercial-entrepreneurial* organizations (such as the National Geographic Society, Educational Testing Service, hospitals, and nursing homes).

Dimensions of the Sector

Number of Entities

On the basis of estimates of proportions between the size of communities and the number of voluntary groups, the Filer Commission (1975, p. 36) estimated that there may be as many as six million private voluntary organizations in the United States (p. 36). The ability to obtain a reliable and valid count of entities has *not* advanced greatly since the commission's report. A meaningful discussion of the total size of the NB–NG sector is confusing at best without a proper count of the total number of entities for several reasons. First, there is no single, authoritative source of information on the NB–NG sector. As a result, different estimators, using different definitions of the sector (mostly according to their own needs and predilections), come up with different counts. Second, the major national data collection agencies—the IRS and the U.S. Bureau of the Census—use different criteria for including or excluding entities in their counts.

According to the IRS count of December 31, 1987 (the most recent count available), there were 881,019 "active" exempt entities, 400,160 of which were in the 501(c)(3) group. This count is inaccurate, in the author's view, because a large number of entities have been excluded. There are two main reasons for the exclusion: (1) some entities are not required by law or regulation to file a return with the IRS (Table 2) and (2) some entities, although required to file, do not bother to file. The following types of organizations are not required to file an annual information return, according to the IRC:

1. A church, an interchurch organization of local units of a church, a convention or association of churches, an integrated auxiliary of a church, or an internally supported church-controlled organization;

Table 2.
National Taxonomy of Exempt Entities

I. **Arts, Culture, Humanities**
   A—Arts, culture, humanities

II. **Education**
   B—Education/instruction and related—formal and nonformal

III. **Environment and Animals**
   C—Environmental quality, protection and beautification (including Environmental Health and Safety)
   D—Animal related

IV. **Health**
   E—Health—general and rehabilitation
   F—Health—mental health, crisis intervention
   G—Health—mental retardation/developmentally disabled

V. **Human Services**
   H—Consumer protection, legal aid
   I—Crime and delinquency prevention–public protection
   J—Employment/jobs
   K—Food, nutrition, agriculture
   L—Housing/shelter
   M—Public safety, emergency preparedness and relief
   N—Recreation, leisure, sports, athletics
   O—Youth development
   P—Human service, other, including multipurpose (also, social services—individual and family)

VI. **International**
   Q—International/foreign

VII. **Public/Society Benefit—General**
   R—Civil rights, social action, advocacy
   S—Community improvement, community capacity building
   T—Grantmaking/foundations
   U—Research, planning, science, technology, technical assistance
   V—Voluntarism, philanthropy, charity

VIII. **Religion**
   W—Religion related/spiritual development

IX. **Other, Including Nonclassifiable**
   X—Reserved for new major group (future)
   Y—Mutual membership benefit
   Z—Nonclassifiable—to be used as a temporary code until information is available to classify entity in one of the major groups A–Y

SOURCE: *National Taxonomy of Exempt Entities*, developed by the author for the National Center for Charitable Statistics (Washington, DC: Independent Sector, 1987).

2. An exclusively religious activity of any religious order;
3. An organization (other than a private foundation) having gross receipts in each tax year that normally are not more than $25,000;
4. A mission society sponsored by or affiliated with one or more churches or church denominations, more than one-half of the activities of which society are conducted in, or directed at persons in, foreign countries;
5. A school below college level affiliated with a church or operated by a religious order, even though it is not an integrated auxiliary of a church;
6. A state institution, the income of which is excluded from gross income under section 115(a);
7. A corporation organized under an Act of Congress that is described in section 501(c)(1);
8. A stock bonus, pension, or profit-sharing trust which qualified under section 401; or
9. A black lung benefit trust described in section 501(c)(21).

As for those entities that are required to file but do not, it would be a mistake to think of them as too small or unimportant. Research by The Urban Institute indicates that thousands of organizations, many of which have revenues in excess of $50,000, may not be found on the IRS master file (see Salamon and Abramson, 1982). Also, a number of these organizations may have never bothered to seek a tax-exempt ruling from the IRS partly because they are not dependent on tax-deductible contributions. In any case, there is a large but unestimatable number of NB–NG entities that are not included in the IRS count.

The U.S. Bureau of the Census studies include only those entities with at least one paid employee. Thus, they exclude all-volunteer organizations. They also exclude, among others, all religious organizations, which are probably the most numerous of all NB–NG organizations.

It should be noted as well that any count of NB-NG organizations would fluctuate from day to day. Some of these entities merge, many dissolve, and others are born daily. The growth during the 1983–87 period was phenomenal. Almost 100,000 new Section 501(c)(3) entities were added to the IRS rolls during that period.

Other Quantitative Measures

Except for students of the NB–NG sector, few Americans know the strength and vitality of this sector in economic terms. The following is a brief summary of just a few of these measures.

Revenue. In 1984, the total revenues of the NB–NG sector from all sources exceeded $250 billion (Hodgkinson and Weitzman, 1986), roughly 27 percent of the total coming from the government and 27 percent from contributions. In 1987, this author estimates that charitable contributions from individual Americans—among the most generous people on this planet—will surpass $80 billion.

Expenditures. Current operating expenditures for the sector exceeded $200 billion in 1984 (Hodgkinson & Weitzman, 1986). The sector represents about 5 percent of the U.S. gross national product (GNP) but 18 percent of all services in the personal-consumption-expenditures component of the GNP (Hodgkinson & Weitzman, 1986). The magnitude of this phenomenon has caused one scholar to observe that the overall budget of the "philanthropic" component (mostly Section 501(c)(3) organizations) exceeds the budgets of all nations of the world (in dollar terms) except the United States, France, West Germany, the United Kingdom, Japan, and, most likely, China and the USSR (Rudney, 1981).

Assets. Total assets of Section 501(c)(3) organizations, excluding religious institutions, exceeded $325 billion in 1982 (Hodgkinson & Weitzman, 1986).

Employment. In 1982, Section 501(c)(3) organizations employed in excess of 6.5 million people, including part-time workers (Hodgkinson & Weitzman, 1986). The author's estimate for employment in the total NB–NG sector is over 8 million workers, or roughly 8 percent of the total U.S. work force.

Volunteer Service. The use of volunteers is a unique dimension of the NB–NG sector. According to a 1985 study entitled *Americans volunteer* (Independent Sector, 1985), about 89 million, or almost one out of two, adult Americans performed some volunteer service. These volunteers contributed an estimated 16 billion hours, the dollar value of which was estimated at $110 billion (Independent Sector, 1985).

Product or Impact Measures

What does the sector produce? Who are its beneficiaries? What is its impact on society? In a sense, depending on the type of entity chosen, the product of an NB–NG entity may be no different from that of a governmental or business entity. For example, the "product" of an NB–NG hospital or university is no different from that of a state-controlled or for-profit hospital or university. However, the products of thousands of institutions and organizations belonging to the NB–NG sector, particularly, the public-interest subsector, are often intangible, and benefits accrue to the society as a whole in the long term. This aspect of the NB–NG sector is well summarized in the Filer Commission report. Referring to the "ultimate beneficiaries" of the NB–NG sector, the commission (Filer Commission, 1975) observed:

> The arithmetic of the nonprofit sector finds much of its significance in less quantifiable and even less precise dimensions—in the human measurements of who is served, who is affected by nonprofit groups and activities. In some sense, everybody is: the contributions of voluntary organizations to broadscale social and scientific advances have been widely and frequently extolled. Charitable groups were in the forefront of ridding society of child labor, abolitionist groups in tearing down the institution of slavery, civic-minded groups in purging the spoils system from public office. The benefits of nonprofit scientific and technological research include the great reduction of scourges such as tuberculosis and polio, malaria, typhus, influenza, rabies, yaws, bilharziasis, syphilis, and amoebic dysentery. These are among the myriad products of the nonprofit sector that have at least indirectly affected all Americans and much of the rest of the world besides. (p. 37)

The Hybrid Sector

What originated as "neither government nor business" in its purest form has evolved into a hybrid with elements of both. The increasing interdependence and intertwining of the three sectors sometimes causes one to wonder whether an agency is governmental, business, or neither—that is, voluntary nonprofit. Increasingly, the boundaries between public and private, profit and nonprofit, governmental and nongovernmental, are blurred.

Nonprofit–Government Connection

On the one hand is the phenomenon of the growing dependence by voluntary nonprofit organizations on governmental funds for the provision of services. The range of dependence on governmental support is from less than 5 percent of the operating budgets of some agencies to more than 95 percent of the budgets of others. Many of these agencies receive over one-half their income from governmental sources. Recent studies by The Urban Institute's Nonprofit Sector Project illuminated this phenomenon. According to Salamon (1987), these studies showed that, in the aggregate, federal government support accounted for 35 percent of the total expenditures of "nonprofit service organizations" (excluding religious congregations) in 1980. A survey of 3,400 nonprofit human service agencies, Salamon also noted, revealed that federal, state, and local governments accounted for 41 percent of the income of these agencies in 1981 and that service fees and charges constituted the second largest source of income at 28 percent of the total. This close operating relationship between the government and NB–NG-sector agencies is further established by the fact that these agencies provided 42 percent of the government-funded human services, whereas governmental agencies provided 39 percent and for-profit companies provided 19 percent of these services (Salamon, 1987).

Nonprofit–For-Profit Connection

More and more NB–NG entities are relying on fees for service and related and unrelated business income for their operating income. Skloot (1983, 1987) gives four major reasons for the spurt in commercial and entrepreneurial activities in the NB–NG sector since 1980: (1) the double-digit inflation of the late 1970s, (2) the reduction in federal domestic spending, (3) the Reagan Administration's call for increased "self-reliance," and (4) stiff competition for foundation and corporate giving.

In particular, because of the federal government's retrenchment in the early 1980s, many NB–NG agencies were required to explore alternative sources of revenue. The increased demand for services, together with the drying up of federal funds, caused some to emulate their for-profit counterparts by adopting a "lean and mean" posture. In short, many of the affected NB–NG entities learned to become more businesslike in their day-to-day operations. Efficiency became a more important value than effectiveness, and quality sometimes was emphasized less than was quantity. Some even delved into for-profit subsidiaries in the hope of providing a steady stream of income to subsidize their nonprofit programs.

In sum, the NB–NG sector is vast and complex—as complex as our society itself. In this chapter, the author has been focusing on a relatively small group of large agencies—those that command adequate human and financial resources. These agencies, for the most part, are hybrids. And it is essential to grasp this peculiar characteristic of these agencies before one can understand how new management ideas can be applied to these organizations.

THE CHANGING SOCIAL ENVIRONMENT:
CHALLENGES AND RESPONSES

In an important sense this world of ours is a new world, in which the unity of knowledge, the nature of human communities, the order of society, the order of ideas, the very notions of society and culture have changed and will not return to what they have been in the past . . . . One thing that is new is the prevalence of newness, the changing scale and scope of change itself, so that the world alters as we walk in it . . . . What is new is that in one generation our knowledge of the natural world engulfs, upsets, and complements all knowledge of the natural world before. The techniques, among and by which we live, multiply and ramify, so that the whole world is bound together by communication . . . . What is new in the world is the massive character of the dissolution and corruption of authority, in belief, in ritual, and in temporal order. Yet this is the world that we have to live in. (Robert Oppenheimer, quoted in Bennis, Benne, & Chin, 1969, p. 1)

The past 25 years have witnessed major changes in the American socioeconomic fabric. Change is the only constant of our times. What has become alarming and overwhelming to many is the velocity of change in a cause-and-effect relationship in which one change leads to another. We are living in a global economy, and mass communication and technology have converted the planet into a global village. No individual or institution of society is immune to this phenomenon. Most of the external environmental forces are beyond the control of individuals or institutions. NB–NG agencies are no exception. However, different forces—social, economic, political, and technological—have a different impact on different types of institutions.

In this section, the author summarizes the key issues and trends that uniquely affect the NB–NG agencies and then discusses some of the new management ideas that these agencies have applied in responding to the issues and environmental conditions—namely, public social policy and the acquisition of resources—they are confronting. Issues related to the regulation of charities (United Way, 1983) and privatization ("Prospects for Privatization," 1987) are somewhat less important and will not be discussed here because of the limitations of space.

The NB–NG Sector and Public Policy

The effect of the policies of the federal, state, and local levels of government on the health of the sector has been of concern to leaders of philanthropy and to social thinkers in general. This discussion is limited to two broad areas: budgetary policies and tax policies.

Budget Policies

The massive infusion of governmental funds into the voluntary nonprofit service sector during the 1960s and 1970s had both a positive and negative impact. It allowed voluntary agencies to provide needed health, educational, and other human services on a scale that would be impossible without these funds.

During that period, the government—particularly the federal government—substantially increased its sphere of responsibility to embrace services and programs that had previously not been considered to be in the realm of "public responsibility." A by-product of this massive infusion of public funds was that the government was able to provide new and expanded services and programs without a parallel expansion of its bureaucracy.

These voluntary agencies became increasingly dependent on governmental support for their sustenance. The higher the degree of dependence on governmental funds, the greater the loss of an agency's independence and ability to develop creative responses to problems. As was already noted, the government funds 35 to 40 percent of these agencies' budgets. For some agencies, governmental funding determines whether they will survive. In these cases, the very distinction between a voluntary nonprofit agency and a governmental agency becomes fuzzy, and a question arises as to what extent the agency is still "voluntary."

The dependence of NB–NG agencies on governmental funds has taken on a new meaning since the early 1980s. Responding to the mandate of the 1980 national elections and keeping faith with his campaign promises, President Ronald Reagan presented a budgetary package in 1981 that called for reductions in federal outlays (for 1981–84) of an unprecedented magnitude. Since then, further reductions have taken place, although not as drastic as those of the early period. Abramson and Salamon (1986) noted the impact of these policies, as follows:

Past Reductions in Federal Spending in Fields where Nonprofits Are Active . . . . Compared to the levels that existed in FY 1980, the inflation-adjusted value of federal spending in these fields, exclusive of Medicare and Medicaid, declined by $70 billion during these five years [1982 through 1986] . . . . These already enacted cuts were concentrated in the fields of employment and training, social services, health services, community development, and higher education, with significant percentage declines also in the field of environment.

Impact of Past Cuts on Nonprofit Providers. These reductions in federal spending in fields where nonprofits were active between FY 1982 and FY 1986 translated into revenue losses totalling $23 billion below what would have been available had FY 1980 spending levels been maintained. This represents a loss of approximately $4.6 billion in nonprofit revenues a year, or 27 percent of what was available outside of Medicare and Medicaid as of FY 1980.

These past cuts fell particularly sharply on community development organizations, which by FY 1986 will have lost 44 percent of the federal support they received in FY 1980; on social service organizations, which will have lost 40 percent of their federal support; on non-Medicare and Medicaid supported health service organizations, which experienced losses of 37 percent. (p. xvii)

In light of the current and projected economic environment—what with trade and budget deficits—prospects of a significant improvement in governmental support for NB–NG agencies are bleak. It is an important point to keep in mind that the negative effect is uneven; although some agencies were almost wiped out, others were unscathed.

Tax Policies

Much has been made of the impact of income tax incentives on charitable giving in the United States (Clotfelter, 1985). Although this author is skeptical about the magnitude of the impact, one should not underestimate the concern expressed by many charity leaders and the prevailing perception that tax policies exert a significant influence on whether people give to charities and how much they give.

Three aspects of the current situation need to be noted. First is the issue of itemizers versus nonitemizers. Effective 1987, nonitemizers are not allowed to claim a deduction for charitable contributions. This change in the tax law has raised a major hue and cry among the leaders of the sector, who have estimated that charities will lose billions of dollars annually because of this rule.

Second, a substantial increase in the standard deduction or zero bracket would likely turn millions of taxpayers into nonitemizers. There is considerable concern that this outcome could result in a significant loss in charitable contributions. The prevailing belief among leaders of the NB–NG sector is that if one is a nonitemizer, one has no incentive to give.

Third, and perhaps most important, is the effect of the lowering of the marginal tax rates, which is to increase the "price" of giving to charities and thus to reduce the incentive to contribute. Econometric studies claim that when marginal tax rates are lowered, people give less to charities even though their after-tax income increases. Here again, many believe that charities will be negatively affected. However, there is no agreement on the magnitude of the impact.

The double whammy of federal budget cuts and reduced incentives for giving has resulted in increased competition among the affected organizations for the philanthropic dollar. The reduction in the rate of growth of income among these agencies comes concurrently with the increase in the demand for services from these same agencies—primarily the human service agencies.

Acquisition of Resources

Governmental agencies obtain revenue from direct and indirect tax levies; for-profit corporations fight it out in the marketplace; and the NB–NG agencies must rely on charitable contributions, tax subsidies, and the marketplace. In that sense, charitable institutions have many masters. They are perennially in search of resources to fund programs. Invariably, the demand—particularly for health and human care services—exceeds the supply. Many agencies must live from hand to mouth. Thus, the acquisition of resources is a major problem that these agencies must confront.

For many agencies, revenue from other sources—contributions, fees, and so forth—has not made up the shortfall that has resulted from the cutbacks in federal funds. Two issues place additional constraints on the acquisition of resources by these agencies: (1) for-profit–nonprofit competition and (2) the costs of fundraising.

Competition

In 1987, a subcommittee of the U.S. Congress held several days of hearings on the unrelated business-income tax. (Much of the material in this section comes from "The Role of Nonprofit Human Service Organizations," National Assembly of Voluntary Health & Social Welfare Organizations [National Assembly] 1987.) The hearings focused primarily on complaints by various small business groups that nonprofit organizations competed unfairly against them because of their tax-exempt status. In 1986, a select committee of the Pennsylvania legislature recommended that property-tax exemptions be denied to nonprofit organizations that compete with commercial enterprises. Similar events in Illinois, Kansas, and Oregon indicate that the NB–NG agencies face a new challenge to their traditional exemptions from state and local property taxes. Such challenges from the small-business lobby, combined with the need of local governments for new revenues, have resulted in a new questioning of the justification of tax exemption for NB–NG agencies—particularly those that charge a fee for services or sell products to generate revenue. This issue may seriously challenge the future well-being of the NB–NG sector.

Fundraising Costs

This is not a new issue. However, of late, it has gained new prominence because of the various investigative reports on charities in the media and the increased interest in the subject among the charities regulation officers of the states (Hopkins, 1980).

The basic problem is that it costs money to raise money, and costs are going up with the increased competition for donors. Thousands of new agencies were born during the 1982–87 period. These agencies must compete for contributions from the same pool of donors. Attempts to place legal limits on fundraising expenses as a proportion of total contributions have resulted in litigation that has culminated in appeals to the Supreme Court. Although these legal attempts have failed, for the most part, many agencies feel intimidated about spending more money on fundraising. Public ignorance complicates this problem. Market research studies conducted by United Way and others have shown that the public has little real information on the subject. Clearly, public education in this important area is necessary if charities are to tap the potential for increased giving that undoubtedly exists.

Volunteer Resources

This discussion of the resource-acquisition issue would be incomplete without mentioning volunteers. The extensive use of volunteers—both in governance and operations—is what distinguishes this sector from the other two sectors. Earlier it was noted that the dollar value of contributed time exceeded the dollar donations. From 1980 to 1985, the total number of volunteers aged 14 and older declined slightly, while the total number of volunteer hours went up 27 percent (Independent Sector, 1986).

The changing socioeconomic environment is likely to make volunteer resources just as competitive as cash contributions. Not that volunteering per se will decline, but volunteers will be more selective about where they volunteer and what kind of volunteer work they choose. The net result of this trend is that NB–NG agencies will have to become more creative and sophisticated in attracting and retaining volunteers.

Dawn of the New Management

Organizations in the voluntary sector have developed many systematic responses to changing environmental conditions. These management systems, as they are now called, were invented to cope with imperfectly understood problems. As is typical with inventions, technical or otherwise, each appeared to be independent of the precedent one. Enthusiastic adherents of the latest system claimed that it replaced and made obsolete all of the preceding ones. (Wilkinson, 1985, p. 189)

The quest for new resources for the NB–NG agencies did not begin or end with their flirtation with commercial and entrepreneurial activities. Ever since the 1960s, many of these agencies—particularly the large and sophisticated ones—have looked for new ways of "doing business." This led them to adopt new ideas, techniques, management tools, and knowledge (and perhaps even fads) from the business and public-management approaches. The study of "management" itself became commonplace, and management training institutes proliferated throughout the sector. United Way of America is one of several organizations to establish training institutes. Its National Academy for Voluntarism trained 24,000 students from 1972 to 1987.

A parade of acronyms—MBO, PBBS, ZBB, PERT—seemed to capture the imagination and curiosity of managers of nonprofit organizations. The next wave of "new" management thinking came during the early 1970s with strategic planning. In the late 1970s and early 1980s, managers were introduced to Theory Z (Ouchi, 1982), quality circles, matrix management, and variations on those themes, including *Megatrends* (Naisbitt, 1982) and *In Search of Excellence* (Peters & Waterman, 1982). These ideas were refined further in the late 1980s by Peters (1987) and Waterman (1987). The latest notions to strike the imagination of nonprofit managers are strategic planning and management and strategic marketing.

Strategic Planning and Management

According to Wilkinson (1985),

strategic planning is often done in non-profit voluntary organizations largely on the basis of intuition. These organizations shy away from structured programs of planning on the premise that they are not in business and that they are not concerned with making a profit. Thus, processes that have evolved from the business sector are often avoided by the non-profit sector.

However, more and more non-profit voluntary organizations have come to recognize that intuitive planning is not enough, and that some business practices do indeed provide a framework for adaptation to the non-profit world. (p. 190)

Strategic management, as defined by the United Way of America (1985b)

is a systematic interactive process for thinking through and creating the organization's best possible future. Its purpose is to enhance the organization's ability to identify and achieve specific, desired results.

Strategic management does not replace traditional management activities such as budgeting, planning, monitoring, marketing, reporting, and controlling. Rather, it integrates them into a broader context, taking into account the organization's external environment, its internal capabilities, and its overall purpose and direction.

Strategic management differs from other forms of management: It insists that the organization not only look at what is but form a vision of what could be or ought to be, and it emphasizes continuous interaction among planning, implementation, and evaluation activities. (p. 3)

The process is made up of six building blocks:

1. External environmental analysis.
2. Internal environmental analysis and assessment.
3. Developing organizational vision and setting direction.
4. Defining and selecting base and contingency plans.
5. Implementing plans and work programs.
6. Evaluating performance.

Several national human service organizations have successfully introduced strategic planning and management processes into their corporate culture and operations. The next section reviews how one non-profit system—the United Way—did so successfully.

Strategic Marketing

With regard to strategic marketing, Kotler (1982) observed:

What does the term "marketing" mean? This question was recently put to 300 educational administrators whose colleges were in trouble because of declining enrollments, spiraling costs, and rising tuition. Sixty-one percent said that they saw marketing as a combination of selling, advertising, and public relations. Another 28 percent said that it was only one of these three activities. Only a small percent suggested that marketing had something to do with needs assessment, marketing research, product development, pricing, and distribution. Most people think of marketing as synonymous with selling and promotion. (p. 5)

As a major strategic concept in nonprofit management, marketing has not received the enthusiastic acceptance accorded to strategic planning and management. In part, at least, terminology may be the obstacle, because, in the minds of many, marketing is closely associated with "selling," if not "hustling." The penchant for using innocent words, such as "marketing," and loading them with heavy management-related connotations often causes semantic arguments.

In a technical sense and in the parlance of the profession, "marketing is the effective management by an organization of its exchange relations with its various markets and publics" (Kotler, 1982, p. xiii). Kotler (1982) provided the following definition:

Marketing is the analysis, planning, implementation, and control of carefully formulated programs designed to bring about voluntary exchanges of values with target markets for the purpose of achieving organizational objectives. It relies heavily on designing the organization's offering in terms of the target markets' needs and desires, and on using effective pricing, communication, and distribution to inform, motivate, and service the markets. (p. 6)

The foregoing definition might lead the uninitiated to exclaim, "Marketing is everything!" Indeed, in a more recent exposition, Kotler and Andreasen (1987) stated that in their view, "marketing is at once a philosophy, a process of management, and a set of concepts and tools for carrying out the marketing management process" (p. xiv). Herein lies the problem. Notwithstanding the definition, marketing jargon is gradually seeping into the vocabularies of nonprofit professionals and volunteers alike. Volunteer board members of these agencies—particularly the corporate types—are quick to understand and appreciate the application of marketing principles borrowed from the for-profit world. Their acceptance has helped integrate the concepts and vocabulary of marketing into the nonprofit world. The author's experience in this area prompts him to observe that many good and wise managers almost instinctively practiced the essence of marketing without knowing it or without calling it by that term. The difference is that now what was implicit has become explicit.

The core concept in marketing is *sensitivity to customers.* That is, identify your customers and potential customers, find out what their needs and wants are, and then meet those needs and wants in the best and most competitive manner possible—the final outcome being customer satisfaction, if not delight. The customer may be a donor, a recipient of service, a volunteer, an agency, a participant in a program, a member of an audience, or the society at large.

Exchange is another core concept; it means that one form of value is exchanged for another between two parties. As long as exchanges are voluntary, both parties obtain something of value to them and thus both win; there are no losers. Once again, to quote Kotler (1982):

> Marketing is not a peripheral activity of modern organizations but one that grows out of the essential quest of modern organizations to effectively serve some area of human need. To survive and succeed, organizations must know their markets, attract sufficient resources, convert these resources into appropriate products, services, and ideas, and effectively distribute them to various consuming publics. These tasks are carried on in a framework of voluntary action by all the parties. (p. 6)

A word of caution may be appropriate here. True believers of marketing may be overselling the concept. Marketing is not a panacea for all the ills of society. An excessive reliance on marketing and its literal transference to the NB–NG world may prove counterproductive in the long run. What is called for is a "marketing orientation"—a sensitivity toward those with whom you expect to enter into an "exchange relationship" of any kind. What the author would advocate here is a marriage of the concepts strategic management and marketing orientation.

The following section describes how the United Way movement adopted strategic management and marketing principles at the national level and among its membership.

THE CASE OF THE UNITED WAY

Over 2,300 independent community organizations are known by some variant of the name United Way—United Fund, Community Chest,

United Appeal, United Good Neighbors—the vast majority of them using "United Way" in their official name. United Way of America is a national association of these independent United Way organizations throughout the United States.

In 1987, the combined fundraising efforts of all United Ways in this country raised in excess of $2.5 billion, affecting the voluntary health and human care industry whose strength in the aggregate exceeds $10 billion—probably the single largest voluntary revenue-producing system in the world.

The community-based and local volunteer-driven system provides partial funding for the greatest variety of health and human care services and agencies in the world—an estimated 37,000 service delivery entities across the country. The funding is focused on personal social services to help individuals of all ages and families. In addition to funding health and human care services, individual United Ways also are catalysts to bring the community together to address identified social problems and to meet human needs.

Prelude

The turbulent times of the late 1960s set the stage for the renewal of United Way in the early 1970s. While experiencing significant growth in resources and recognition, United Way was beset by demands from the increasing number of special-interest groups and neighborhood-based services, as well as from the rise in consumerism.

As American society underwent tremendous changes, the individual United Ways saw a corresponding need to offer new types of services and to do more than just raise funds. They responded by urging the traditional agencies to offer new and relevant services and by seeking to bring in and fund more and more nontraditional programs.

In 1970, a new team of dynamic professional and volunteer leaders set a new direction for United Way. Two significant initiatives were the development of a set of standards for and the adoption of strategic planning programs in United Ways.

Standards of Excellence (United Way, 1973) spelled out the major objectives of United Way and represented what United Ways ought to aspire to in their programs and services to communities. It also provided a framework for the raison d'être of United Way. The development of this involved thousands of volunteers and professionals throughout the country.

To help United Ways adopt the standards, United Way of America launched a nationwide effort of education and technical assistance. Many United Ways revamped their mission statements and bylaws to incorporate some of the language of the standards and used the document as a benchmark by which to assess their performance. The system was now primed for entering the strategic planning phase.

Strategic Planning

In 1976, United Way of America launched a strategic planning program, whose initial aims were to develop a rationale for United Ways to adopt long-range planning and to define the most pressing issues facing the United Way movement. A survey of United Ways identified numerous issues that were then grouped into five major areas: areawide arrangements, agency relations, voluntarism and public policy, inclusiveness, and personalization. Subcommittees studied each of the five areas and published their reports in 1978. The reports received extensive exposure and were debated throughout the movement.

Since 1976, the strategic planning program has benefitted from the continued involvement of some of this nation's top leaders, including the chief executive officers of major national corporations. With the guidance of these leaders, a number of thoughtful products have been developed and disseminated among United Ways and other interested parties: environmental scanning reports, critical issue reports, and "how-to" manuals (United Way, 1985b; 1987).

Most major United Ways now have their own local strategic planning programs. These programs, together with the national program, have given the movement a capacity to develop strategies for change in a planned and organized manner.

Strategic Vision and Direction

Several years of experience with strategic planning and management helped United Way develop *Rethinking Tomorrow and Beyond* (United Way, 1985a), which furnished a strategic vision for and set the future direction of United Way into the 1990s. This document proposed five core strategies and eight supportive programs for consideration by individual organizations. The five core strategies are (1) community problem solving; (2) inclusiveness of people (especially women and minorities), agencies, and geographic service areas; (3) a single community-wide campaign; (4) a year-round communications program in the community, particularly in the workplace; and (5) a flexible fund distribution system. The eight supportive programs are in the areas of (1) professional development, (2) volunteer development, (3) management assistance, (4) information and referral, (5) governmental relations (public policy), (6) agency relations and outreach, (7) strategic planning and management, and (8) research and information processing.

A Market-Oriented United Way

In May 1987, the United Way launched a new program, which it called Second Century Initiative. The major goals of this program are to double the capacity of United Way to provide services and to double the volunteers and financial resources of United Way from 1987 to 1991.

The program agenda of the Second Century Initiative Committee is to be driven by a number of functional working committees, among them the high-level Marketing Committee. Both the Second Century Initiative and the new "marketing" thrust grew out of the strategic planning and management processes that were launched in 1976. They were a natural culmination of years of systematic thinking about United Way's role and mission in the context of a fast-changing social environment.

Thus, a new modern management discipline—marketing—was injected into the bloodstream of a 100-year-old movement. Operationally, implementation strategies were developed for the national and local United Ways in an integrated manner. The challenge was to inculcate a new marketing culture and mindset among the thousands of United Way professionals and volunteers in the movement.

A marketing plan, developed under the direction of top corporate volunteers, focused on three major approaches: (1) to present United Way as "the way to care," not just a way to give; (2) to provide marketing leverage, tools, and technical assistance to local United Ways; and (3) to develop a market research capacity to help United Ways achieve a marketing orientation. On a parallel track, United Way of America began to reorder its priorities to become marketing oriented through retraining employees to think in terms of marketing, a reorganization and reorientation of the staff after a comprehensive study by a major outside consulting group, and the reallocation of resources to support the marketing plan.

NONNEGOTIABLE VALUES

What assures the survival of voluntarism with increased strength, in our view, are the values of which voluntary action is the visible expression, and the momentum which voluntarism has maintained over the centuries. The persistence of people of every race, color, creed, age, economic condition, and sex to involve themselves in service to others and to improve the conditions under which all live, will not be denied or diverted. Neither governments, nor inflation, nor temporary privatism will stand in the way.

Yet survival does depend, at last, on those persons of good will who will support diligently that which they deem to be precious, and who know that, despite its strength, voluntarism, like freedom, is fragile and can be eroded silently, and soon lost. (Academy for Educational Development, 1979, p. 31)

The nonprofit sector in the United States is like the nonprofit sector of no other place on earth. The sector—particularly the public interest subsector—has something unique and precious to contribute to society that neither the government nor commercial enterprise can achieve.

It is incumbent on managers of complex modern institutions in this complex, industrial society to remain alert to new ideas and opportunities that would enhance their ability to serve their constituencies more efficiently and effectively. They must cultivate an attitude of openness and receptivity and be skeptical about any new fad that comes along. Everything new and modern is not automatically appropriate for the nonprofit sector. Much can be learned from business but much is not appropriate for the nonprofit sector and is best left to business.

The fundamental values that undergird the nonprofit sector are, in a sense, "nonnegotiables." In the event of conflict, these values must prevail, or society will be the loser.

REFERENCES

Abramson, A. J., & Salamon, L. M. (1986). *The nonprofit sector and the new federal budget.* Washington, DC: The Urban Institute Press, p. xvii. Reproduced by permission.

Academy for Educational Development. (1979). *The voluntary sector in brief.* New York: Author.

Anthony, R. N. (1978). *Financial accounting in nonbusiness organizations: An exploratory study of conceptual issues.* Stamford, CT:

Financial Accounting Standards Board.

Bennis, W. G., Beene, K. D., & Chin, R. (1969). *The planning of change.* New York: Holt, Rinehart & Winston.

Clotfelter, C. T. (1985). *Federal tax policy and charitable giving.* Chicago: University of Chicago Press.

Commission on Private Philanthropy and Public Needs. (1975). *Giving in America: Toward a stronger voluntary sector.* Washington, DC: Author.

Hall, P. D. (1987). A historical overview of the private nonprofit sector. In W. W. Powell (Ed.), *The nonprofit sector* (pp. 3–26). New Haven, CT: Yale University Press.

Hansmann, H. B. (1987). Economic theories of nonprofit organization. In W. W. Powell (Ed.), *The nonprofit sector* (pp. 27–42). New Haven, CT: Yale University Press.

Hodgkinson, V., & Weitzman, M. (1986). *Dimensions of the independent sector, 1986.* Washington, DC: Independent Sector.

Holtman, A. G. (1983). A theory of non-profit firms. *Economics, 50,* 439–449.

Hopkins, B. R. (1980). *Charity under siege: Government regulations of fund raising.* New York: Ronald.

Independent Sector. (1986). *Americans volunteer, 1985.* Washington, DC: Author.

James, D. (1987). Political theories of nonprofit organization. In W. W. Powell (Ed.), *The nonprofit sector* (pp. 43–54). New Haven, CT: Yale University Press.

Kotler, P. (1982). *Marketing for nonprofit organizations.* Englewood Cliffs, NJ: Prentice-Hall.

Kotler, P., & Andreasen, A. R. (1987). *Strategic marketing for nonprofit organizations* (3rd ed.). Englewood Cliffs, NJ: Prentice-Hall.

Naisbitt, J. (1982). *Megatrends.* New York: Warner Books.

National Assembly of Voluntary Health & Social Welfare Organizations. (1987). *The role of nonprofit human service organizations* (draft report). Washington, DC: Author.

Newhouse, J. (1970). Toward a theory of non-profit institutions: An economic model of a hospital. *American Economic Review, 60,* 64–74.

Ouchi, W. G. (1982). *Theory Z: How American business can meet the Japanese challenge.* New York: Avon Books.

Peters, T. J. (1987). *Thriving on chaos: Handbook for a management revolution.* New York: Alfred A. Knopf.

Peters, T., & Waterman, R. H., Jr. (1982). *In search of excellence: Lessons* from America's best-run companies. New York: Harper & Row.

Prospects for Privatization: Proceedings of the Academy of Political Science. (1987). *36.*

Rudney, G. (1981). *A quantitative profile of the non-profit sector.* Unpublished manuscript, Yale University, Program on Non-Profit Organizations, New Haven, CT.

Salamon, L. M. (1987). Partners in public service: The scope and theory of government nonprofit relations. In W. W. Powell (Ed.), *The nonprofit sector* (pp. 99–117). New Haven, CT: Yale University Press.

Salamon, L. M., & Abramson, A. J. (1982). *The federal budget and the nonprofit sector: Implications of the Reagan budget proposals.* Washington, DC: Urban Institute Press.

Skloot, E. (1987). Enterprise and commerce in nonprofit organizations. In W. W. Powell (Ed.), *The nonprofit sector* (pp. 380–393). New Haven, CT: Yale University Press.

Skloot, E. (1983). Should not-for-profits go into business? *Harvard Business Review, 61.*

Sumariwalla, R. D. (1983). Preliminary observations on scope, size and classification of the sector since the Filer Commission. In *Working papers for spring research forum* (pp. 181–228). Washington, DC: Independent Sector.

United Way of America. (1973). *Standards of excellence.* Alexandria, VA: Author.

United Way of America. (1974). *Accounting and financial reporting: A guide for United Ways and not-for-profit human service organizations.* Alexandria, VA: Author.

United Way of America. (1975). *Budgeting—A guide for United Ways and not-for-profit human-service organizations.* Alexandria, VA: Author.

United Way of America. (1976). *UWASIS II: A taxonomy of social goals and human service programs.* Alexandria, VA: Author.

United Way of America. (1983). *Some aspects of philanthropy in the United States: Scope and trends.* Alexandria, VA: Author.

United Way of America. (1985a). *Rethinking tomorrow and beyond: A strategic vision of the modern United Way.* Alexandria, VA: Author.

United Way of America. (1985b). *The strategic management and United Way Series.* Alexandria, VA: Author.

United Way of America. (1987). *What lies ahead—Looking toward the '90s.* Alexandria, VA: Author.

Waterman, R. H., Jr. (1987). *The renewal factor: How the best get and keep the competitive edge.* New York: Bantam Books.

Weisbrod, B. (1974). Toward a theory of the voluntary non-profit sector in a three-sector economy. In E. S. Phelps (Ed.), *Altruism, morality, and economic theory* (pp. 171–195). New York: Russell Sage Foundation.

Wilkinson, G. W. (1985). Strategic planning in the voluntary sector. In G. A. Tobin (Ed.), *Social planning and human service delivery in the voluntary sector* (pp. 189–207). Westport, CT: Greenwood.

12

▲

New Management Concepts in Family and Children's Services

James N. Miller

THE APPLICATION OF MODERN MANAGEMENT PRINCIPLES to any field of practice requires some examination of the management problems and issues that field of practice faces. Although the problems examined in this chapter may not include all those that might appear on some managers' lists of most critical problems, they are common to family and children's service agencies. These problems and issues are not unique to this field of practice, but the history and values of the family and children's field may provide a special perspective to the applicability of new management theories and practice to human service agencies.

PROBLEMS AND PRESSURES

Survival

Survival is an issue that has occupied increasing attention and caused some anxiety among administrators of family and children's agencies in recent years. The deinstitutionalization movement has affected many children's institutions. Governmental sources of revenue, which supported the substantial growth of agencies in the 1970s, are now setting ceilings on contract rates, holding total contract values to the level of previous years, or reducing or eliminating some contracts. The growth in United Way funding has increased more slowly than has the cost of doing business and has not replaced the cutbacks in governmental funds.

These problems, as well as other issues, have focused a great deal of management attention on the need to survive.

Whether the threat to survival is real or only perceived is open to some question. On the one hand, going out of business is no longer an unthinkable option, and some agencies are giving this alternative serious consideration (Tietyen, 1987). Other agencies are at the point of being taken over by hospitals or new health care systems that have a growing interest in a variety of outpatient services and broader approaches to health care. Still others are losing clients and programs to health maintenance organizations, private practitioners, and for-profit agencies that are discovering markets for services that traditionally were provided by not-for-profit or governmental agencies. On the other hand, family service agencies have grown phenomenally in the past 10 years. Data gathered by Family Service America (Rice, 1987) showed that, as a group, its member agencies have experienced faster growth than the economy as a whole. Perhaps the threat of losing out to competitors has unleashed the survival instincts of not-for-profit corporations and produced a new era of growth.

In any case, rapid change is taking place in the environment of most not-for-profit organizations. Rapid change means that some familiar patterns of living and working are left behind. The farewell to the familiar and introduction to the unfamiliar are often accompanied by feelings of loss or abandonment, not unlike the fears associated with threats to personal survival. At a minimum, one of the problems that managers of family and children's agencies must cope with is the perception, if not the reality, of a threat to their organizations' survival.

The concern that many managers have about their *own* survival may be just as much of an organizational problem. Experienced managers in the field believe that a large and growing number of executives have been dismissed or allowed to resign in lieu of being dismissed. Some of the managers who are employed are vulnerable to dismissal because they are mismatched with their boards of directors or have stress-related health problems that impede the performance of their jobs.

Competition

A second problem faced by not-for-profit agencies is competition. This problem is different from but closely related to survival. Some individuals and organizations avoid competition and believe it is incompatible with serving humanity. They also view their work as being incompatible with ideas about marketing, creating a demand for products, abandoning unprofitable service programs, or creating images of services that appeal to certain types of potential clients more than to others.

Nevertheless, competition is part of the social agency environment, and it appears to be here to stay. Private practitioners compete with agencies for clients who are able to pay the highest fees. For-profit agencies and health-care providers compete with each other and with traditional counseling agencies for contracts with business and industry for employee assistance plans. All types of agencies compete with one another for governmental contracts. United Way-supported agencies compete with each other for increases in the allocation of contributed dollars. Agencies compete with each other for board members and officers with the most "clout," for volunteers who are best able to organize fundraising events, for access to the mass media, for "favorite charity" status with the most wealthy and generous donors in the community, for the most capable and charismatic staff, and so on. Thus, it is obvious that agencies have been competing with each other for years. What is new about competition among agencies is its pervasiveness, its acceptance as a way of life, and its extension to competition for the clients themselves.

Efficiency and Cost Containment

A third closely related problem is the pressure for efficiency and cost containment. Funding sources tend to award resources to providers with the lowest costs. In a labor-intensive field such as the social services, the obvious pressure on agencies is to contain salaries and fringe benefits and to demand high productivity from employees. This author's experience does not substantiate the common claims of practitioners that there is an inverse ratio between high quality and a high volume of service. Nevertheless, cost containment comes with a price.

One of the problems associated with containment of salaries is that those staff members who are often the most competent and charismatic are recruited by other employers whose resources enable them to pay higher wages. Generally governmental agencies; health-related agencies that collect reimbursements from private insurers; agencies that serve affluent, paying clients; or agencies that receive considerable funds through fundraising are able to pay higher salaries. Such agencies are deemed successful because they have the most money and, except for the governmental agencies, are the most independent. They do not tend to have a high proportion of disadvantaged persons on their caseloads. Thus, the most competent staff tend to be attracted to the agencies that pay the highest salaries and whose clients tend to have substantial personal, financial, educational, and social resources.

In contrast, agencies that serve clients whose functioning is the most severely disorganized and who have the lowest reservoirs of coping resources tend to be most dependent on funds allocated by funding authorities and, therefore, the most vulnerable to the pressures to contain the cost of salaries. Unless money is not their major consideration, staff members who remain with these agencies tend to be unsuccessful in obtaining higher-paying jobs and have low morale and self-esteem because of their comparatively low pay and because their clients are identified more with failure than with success. This situation might promote mediocrity in services to the poor and lead clients with the most complex and severe problems and the least resources to be served by practitioners who are the lowest paid and perhaps least competent; the most highly skilled practitioners with the higher paying jobs would serve people with greater resources and motivation. Fortunately, money is not the only factor that affects the distribution of competence among service providers.

Another way in which communities and agencies pay a high price for cost containment is in the sacrifice of coordination and cooperation among agencies. Communities still expect human service agencies to work together efficiently and effectively. Cost containment is only one of the reasons that services become fragmented and uncoordinated, but it is a significant one. The services of several providers cannot be coordinated and integrated without regular communication among providers. Staff members who are faced with demands for providing a high number of billable direct-service units to clients have a disincentive for spending time planning and holding case conferences. Coordination runs a collision course with cost containment. When high unit costs negatively affect the award of contracts or the allocation of money from the United Way, managers generally will choose cost containment.

Expectations of Boards of Directors

A fourth problem that managers who are in family and children's agencies face is coping with inconsistent and contradictory expectations from boards of directors. In his "Report from the Field," Rice (1986) referred to a "new wave" of board members who are data oriented, entrepreneurial, and competitive; have a specialized approach to board work; are pressed for time and have limited time for agency work, seek systematized information; and are results oriented, interested in efficiency, and focused on the environmental conditions facing the agency. Often, they come from large corporations.

The interests of these board members contrast with those of more traditional board members who are program oriented, conceive of the agency as an enterprise that cooperates with other organizations, are broadly knowledgeable about the agency and the problems it faces, and are generous with their time. These traditional board members seek information about the effectiveness of programs from professionals or direct information as volunteers. They are mission oriented and interested in the philosophical underpinnings of agency activities. They are often interested in "quality" more than efficiency and have a underlying set of assumptions about what quality is. They have affection and regard for the family service organization and are focused on the agency, rather than on the environmental conditions it faces. Often they are housewives, retired persons, or owners of small businesses.

Professional Expectations

What are the executive's options for responding to these competing and sometimes contradictory interests? Is it a proper administrative role to reconcile differences among board members? If the administrator takes a stand on one side or the other, how will his or her future executive-board relationships be affected when, for example, a person with an opposing view becomes an officer of the board? If the executive maintains neutrality in the midst of the different perspectives of the board members, can he or she continue to provide effective leadership? What should be the administrator's role in the process of selecting board members and officers? Will the administrator's influence in shaping the composition of the board contaminate the principle of governance by a representative board that expresses the will of the community? What guidelines are available to help the executive weigh the risks and potential benefits of the various positions that might be taken with reference to new wave versus traditional styles of board leadership?

If there are problems in communication involving board members with different perceptions, needs, and interests, the same is certainly true of the staff. Gone are the days when work in agencies, particularly voluntary agencies, was the only destiny of professional social workers. More lucrative options, such as private practice, are now available (Skloot, 1987). Many social workers who seek employment in the family and children's field want to specialize. Furthermore, certain funding and regulatory bodies demand specialization, such as certification in the treatment of alcohol or chemical dependence. "Clinical" social workers prefer to be distinguished from those who do other types of social work. Some prefer to do family therapy, to practice only the Gestalt methodology, or to work just with children. Others prefer specific areas of management. For many new graduates of schools of social work, employment represents a second family income. Thus, to some, the salary may be less important than interesting, stimulating duties, favorable work schedules, and vacation benefits.

Another problem with regard to the staff of agencies is that family service agencies often lack adequate career ladders. Thus, they are forced to turn to inexperienced personnel and find it necessary to give them their initial experience in the field, when they are likely to be the least productive. Many agencies report that their professional positions are less satisfying than they might have been in the past. The work is less leisurely because practitioners are pressed to use their time more efficiently and hence are less able to pursue their own interests.

Changes in Clientele

An additional problem faced by family and children's agencies is that of responding appropriately to rapid changes in the characteristics and needs of clients. Many agencies, for instance, are unprepared to cope with the wave of drug and alcohol addiction among elementary school children or have the resources to deal with the needs of the rapidly increasing population of elderly people. Service to the aging has not captured the interest of many family agencies, some of which limit their services to marital and parent–child relationships. However, few agencies are well equipped to cope with the complexities of family life that is strained by teenage parenthood.

Even the definition of *who* is the client is becoming more and more ambiguous. For example, when a corporation contracts with an agency to provide counseling services to its employees, is the client, the company, or the employee receiving the counseling? Companies may feel they have a right to know the names of their employees who use the company-paid service, at least to verify the legitimacy of claims for the payment of services. Employees, however, may fear that such information will be entered into their personnel records and negatively affect their potential for advancement. Similarly, governmental agencies that pay for the service frequently want to inspect clients' records and other documents to verify the agency's compliance with contractual obligations. Many providers believe that such requirements violate the principles of client confidentiality and privacy.

Agencies that serve families who have run afoul of legal authority for child abuse or neglect, the sexual abuse of children, spouse abuse, drug abuse, juvenile delinquency, or other problems have found that their traditional definition of "client" applies more to the referring agency than to the family that will receive the service. Often the family members are resistant, if not hostile, and see the service agency as an extension of the legal authority with whom they are in trouble. Treatment relationships involve not only agency staff members and clients, but the third parties who have authority over the clients. Coordination with these agencies often is difficult because of their high rate of staff turnover, expectations for quick and irreversible results, and instant and unpredictable need for information. The failure to attend to such coordination, however, may mean the premature termination of services to the client by the referring agency, the cessation of further referrals, or negative perceptions of the provider.

Even clients who apply for services appear to expect quick results with a minimal expenditure of time, effort, and money. They think that solutions to problems derive from the social worker's knowledge and skills, rather than from their (the clients') efforts. Many clients and social workers do not think there is time—or that it is worth the time—to become thoroughly acquainted with the client and his or her background before making specific recommendations for corrective actions.

Other Important Issues

According to Tietyen (1987), the primary issue identified in her discussions with executives, board members, and staff of family service agencies is the alleged *unfair competition* by not-for-profit agencies with the private profit-making sector (*see also* Welford & Gallagher, 1985). In her report, Tietyen noted that 35 states have legislation pending or written that would tax nonprofit agencies or change their tax-exempt status. The rationale for this legislation is that nonprofit agencies have an unfair competitive edge because of their exemption from property, sales, and corporate income taxes. The issue is particularly volatile in the area of bidding for governmental contracts and has been joined in favor of the for-profit sector by the Small Business Administration. Some legislators, eager for new sources of tax revenues, are taking a fresh look at the tax exemption of nonprofit agencies.

The second most important issue that Tietyan identified is *competition-partnership* with the health care system. The health care system is defining itself more broadly as part of the human service industry and is beginning to provide services that were traditionally offered by nonprofit agencies outside the health care field.

The third most important issue, according to Tietyen, is *family policy*, as represented by the reform of the welfare system. With the growing concern about the many failures of the current welfare system and the imperative to conserve public funds that are allocated to the human services, there is a new opportunity to promote the development of a coherent national family policy to undergird specific welfare programs.

Other issues of concern to family service agencies that Tietyen reported are economic difficulties, changes in the philosophy of United Way and in its methods of allocating funds, and the opportunity for family agencies to become a national delivery system for packaged or standardized services. Tietyen also noted the problems that family service agencies have in responding to the needs of families of "special commitment" (those who care for members who are developmentally disabled or mentally ill or who have Alzheimer's disease) who exert extraordinary efforts—physical, psychological, and financial—that are out of proportion to the resources available to them. Also, these agencies are concerned about developing a "teachable practice framework" for assisting executives to integrate concepts of social responsibility and the new demand for bottom-line business approaches in the management of social agencies.

CHARACTERISTICS OF MANAGEMENT

The problems just described provide a context in which to consider certain aspects of the philosophy and style of management that may prove helpful in coping with the new complexities that confront decision makers. As Lilienthal (1967) stated:

> It's worth reminding ourselves that management does not really exist. It is a word, an idea. Like science, like government, like engineering, management is an abstraction. But managers exist. And managers are not

abstractions; . . . they are human beings. Individuals with a special function: to lead and move and bring out the latent capabilities and dreams of other human beings. (p. 18)

If management is an "art," practiced by individual human beings, the management of each organization will have its unique brush strokes that reflect the particular character and personality of the manager. Is effective management then achieved only by selecting the "right" manager for a particular organization (getting a "good fit" between manager and organization)? Or is there some accumulation of knowledge and experience, some science, that will help individual managers know how to manage?

For several decades, dozens of graduate programs and hundreds of management seminars and training courses have probed the depths of management as a scientific endeavor. Graduates who are schooled in the science of management have been in great demand. Moreover, managers of human service agencies tend to feel embarrassed when they have to fulfill managerial responsibilities without the requisite training in the science of management. In recent years, however, some corporations have begun to question the effectiveness of management science and have pursued the even more elusive qualities of leadership. Without discarding all that has been learned about management as a science, the remainder of this chapter will emphasize some ideas about leadership, in the context of the history and culture of not-for-profit family and children's agencies.

HISTORY AND CULTURE OF AGENCIES

A few key elements of the history and culture of not-for-profit family and children's agencies are relevant to an examination of the applicability of modern management principles to this field of practice. One of the cardinal features of most not-for-profit agencies, and certainly of those in the family and children's field, is *ownership by volunteers*. These agencies were founded by groups of concerned volunteers who perceived some social need and had a vision regarding its remediation. Typically, these volunteers not only governed the organization but financed it and did the work. As the agencies grew in size, complexity, and resources, the volunteers delegated the responsibility for operating the agencies to paid executives and accepted funds from the United Way and from the government (in the form of grants and contracts). They retained clear ownership of the agencies, however.

Now, another transition seems to be under way—toward the assumption by executives of greater control over and responsibility for the direction and destiny of agencies. It still is understood generally that boards should establish policies and objectives, but there appears to be a shift in what is defined as policy and what is defined as management. Decisions about fringe-benefits packages, for example, once considered exclusively a policy-development responsibility of the board, are now defined by some agencies as an operational responsibility of the chief administrator. Many agencies have changed the title of their chief administrator from executive director to president, and some have identified their administrator as the chief executive officer.

Although the new models of executive leadership may be consistent with the increasing demands of efficiency and quick and decisive responses to changing conditions (the "businesslike" approach), they may be inconsistent with the agencies' history and culture of ownership by volunteers. Thus, a major administrative task often is to provide effective leadership within the context of agency ownership by volunteers.

A second important cultural characteristic of most family and children's agencies, if not of other types of not-for-profit organizations, is responding to the needs of the community. This tradition is still the raison d'être of most social agencies. The current market-driven competitive environment has begun to push agencies in the direction of doing whatever is necessary for the organization to survive. Meeting the needs of the community may become a secondary consideration. How many such needs will be met, managers ask, if the organization does not exist?

A third, closely related cultural characteristic is an organizational structure that is designed to maximize the participation and involvement of as many people as possible. It is true that some agencies were begun and still are maintained by a small elite group of individuals and that in many agencies the real power is invested in a small self-perpetuating group while nominal involvement is sought from a much larger constituency. Nonetheless, the archetypal not-for-profit family or children's agency seeks a large, informed, supportive constituency from which it draws financial support, influence, prestige, and the people to assume positions on its governing body and its working committees. The constitutionally defined size of the board of directors illustrates this inclination toward maximum involvement and participation. Boards of directors of agencies commonly comprise 18 to 36 members, and boards of 60 to 150 members are not unheard of. In contrast, the typical business corporation has five to seven directors.

It could hardly be argued that efficiency and tight accountability are the organizing principles behind the establishment of large boards. But agencies are now scrambling to make the processes of governance and management more efficient, more highly accountable, and less "wasteful" of time and talent. Thus, the trend is toward reducing the number of standing committees, reducing the size of boards, and vesting authority in the hands of fewer people.

The traditional structures of such agencies may no longer be defensible under current conditions. Nevertheless, the historical traditions and the value placed on involvement must not be neglected if these agencies are to maintain their influence and reputation in their communities, their base of financial support, and their reservoir of talent.

Finally, a factor that often is overlooked as a historical function of not-for-profit organizations is their ability to develop a consensus from among opposing philosophical, economic, and political viewpoints in the community. For instance, several years ago, the Personnel Committee of the Family Service Association of Indianapolis devoted a number of meetings to debating what the executive (the author) thought to be a minor but controversial issue affecting employer–employee relations. On the committee were several corporate attorneys, a college professor, and the personnel managers of two major corporations in the community. After the issue was resolved, the executive asked the chairperson of the board for his opinion about why the committee had spent so much time on such a minor issue. The chairperson explained that the issue was of concern to each member of the committee in his or her own business and that the committee provided a forum for those persons to discuss points of view. The committee discussions performed a valuable service to the members and, indirectly, to the community, as well as the agency.

PARALLELS IN BUSINESS AND INDUSTRY

It is interesting to note that large corporations are focusing increased attention on similar factors. For example, Richard D. Wood, chief executive officer of Eli Lilly Company of Indianapolis, attributed the success of the company to four factors (as quoted in Burke, 1981):

(1) emphasis on research and development, (2) *maintaining the company's central values* [italics added], which focus on high ethical standards in product manufacture and marketing and in the treatment of employees, (3) careful selection of employees and promotion predominantly from within,

and (4) fair and equitable treatment of employees, especially with reference to compensation. (p. 23)

Commenting further on the company's values, Wood stated:

The [Lilly] family always believed in doing what was right in every aspect of the corporation—not just the people side, but in terms of our business practices, in terms of our everyday conduct, and certainly in terms of the products we produce, which are really top quality, and not over-promoted. With respect to our pharmaceuticals, we tell the physicians exactly what the product is, and often what it isn't, so that a fair story is presented. Of course, this task is a little hard for the typical marketing group to accept. Certainly, the natural tendency is to tell the doctor all the good points—but our job is to make sure that the other side is put forward as well. (Burke, 1981, p. 24)

. . . organizational members believe more in these principles today than they did back, in, say, the sixties. This may be because the younger generation was more skeptical then, and more inclined to go their own way without concern for tradition . . . what may have appeared to be a stodgy, rigid business approach is really the best one in the long run. (Burke, 1981, p. 25)

According to Sathe (1983),

culture is both an asset and a liability. It is an asset because shared beliefs ease and economize communications, and shared values generate higher levels of cooperation and commitment than is otherwise possible. This is highly efficient . . . If culture guides behavior in inappropriate ways, we have efficiency but not effectiveness. Culture is a liability when the shared beliefs and values are not in keeping with the needs of the organization, its members, and its other constituencies. (pp. 9–10)

Thus, it would appear that managers must assess and be attentive to the cultures of the organizations they manage. They also must serve as catalysts for deliberate cultural change when the needs of the organization require some modification of past behavior and approaches. This is not a new challenge for family agencies. Substantial cultural change in these agencies was induced in the 1930s after the Social Security Act was passed and the federal government, instead of voluntary agencies, became the major resource for direct financial assistance to individuals. In the ensuing years, family agencies shifted their concern to family relationships and the mental health of individual family members. Their basic beliefs about the needs of families and about the ways families contribute to the well-being of the larger society did not change significantly, however. What altered was the behavior of the agencies in response to changed conditions and new opportunties. Old beliefs and values found new expression in these behavioral changes.

OPERATIONAL THEMES AND PRIORITIES

This section briefly examines some common driving forces or themes that are applied by managers of organizations who are faced with changing external demands. Although the author's observations and experiences have been primarily in not-for-profit agencies, the literature indicates that these same forces influence managers' actions in the for-profit sector as well.

Mission-Driven Organizations

Some organizations and managers view their basic mission and purpose as the dominant force influencing organizational behavior. The essential question that these mission-driven organizations pose regarding any contemplated action is whether it is consistent with the agency's basic mission. The intent to act comes from within the organization. The mission, like the Constitution, may undergo amendment and reinterpretation to adapt the organization to changing conditions and needs, but the basic values of mission-driven organizations seldom undergo radical change. Such organizations tend to be stable (their critics may call them rigid); have a clear sense of their own identity; have little difficulty setting organizational goals; and feel in charge of their own destiny. In the extreme, mission-driven organizations are willing to dissolve if their mission becomes outdated and no longer relevant. Most, however, will find new applications for their basic values and beliefs.

History is replete with examples of the failure of organizations that were unclear about their missions or defined them too narrowly: the railroads that failed to see themselves as being in the transportation business instead of just the railroad business, maternity homes that confined their vision to residential care, and churches that refused to consider expanding their constituency despite an eroding membership base. Although these examples also illustrate the failure to apply the fundamentals of marketing, they represent even more basically a conceptual deficit in understanding why the organization exists—its mission. Many mission-driven organizations have no difficulty in assessing and responding to market conditions. Market-driven organizations, however, tend to be less concerned with *why* they are in business than they are with *being* in business.

Need-Driven Organizations

The need for service is closely related to mission as the determining factor in decision making by organizations. Agencies that are need driven are most apt to place a high priority on the assessment of needs. Need-driven agencies tend to be dynamic, innovative, and relevant, and tend to maintain good public relations. The intent to act comes from the agencies' perception or assessment of what is needed in the world outside the organizations.

Unfortunately, new needs do not fall necessarily within the scope of the agency's mission or within the capacities of the staff of experts that were assembled to meet a former need addressed by the agency. Furthermore, *need* is not necessarily matched by *demand*. An inner-city minister once told the author that he has no confidence in the assessment of needs of a neighborhood because every respondent would answer that the service was required because a neighbor needed it, but few would think that the service was relevant to their needs or would use the service. Although this remark is hardly sufficient to cast doubt on all surveys of needs, it seems to contain some truth.

Market-Driven Organizations

The goals of market-driven agencies come from outside the organization and are expressed in the form of a demand for services. Sometimes, there is little or no demand (or no funding) for services that the community needs. At other times, there may be a high demand for services that, from a rational perspective, are not needed so badly. The questions asked by market-driven agencies tend to be "Is it funded?" "Will the program sell?" "Are there people who will use it?" "Can a demand for the service be created?"

Skloot (1987) stated that the reduction in federal funds, changes in the tax code that are likely to reduce charitable contributions by billions of dollars, the privatization of services, the resurgence of entrepreneurship, and the trend toward deregulation have moved nonprofit organizations into a "market economy." The "rules of the game" are, he suggested, sharply different in this new environment from those to which nonprofit agencies are accustomed. "The problem," Skloot contended, is that many nonprofits are need-driven rather than market-driven and some weigh mission more highly than money" (p. 41). Skloot also observed that many non-for-profit agencies are ill equipped for the market economy because they are undercapitalized. Their reliance on charitable dollars and governmental contracts makes it difficult to accumulate operating reserves, and they cannot raise equity capital for growth or expansion. "Without substantial fund balances," Skloot (1987) noted, "nonprofits cannot easily . . . compete with well-heeled private sector vendors . . . . Many have a difficult time breaking away from assumptions based on service desirability and moving toward dollar-and-cents calculations of the long-term costs of service delivery" (p. 41).

Expediency-Driven Organizations

Some not-for-profit agencies seem to be driven by expedience, doing whatever it appears needs to be done to "get through" another year. These organizations do little planning, rarely review or update their mission statements, and are only marginally concerned with a serious assessment of the needs of their communities. Rather, they tend to be power and influence brokers, attempting to use influential businesspersons or political leaders to help them cut through the red tape of the contracting or fund-allocating process. In such organizations, programs and services are ad hoc, fundraising events that receive a lot of publicity are favored, grant- and proposal-writing capabilities are highly developed, and grants, contracts, and projects are sought constantly.

Such organizations tend to become dominated by their staffs. The executives who gravitate to these agencies tend to be opportunists who hop from one better-paying job to another; their resumes emphasize the size of the budgets they administer and the dollar amounts of the grants they have secured. The author knew one such executive who found a "better opportunity" after a governmental agency asked for a reimbursement of several hundred thousand dollars worth of claims that it found on audit did not fully comply with the contracting agency's requirements. This executive failed to inform his board of this problem and left his successor to deal with it.

STRATEGIES FOR EFFECTIVE MANAGEMENT

Attention to the Organizational Culture

An awareness of the agency's organizational culture is an appropriate starting point for planning a strategy to deal with the challenges the agency facts. The analysis of this culture is by no means an exact science, however. Some important aspects of an organization's culture are not readily observable, and the actual behavior of an organization's system is not always consistent with its stated rules and objectives.

The literature on the intricacies of organizational culture affords meaningful insights into its importance. For instance, Schein (1986) explored what culture is and does, how cultures begin and develop, and how cultures change. He presented the following guidelines for managers who attempt to analyze their organization's culture:

1. Do not oversimplify and do not confuse culture with other useful concepts, such as "climate," "values,"or "corporate philosophy." Culture operates at one level below these others and largely *determines* them . . . .

2. Do not assume that culture applies only to the human side of an organization's functioning . . . . Focusing on how people relate to each other in the organization and labeling that aspect "the culture" can be a dangerous trap because it draws attention away from shared basic assumptions about the nature of the product, the market, the organization's mission, and other factors that may have far more influence on how effective the organization is ultimately.

3. Do not assume that culture can be manipulated like other matters under the control of managers. Culture controls the manager more than the manager controls culture . . . .

4. Do not assume there is a "correct" or better culture, and do not assume that "strong" cultures are better than weak cultures. What is correct or whether strength is good or bad depends on the match between culture assumptions and environmental realities . . . .

5. Do not assume that all aspects of the culture are relevant to the effectiveness of the organization. Any group with any history will have a culture, but many elements of the culture may be essentially irrelevant to that group's functioning . . . .

In working papers of the Lilly Endowment Leadership Education Group (1987, p. 3) four areas were identified as being pivotal determinants of an organization's vitality and effectiveness:

1. An awareness of the organization's history and an understanding of its influence and value.

2. Clear articulation and understanding of organizational mission and consensus about the nature of the mission and its importance.

3. Purposeful identification of the publics served by the organization—not only the clients served directly, but the "stakeholders" whose interests are served by agency activity.

4. A vision of the future, including not only those factors which shape the organization such as demographic and economic trends, but a vision of how the organization can shape its own future and that of its surrounding environment. (pp. 314–315)

Selection of Personnel

Whatever the history, mission, clientele, and future of an organization, it is essential to select personnel whose values are consistent with those of the organization. Obviously, a board's selection of a chief administrator who identifies with the agency's mission and values is essential to the agency's successful operation and development. The choice of board members with similar beliefs and commitment to the agency's mission and goals is equally important. The author believes that the chief administrator has the most comprehensive knowledge of the skills that are needed by his or her agency and thus should play a key role in selecting new board members.

Orientation and Socialization of Personnel

The orientation process complements the selection process. It also may be called the socialization process, for it transmits the organization's values and norms (its *culture*) to its new staff members, board members, and volunteers. Formal orientation programs usually are brief and are focused on policies, procedures, and work requirements. It takes a much longer time, however, to absorb the organization's values, norms, and beliefs and the ways in which the agency's mission is translated into practice.

The orientation-socialization process is ongoing, dynamic, and aimed at integrating the individual into the life of the organization. A clearly articulated mission, philosophy, and statement of goals is obviously necessary if the orientation and socialization process is to achieve its aims. Otherwise, the process tends to become random, fragmented, and even divisive. As Hatvany and Pucik (1981) observed:

A primary function of the company's socialization effort . . . is to ensure that employees have understood the philosophy and seen it in action. Close attention is given to hiring people who are willing to endorse the values of the particular company and to the employees' integration into the organization at all stages of their working life. (p. 11)

Focus on Human Resources

Another strategy for effective management is to maintain a focus on the agency's human resources. Hatvany and Pucik's (1981) quotation from the in-house literature of a Japanese-owned electronics component maker in California illustrates this point:

> Our goal is to strive toward both the material and the spiritual fulfillment of all employees in the company, and through this successful fulfillment, serve mankind in its progress and prosperity.
>
> Our purpose is to fully satisfy the needs of our customer and in return gain a just profit for ourselves. We are a family united in common bonds and similar goals. One of these bonds is the respect and support we feel for our fellow family co-workers. (p. 11)

In a similar vein, Hollis (1954) wrote:

> On the whole, caseworkers believe that in the good society, the welfare of the individual and of society go hand in hand, that what is good for the one is good for the other. They believe that individuals, separately and collectively, have responsibility for the welfare of each other, as well as the right to pursue with vigor their own goals. (p. 475)

Security of employment is obviously one of the most basic ways to recognize and respect the needs of employees. Equally fundamental is *adequate compensation.* As was noted earlier, the growth in family service agencies in the past 10 years has been faster than the growth in the rest of the economy. One would thus presume that employment in family agencies has been relatively stable. Compensation levels, however, have not shown commensurate growth. This condition continuously destabilizes employment in family and children's agencies because employees leave to seek higher salaries with other employers.

Hatvany and Pucik (1981) identified several other aspects of the focus on human resources in an agency: slow promotion, job rotation, internal training, a complex appraisal system, emphasis on work groups, open and extensive communication, consultative decision making, and concern for employees. It commonly is understood that slow promotion, job rotation, and internal training are designed to develop managers who have been thoroughly socialized in an agency's values and philosophy and who understand all aspects of its operations.

The long waiting period for advancement (*slow promotion*) can be used to help the employee gain a thorough understanding of the current assignment and its relationship to other departments and programs;

develop the job to its fullest potential; and prepare, through training, further education, and experience, for a position of greater responsibility. *Job rotation* also can occur while the employee is waiting for a promotion. It not only acquaints aspirants with all aspects of the agency's operations, but promotes integration of the staff and mutual understanding and appreciation of the jobs of others in the organization. When employees have done the jobs of other staff members or know that they are likely to do so, mutual appreciation, cooperation, and communication are enhanced, and misunderstanding, competitiveness, and criticism are reduced.

The current pressure for efficiency and high productivity may militate against the rotation of jobs, as may the attitudes of some staff members, especially if the rotation is into an area of concrete or direct care services from an area that affords more opportunities for "therapy" or "clinical work." Comments such as "I'm being stretched too thin," "there are too many new forms and procedures to learn," and "I don't like to feel like a beginner again" are heard when rotation or any other techinque is proposed that moves in the direction of a generalist rather than a specialist approach.

Complex appraisal systems measure not only an individual's performance against predetermined standards and goals, but address "various desirable personality traits and behaviors—such as creativity, emotional maturity, and cooperation with others as well as team performance results" (Hatvany & Pucik, 1987, p. 13). Attention to these traits and behaviors, according to Hatvany and Pucik, make the evaluation process more "self-selective" because of the motivation and commitment required to make it obvious to superiors that the employee possesses such desirable personality traits and exerts unusual effort in behalf of the organization.

Equity is essential to the maintenance of group cohesiveness and cooperation. As Ouchi (1981) wrote:

> An organization is any stable, patterned set of transactions among a set of individuals or units. This pattern of transactions will remain stable, without defections, only so long as each party to the transaction is satisfied that he or she is receiving an equitable share of rewards. Therefore, the problem of organization is the problem of finding the least-cost method of maintaining equity among trading partners. (p. 41)

Hatvany and Pucik (1981) quoted the personnel director of a major company, who commented on slow promotion, as follows: "The secret . . . is to make everybody feel as long as possible that he is slated for the top position in the firm—thereby increasing his motivation during the most productive period of his employment" (p. 13). Hatvany and Pucik added that "the public identification of 'losers,' who of course far outnumber the winners in any hierarchical organization, is postponed in the belief that the increased output of the losers who are striving hard to do well and still hoping to beat the odds, more than compensates for any lags in motivation of the impatient winners."

Such schemes for keeping productivity high while developing a cadre of well-qualified and well-socialized managers, however, require a high level of finesse by managers in any environment and are hazardous particularly in a field that is historically and culturally rooted in remediating the failures and injustices suffered by the underclass. According to Ouchi (1981),

> . . . it is an underlying acceptance of the legitimacy of the hierarchy that creates a perception of equity. A bureaucracy succeeds only if employees at lower levels regard their superiors as being fair and evenhanded in evaluating their work and providing them with appropriate rewards . . . short-run sacrifices will be made because all parties know that they will be there for the long run—and they know that in the long run equity will be restored. (pp. 41–42)

Is it realistic and appropriate to expect historically disadvantaged groups, such as women and minorities, to have an "underlying acceptance of the hierarchy"? Similarly, when low salaries continue to destabilize the work force in family and children's agencies, will most staff members be willing to make such "short-run sacrifices" because they "know" that they will belong to the organization long enough for "equity to be restored"? The author thinks not. In this field, it is not Ouchi's "impatient winners" who have "lags in motivation"; it is the impatient "losers" who assume, on the basis of historical and current circumstances, that they are disadvantaged before they are put off further by slow promotion, lateral transfers, and comprehensive evaluations. Rebellion, burnout, and defection are more common responses to inequity by those who do not see a clear path to advancement. In the typical family and children's agency, the author has observed, the willingness to make short-term sacrifices comes more from the congruence of the staff member's and agency's values than from confidence in the restoration of equity in the long term.

The difficulties in implementing sound management principles do not negate their value. Problems of execution can and should challenge administrators to find applications that are appropriate and specific to their organizations. Scrupulousness in defining equitable personnel policies and fringe benefits can go far toward establishing "underlying acceptance of the legitimacy of the hierarchy" (Ouchi, 1981, pp. 41–42).

Hatvany and Pucik (1981) stated that *work groups* influence their members directly through the enforcement of norms and indirectly by affecting the values and beliefs of members. Tasks are assigned to groups rather than to individuals, and group cohesion is stimulated by delegating responsibility to the group not only for getting the tasks performed, but for designing the way in which they get performed.

Open and extensive communication also is important. Staff members need to know, at a minimum, information that affects them personally and affects their job. If staff members are expected to coordinate their work with others, they must know about the functions and roles of others and what problems and pressures they face. If staff members are expected to be committed to the organization, its mission, and its goals, they must know as much about the organization as possible.

Still, there are constraints on the nature and amount of information that should be shared. Should staff members know how the agency invests its endowment funds? Should threats of cuts in funding—and therefore in personnel—be made known to staff, or should the sharing of such information be postponed until it is time to make the cuts? Should administrative difficulties with other agencies or funding sources be revealed to staff members? How much time should be spent in communication with staff? How much time should be given to feedback? These and other questions plague administrators who seek that level and style of communication that is at once efficient, inspirational, and acceptable to staff members and that enhances the effective operation of the agency. The effectiveness of extensive face-to-face communication must be balanced against spending too much time in meetings. Consideration must be given to the type of information that must be communicated through informal, casual channels. The balance between oral and written communication is similarly important.

Open and extensive communication is a prerequisite to *consultative decision making*. Without clear, open communications, both the nature of problems and the advice concerning their resolution are at serious risk of being misunderstood. Without all the available information, understood in the proper context, decision makers are not informed fully and are vulnerable to making poor decisions.

A concern for the employee must pervade all aspects of management. In many companies, it is manifested by special gifts and bonuses, company-sponsored social events and recreational facilities, or the provision of educational scholarships and awards. It also is demonstrated in the managers' attention and responsiveness to the everyday problems, needs, and interests of employees. As Peck (1978) noted:

> When we love another we give him or her our attention. We attend to that person's growth. When we love ourselves we attend to our own growth. When we attend to someone we are caring for that person. The act of attending requires that we set aside our own preoccupations . . . and actively shift our consciousness. Attention is an act of will, of work against the inertia of our own minds. (pp. 120–121)

MODERN MANAGEMENT PERSPECTIVES

Douglas McGregor summarized a great deal of research in saying that "effective peformance results when conditions are created such that the members of the organization can achieve their own goals best by directing their efforts toward the success of the enterprise" (as quoted in Hatvany & Pucik, 1981, p. 20). And as Richard D. Wood of Eli Lilly Company put it (as quoted in Burke, 1981),

> I think that, for the corporation to be coordinated properly and to help make sure that we give priority to the right thing, it is really necessary for me to have a pretty good feel for what is going on in all pieces of the business. On the other hand, I don't try to tell them every day how to run their shop.
>
> I think our employees in the company understand the conditions under which we operate and they respect them—and I think they also respect the honesty and integrity of management in the decision-making process, particularly as it applies to them as individuals. And if we can maintain that kind of feeling in that kind of atmosphere, everything else will fall into place. (pp. 34–35)

The author has developed the following four questions that managers may want to ask themselves periodically:

1. Am I doing my job as well as it needs to be done?
2. Am I doing my job as well as I can do it?
3. Am I doing my job as well as someone else can do it?
4. Am I doing my job to the satisfaction of my employer?

Finally, the words of Watson (1963) of IBM are an appropriate summary of modern management perspectives:

I firmly believe that any organization, in order to survive and achieve success, must have a sound set of beliefs on which it premises all its policies and actions. Next, I believe that the most important single factor . . . is faithful adherence to these beliefs, and finally, I believe if an organization is to meet the challenge of a changing world, it must be prepared to change everything about itself except those beliefs. (p. 5)

REFERENCES

Burke, W. W. (1981). Conversation: An interview with Richard D. Wood. *Organizational Dynamics, 9*, 22–35.

Hatvany, N., & Pucik, V. (1981). Japanese management practices and productivity. *Organizational Dynamics, 9*, 5–21.

Hollis, F. (1954). Social casework. In R. Kurtz (Ed.), *Social work yearbook* (pp. 474–480). New York: American Association of Social Workers.

Lilienthal, D. E. (1967). *Management: A humanist art.* New York: Columbia University Press.

Lilly Endowment Leadership Education Program. (1987). *A rich tradition of service: Volunteer leadership for the public good.* Unpublished manuscript.

Ouchi, W. G. (1981). Organizational paradigms: A commentary on Japanese management and theory Z organizations. *Organizational Dynamics, 9*, 36–43.

Peck, S. (1978). *The road less travelled.* New York: Simon & Schuster.

Rice, R. M. (1986). *Report from the field.* Unpublished manuscript. Milwaukee, WI: Family Service America.

Sathe, V. (1983). Implications of corporate culture: A manager's guide to action. *Organizational Dynamics, 12*, 5–23.

Schein, E. H. (1986). *Organizational culture and leadership.* San Francisco: Jossey-Bass.

Skloot, E. (1987). Survival time for nonprofits. *Foundation News, 28*, 38–42.

Tietyen, J. (1987). *Memorandum to mid-America chief executive officers and chief volunteer officers.* Unpublished manuscript.

Watson, T. J. (1963). *A business and its beliefs: The ideas that helped build IBM.* New York: McGraw-Hill.

Welford, H., & Gallagher, J. (1985). *The myth of unfair competition by nonprofit organizations.* Washington, DC: National Assembly of National Voluntary Health & Social Welfare Organizations.

13

▲

Modern Management
in Day Care and
Early Childhood Education

Todd Boressoff

A GREAT DEAL OF EXCITEMENT has been generated in the business community about the success of Japanese industry in the American market-place. Although some attention has focused on tariffs and quotas, much of the recent writing has stressed the importance of Japanese management principles, which are strikingly similar to those of modern "excellence" management (Alston, 1986; Hatvany & Pucik, 1981; Ouchi, 1981; Pascale & Athos, 1981; Peters & Austin, 1986; Peters & Waterman, 1982).

For those who are well versed in child development, the extent to which certain themes of modern management parallel the root concepts of day care and early childhood education is striking. One common theme is trust—in group process, in the eagerness of individuals to learn about and take charge of their world, and in the capability of workers in the workplace and of children in the classroom. Other common themes are learning through action, a holistic concern for the employee and for the child, and shared responsibility for decision making. If there are important parallels between modern management principles and practice in early childhood development, then it follows that the early childhood education program/day care center might be a fertile ground for the implementation of these new management techniques. Some of the key principles of modern management are examined in this chapter and the extent to which they relate to the core concepts of day care and early childhood education are considered. Also, how directors of day care and early childhood programs may use these strategies in their daily work is described.

KEY PRINCIPLES OF MODERN MANAGEMENT

Some of the principles of modern management may have less relevance in the day care and early childhood environment than do others. Although these less-relevant principles are noted, the primary emphasis in this section is on those concepts that translate most directly to the environment of early childhood programs. The aspects of modern management that are most appropriate to day care/early childhood education are examined.

Orientation to People

Ouchi (1981) noted that "what is distinctive about Japanese companies is their devotion to their human assets" (p. 37). Pascale and Athos (1981) identified "careful attention to their human resources from recruitment all the way through retirement" (p. 204). Peters and Waterman (1982) devoted a chapter to "Productivity Through People." Moving even further in this direction, Peters and Austin (1985) advocated a "bone-deep belief" in people. But how is this orientation to people reflected in modern companies? Alston (1986) described four basic principles of Japanese management. The first two are as follows:

1. The worker who is able to perform any work duty is intelligent enough to improve the productivity and quality of that work.
2. Given the chance, workers want to improve the quality of their work (p. 23).

An orientation to people permeates the Japanese and excellence-oriented American companies. It is reflected in the trust in the capability of workers, the dignity accorded the individual, the holistic concern for the worker, and the many opportunities for face-to-face interaction and communication between workers and between workers and managers.

Two factors affect the concept of *worker capability*. One is the belief in the intrinsic intelligence of the worker—that "the worker is not stupid" (Alston, 1986, p. 24). The other is the unique position that each worker holds in the organization. Each worker is uniquely qualified to understand the subtleties of his or her job and, therefore, should be given wide latitude in making day-to-day decisions and should be looked to for information. As Peters and Austin (1985) stated: "If you are asking for practical innovation from everyone—receptionist as well as designer—you are turning every employee into an outward-focused, adaptive sensor" (p. 7). Of course, along with the perception that the worker is capable and uniquely situated is the concept that the worker is responsible for what happens at that position (Hatvany & Pucik, 1981, p. 20).

An orientation to people is visible in the assertion of *individual dignity*, which echoes throughout these works. "IBM's philosophy is largely contained in three simple beliefs. I want to begin with what I think is the most important: *our respect for the individual . . . .* We devote more effort to it than anything else" (Peters & Waterman, 1982, p. 238). With this quote from Thomas Watson, Jr., chairman of IBM and son of its founder, Peters and Waterman pointed out that "there was hardly a more pervasive theme in the excellent companies than their respect for the individual (p. 238). Even in Japanese corporations, where the individual is encouraged to make his or her individual needs subservient to those of the work group, the basic respect for the individual remains. New employees are seen as human resources to be cultivated. Workers are defined as "persons who, if given the opportunity, will develop their skills and talents" (Alston, 1986, p. 172).

The *holistic concern for the employee* is evident especially in the Japanese concept of lifetime employment. Although the term applies only to some employees in the larger corporations, "permanent" workers have almost total job security (Alston, 1986, p. 223). And lifetime employment cuts both ways. It provides the worker with job security and substantial benefits and ensures that the time and energy the company invested in developing the skills of the employee will not be wasted. The employee will reinvest these capabilities in the organization. The total concern for people in the "excellent" organizations is evident in Peters and Austin's (1985) listing: "People involvement in all plant activities: budgeting, inventory management, layout and design, day to day problem solving (100 percent). Gain-sharing/productivity-sharing programs; employee ownership programs . . . . Creation of . . . 'heroes' . . . down the line" (p. 550).

As Peters and Waterman (1982) noted, "the point, then, is the *completeness* of the people orientation in the excellent companies." This orientation is also evident in the emphasis on face-to-face interactions and open communication (p. 240). Alston (1986) described the use of open space in the typical Japanese corporation: "Offices are large and contain desks and work space for every member of the department. All workers are visible to each other and interaction is easily accomplished" (p. 163). Tasks that might require memorandums in a more compartmentalized environment can be accomplished with a glance across the room. When the telephone of an absent colleague rings, the worker at the next desk can answer it. "Telephone conversations are overheard, files are kept in common cabinets, and dealings with visitors are visible to co-workers" (Alston, 1986, pp. 163–164). Even meetings take place in a common area, in an open space visible to everyone else. Coffee, tea, and snacks are available throughout the day, and it is common for employees to congregate informally. As another example, when Rene McPherson took over the leadership of the Dana Corporation, one of his first steps was to destroy the "22½ inches of policy manuals" and replace them with a one-page statement of philosophy. The first point in the statement was, "Nothing more effectively involves people, sustains creditability or generates enthusiasm than face-to-face communication" (Peters & Waterman, 1982, p. 248).

These people-oriented themes are summarized in the following statement from Bill Hewlett, co-founder of Hewlett-Packard:

I feel that . . . it is the policies and actions that flow from the belief that men and women want to do a good job, a creative job, and that if they are provided with the proper environment, they will do so. It is the tradition of treating every individual with consideration and respect and recognizing personal achievements . . . . The dignity and worth of the individual is a very important part. (Peters & Waterman, 1982, p. 244)

Hewlett went on to describe the elimination of time clocks, the evolution of flexible work hours, the policy of allowing personnel to take home expensive laboratory equipment for their own use, the use of first names, and other examples of Hewlett-Packard's person-centered approach. However, he concluded: "You can't describe it in numbers or statistics. In the last analysis it is a spirit, a point of view. There is a feeling that everyone is part of a team . . . [and] it is an idea that is based on the individual" (Peters & Waterman, 1982, p. 244).

Group Harmony/Group Process

Although "devotion to their human assets" or "productivity through people" reflect the understanding of and commitment to the capability of individuals, both the Japanese and the excellence-oriented American companies share a view of the importance of group process and teamwork. As Hatvany and Pucik (1981) noted, "Japanese organizations devote far greater attention to structural factors that enhance group motivation and cooperation than to the motivation of individual employees" (p. 14). Tasks are assigned to groups rather than to individuals. Group cohesion is encouraged through the expectation that the group will be responsible for designing the methods to accomplish its task. The group is evaluated on its accomplishments.

The Japanese use the term *wa* to describe the concept of group harmony or consensus. Wa "refers to a balance or limitation of individual needs and desires in favor of the good of the group" (Alston, 1986, p. 40). Shared values, quality circles (in which work groups come together to improve their efforts); consensual decision making; and management for group harmony are some of the ways in which the Japanese endeavor to establish wa. "In this context," Alston stated, "production goals are secondary. It is assumed that group morale results in high production and quality performance" (p. 23). Pascale and Athos (1981) noted that the work group is the "major building block of Japanese organizations" (p. 125). This emphasis on interdependence (as opposed to independence) and group success (as opposed to individual heroics) permeates even Japanese baseball, in which, according to Pascale and Athos "neither the spectacular batter nor the brilliant infielder is recognized as truly valuable until he acquires this capacity to blend into the harmonies of the team" (p. 130).

In successful American organizations, the concept of wa is more likely to be called team spirit. The importance of the work group is evident throughout *In Search of Excellence* (Peters & Waterman, 1982). For example, the authors quote Lee Smith in *Fortune* on the 3M Corporation: It is "so intent on innovation that its essential atmosphere seems not like that of a large corporation, but rather a loose network of laboratories and cubbyholes populated by feverish inventors and dauntless entrepreneurs" (p. 14). The enthusiasm for groups is reflected in *A Passion for Excellence* as well, in which Peters and Austin (1985) quoted Gerhard Newman, the guiding force in General Electric's program of jet engine development, on aspects of teamwork: "All of us were one team: workers, managers, foremen and engineers . . . ." (p. 197). "The project reminded me of the Flying Tigers . . . undermanned, overworked, and successful" (p. 132). Peters and Austin continued to discuss the sense of commitment that develops in small groups working together by quoting from Data General's Tom West, hero of Tracy Kidder's *The Soul of the New Machine:* "There's thirty guys out there who think it's their machine. I don't want that tampered with" (p. 166).

Shared Values/Superordinate Goals

All the works on modern excellence-oriented organizations stress the importance of a shared philosophical thrust or superordinate goal. This shared orientation becomes the glue that holds these decentralized, action- and people-oriented organizations together. Pascale and Athos (1981) referred to "superordinate goals," noting that "Great Companies Make Meaning." Peters and Waterman described modern companies as hands-on and value driven. Peters and Austin (1985) wrote of symbols, drama, vision, and even love. And Ouchi (1981) stated, "In every Type Z ("excellent") company there is a distinctive philosophy of management. That philosophy supplies the underlying premises for decision making." Each of these organizations has a sense of uniqueness that "derives from an underlying, common understanding of both the purpose and appropriate methods of management" (p. 40). Ouchi went on to say that this philosophy needs to be "explicitly stated in a cogent and integrated statement" (p. 40). The following are a few examples of this kind of statement in excellence-oriented companies.

A one-page operational philosophy was evolved by a group of employees at the Dana Corporation. Some of their "40 Thoughts" included these:

■ Recognize people as our most important asset.
■ Help people grow.
■ Encourage entrepreneurship.
■ Make every employee a manager.
■ Decentralize.
■ Remember—people respond to recognition. (Peters & Austin, 1985, p. 402)

Johnson and Johnson's one-page credo makes some of the following points:

We believe our first responsibility is to the doctors, nurses and patients, to mothers and all others who use our products and services.

Everyone must be considered as an individual. We must respect their dignity and recognize their merit . . . . Employees must feel free to make suggestions and complaints.

We are responsible to communities in which we live. (Peters & Austin, 1985, p. 392)

At Tandem Computer, the core philosophy is

(1) all people are good;
(2) people, workers, management and company are all the same thing;
(3) every single person in the company must understand the essence of the business;
(4) every employee must benefit from the company's success;
(5) you must create an environment where all of the above can happen. (Peters & Austin, 1985, pp. 241–242)

Former Mayor of Baltimore William Donald Schaefer (now Governor of Maryland) stood before his cabinet and wrote on an easel "People," or "Pee-Pull!," or "What if you lived There?" (Peters & Austin, 1985, p. 13). Each of these organizations or people takes pains to establish an overarching framework of clearly articulated values.

Action Orientation

Explicit in discussions of the excellent American corporations and implicit in the writing about Japan is what Peters and Waterman (1982) termed "a bias for action." The use of task forces, project teams, and innovation through *skunk-works*—small independent work projects that are given great leeway for brainstorming and production models—are explored in depth by Peters and Waterman (1982) and Peters and Austin (1985).

Not at all facetiously, Peters and Waterman (1982) sprinkled their discussion of action with such quotes as "Ready. Fire. Aim" (p. 119), by an executive at Cadbury's; "But above all try something" (p. 119), by Franklin Delano Roosevelt; their own favorite axiom, "Do it. Try it. Fix it" (p. 134); "Chaotic action is preferable to orderly inaction" (p. 134), by Karl E. Weick, a social theorist at Cornell University; and, finally, Woody Allen's "Eighty percent of success is showing up" (p. 119). A propensity for getting started, for getting down to a problem, and for experimenting characterizes most of the excellent companies. The thrust is, let us see what happens if, rather than ideas first and action later. This is the hands-on part of the hands-on/value-driven organizations described by Peters and Waterman (1982).

Although the writers on Japanese management are less direct in this regard, the focus on the work group (Alston, 1986), delegation, quality control circles, participative planning and control (Pascale & Athos, 1981), and decentralization all underline the relative action orientation of these corporations.

Quality for the Customer

Concern for quality, or excellence, in a product or service and a "bone-deep" belief in the importance and value of the customer are two concepts that are inextricably intertwined in modern management approaches. Pascale and Athos (1981) traced the evolution of IBM's basic beliefs (shared values), beginning in 1940 with Thomas J. Watson, Sr.'s first aphorisms to himself: "Aim high and think in big figures; serve and sell; he who stops being better stops being good" (p. 181). In 1962, Thomas Watson, Jr., was espousing the following set of beliefs. Note that two of the three have to do with quality and a focus on the customer, with an orientation to people, of course, being the first belief.

> Respect for the individual. Respect for the dignity and rights of each person in the organization.
> Customer service. To give the best customer service of any company in the world.
> Excellence. The conviction that an organization should pursue all tasks with the objective of accomplishing them in a superior way. (Pascale & Athos, 1981, p. 185)

In their chapter "Close to the Customer," Peters and Waterman (1982) keyed in on a shared passion of excellent companies, what they termed "quality obsession." They quoted from an article in *Fortune* about Caterpillar Tractor as follows: "The main principles are excellence of quality, reliability of performance, and loyalty in dealer relationships (with the customers)" (p. 170).

The use of quality control circles in Japan is a reflection of the emphasis on the work group, team responsibility and capability and of the concern for quality. "Quality of work and speed of job execution are key concerns" (Hatvany & Pucik, 1981, p. 15). Alston (1986) noted that manufacturers see quality and productivity as one and the same: "A good product is both error-free and made as cheaply (efficiently) as possible." The Japanese view a "perfect" product as one that is error free, but a high-priced error-free product is not considered perfect. To this end, "workers are expected to be *personally concerned* with making *every* product they make *better* and *more cheaply*" [Italics added] (p. 260).

Quality circles and other quality-oriented devices are valuable, according to Peters and Austin (1985), only if managers—at *all* levels—are living the quality message, paying attention to quality, spending time on it . . . And if managers understand that quality . . . . comes from people who care and who are committed. Finally, quality comes from the belief that *anything* can be made better, that beauty is universally achievable. (p. 115)

Quality and quality at a fair price are nothing if they are not a reflection of the importance of the human being who receives the product or service—the customer. Peters and Waterman (1982) devoted a full chapter to being close to the customer, and Peters and Austin (1985) stated that customers are fully one-quarter of their structural formula for successful management (p. 5). In many ways, the care of customers is simply the logical extension of the orientation to people inherent in the modern management approach. In all respects, the thrust is to humanize the relationship between the organization and its customers. Peters and Austin (1985) summarized this view by quoting from the following prominently displayed poster at L.L. Bean:

What is a Customer?

A Customer is the most important person in this office . . . in person or by mail.

A Customer is not dependent on us . . . we are dependent on him.

A Customer is not an interruption of our work . . . he is the purpose of it. We are not doing him a favor by serving him . . . he is doing us a favor by giving us the opportunity to do so.

A Customer is a person who brings us his wants. It is our job to handle them profitably to him and to ourselves. (pp. 111–112)

Thus, an orientation to people, group process, shared values, an action orientation, and quality for customers are some of the philosophical principles of modern management. Before examining the related techniques that directors of day care and early childhood programs might use, some thought must be given to the parallels between these principles of modern management and the root philosophies of developmental early childhood education.

PARALLELS: MODERN MANAGEMENT AND EARLY CHILDHOOD THEORIES

This section draws parallels between modern management and the core philosophies of developmental, interactive day care and early childhood education. Of course, there are many differences between the two, not the least of which is self-evident—namely, that one field is concerned with the work of adults and the other with the growth of children. Some might feel that drawing such parallels implies a demeaning view of the adult, but the intention here is the opposite. Modern, developmental early childhood theory has already covered the ground that modern business is only discovering. For years, it has exalted action-oriented discovery by individuals and groups.

A 1986 position paper of the National Association for the Education of Young Children (NAEYC) helps provide continuity throughout this section. On the basis of "both laboratory and clinical classroom research to document the broad-based literature that forms the foundation for sound practice in early childhood education," the position paper lists 129 references in its bibliography (NAEYC, 1986b, p. 28).

People-Oriented/Child-Centered Views

Capability, dignity, a holistic view of the individual, and the importance of face-to-face interactive communication are some aspects of the orientation to people that already have been examined. In the world of day care and early childhood education, this orientation to people is reflected in the term *child centered*. The people-oriented classroom focuses on the child. "Children's natural curiosity and desire to make sense of their world are used to motivate them to become involved in learning activities" (NAEYC, 1986b, p. 26). Similar to the Japanese view of workers—that they "want to improve the quality of their work" (Alston, 1986, p. 23)—NAEYC (1986b) holds that "children do not need to be forced to learn; they are motivated by their own desire to make sense of the world" (p. 21).

Children are trusted and treated with dignity, but this trust is not frivolous. One does not naively set the child adrift and expect competence; rather, one understands that with supportive supervision in an appropriate environment, children flourish and are, relative to their developmental level, supremely competent. "Each child is viewed as a unique person with an individual pattern of timing of growth and development" (NAEYC, 1986b, p. 23).

Similar to the Japanese holistic view of the employee is the early childhood concept of the "whole child" (Biber, 1984, pp. 4–5). Programs are designed to "meet children's needs and stimulate learning in all developmental areas—physical, social, emotional, and intellectual" (NAEYC, 1986b, p. 23). Cohen, Stern, and Balaban's (1983) view demonstrates dignity toward children and clarifies the holistic view. Rooted in the child study movement, their classic early childhood work sees children as a profound source of knowledge about children. These authors lead teachers through the techniques of observation: how to observe children during routines, relating to one another, using materials, at fantasy play, and relating to adults. They help teachers learn from children about how children learn.

As Biber (1984) noted, "the child is the major actor in this environment" (p. 253). NAEYC (1986b) emphasized the importance of face-to-face interaction: "Children acquire knowledge about the physical and social worlds in which they live through playful interaction with objects and people" (p. 21). According to Stone and Church (1973) "the teacher needs to be an alert observer, but a participant observer who can interpret and clarify the child's intellectual and emotional experiences, and who capitalizes on the fortuitous occasions for learning which arise" (p. 329).

Action Orientation/Learning by Doing

In early childhood education, the concept of learning by doing is equal in importance to the term "child centered" and is the direct equivalent of modern management's bias for action. As NAEYC (1986b) stated:

> Young children learn by doing. The work of Piaget, Montessori, Erikson, and other child development theorists and researchers has demonstrated that learning is a complex process resulting from the interaction of children's own thinking and their experiences in the external world. (p. 20)

Children develop knowledge through "playful interaction" (p. 21), from "self-directed problem solving and experimentation" (p. 24), and through "concrete learning activities with materials and people relevant to their own life experiences." They are expected to be "mentally and physically active" (p. 23).

In the preschool or day care classroom, children's action is termed play. Biber (1969) documented the emphasis on play by quoting Harriet Johnson, a theorist in the 1920s:

> "We do not believe that sense experiences should be given by training, but by providing materials the use of which leads to sense discrimination because again we are convinced that *with self-initiated use comes power.*" [Italics added] (p. 28)

The concept of hands-on interaction through play permeates the literature on early childhood education. "Play is the fitting of the half-formed concept in the child's mind with a garment, not of words, but of representation" (Lowenfeld, 1967, p. 158). Play "requires the child to: (1) create a context for play rather than finding it; (2) deal with reality and scale in translating ideas to the medium; (3) gradually step outside of self to symbolize self in play" (Cuffaro, 1984, p. 72). The history of the importance of play is indeed a long one, and dates back to Plato:

> Arithmetic, then, and geometry and all branches of preliminary educa-
> tion . . . should be introduced in childhood; but not in the guise of com-
> pulsory instruction, because for the free man [and woman] there should
> be no element of slavery in learning. Enforced exercise does no harm to
> the body, but enforced learning will not stay in the mind. So avoid com-
> pulsion, and let your children's lessons take the form of play. (Plato, *The
> Republic of Plato*, 1941, p. 258)

Group Harmony/Group Process

According to the NAEYC position paper (1986b), children need to work individually "or in small groups" (p. 23) and should be "provided many opportunities to develop social skills such as cooperating, help-ing, negotiating, and talking with the person involved to solve interper-sonal problems" (p. 24). Although a focus on the individual is impor-tant in the early years of development, the classroom is, by definition, a group experience. The classroom is a laboratory for life, and early childhood theorists never hesitate to look at the importance of evolving group harmony. As Rudolph and Cohen (1984) indicated, "our ready focus on the individual must be balanced by an equal concern for the individual as a member of the group" (p. 49). Some key goals of early childhood programs are "to help the children establish mutually support-ing patterns of interaction. Building informal communication channels, verbal and non-verbal . . . . Cooperative and collective child-group relations: e.g., discussion periods, joint work projects" (Biber & Franklin, 1967, p. 19). Replace the word "child" with the word "employee" and this quote might have come directly from any of the works on modern management discussed in the first part of this chapter. Innovative skunk-works, establishing wa, and work teams—are much of what the early childhood classroom is about.

Quality for Customers/Caring about Parents and Children

Parents and children are the customers in the early childhood or day care program. Quality at this level means the coaxing of excellence from children and the provision of concerned care to parents and children. According to NAEYC (1986b), a high quality early childhood program provides a safe and nurturing environment that promotes the physical, social, emotional, and cognitive development of young children while responding to the needs of families (p. 6).

> The quality curriculum is developmentally appropriate both to the individual and the particular age level; it integrates physical, social, emotional and intellectual development; it is based on observations of children; it emphasizes hands-on interactive learning which is concrete, real and relevant to children's lives; and it provides a variety of activities of increasing difficulty, complexity and challenge (pp. 6–7). This increased challenge is at the same time in response to and stimulating of the child's developing understanding and skill. (p. 8)

Whereas American excellence-oriented companies and Japanese companies have learned the importance of obtaining feedback from customers, high-quality day care programs encourage the involvement of parents. "Parents have both the right and the responsibility to share in decisions about their children's care and education." They "should be encouraged to observe and participate" (NAEYC, 1986b, p. 15). Programs need to "work in partnership with parents, communicating regularly to build mutual understanding and greater consistency for children" (p. 27).

Shared Values/Superordinate Goals

The shared values that drive the high-quality day care and early childhood programs are focused on developing the vital potential of whole children. These values, of course, are reflected in a child-centered, action-oriented concern for children—a concern that nurtures excellence and remains wholly in touch with children and their parents. According to Biber (1984), the following developing processes are the superordinate goals of developmental, interactive early childhood programs:

> 1. There is the process of becoming competent, as a body and a mind, able to make and do and think, registering in the inner self the feelings of being able to overcome obstacles, master confusion, solve problems and feel one's self a doer and maker in the world of objects and ideas . . .

2. There is the process of building personal and interpersonal strength, the course by which a child can become . . . a person capable of acting autonomously—making choices, developing preferences, taking initiative, setting his [or her] own course for problem solving, evolving a code of ethics . . . [A process that evolves] from the impulse-ridden stage of infancy to the approximation of the integrated stage of maturity in which . . . individual differences are not only tolerated, but cherished, and a sense of identity can be achieved.

3. [There is the process of developing] an open, expanding system of sensitivity and responsiveness that makes it possible to perceive and respond to a wide range of phenomena . . . . Maturity in this developmental process . . . can be characterized in having available multiple modes—logical and alogical, reasoned and intuitive—for interacting as a self with the environment. (p. 128)

IMPLICATIONS FOR DIRECTORS

In the earlier parts of this chapter, significant parallels between modern management principles and those of day care and early childhood education were highlighted. The orientation to people of the mangement philosophy parallels the child-centered character of early childhood education. The bias for action aspect of managers parallels the hands-on, interactive, play-oriented approach of practitioners of early childhood education. Readings from both fields emphasize the importance of group harmony and social interaction and their necessary skills and reflect a deep commitment to quality and care, or even love, for customers and parents and children. These are some of the shared values that drive exemplary programs for both fields. As the key manager in day care and early childhood programs, the director is in a position to take special advantage of this confluence of philosophies.

A great many techniques are highlighted in the works on management already considered. One technique, management by wandering around, is key to the process of modern management. Although the central focus of this final section is on the roles of the director in this people/child-centered, action/play-oriented, caring environment, the chapter concludes with a thorough discussion of practical management by wandering around techniques.

The roles that will be considered are the director as role model, as facilitator/enabler, and as tone setter. In keeping with the modern management philosophy, however, it is necessary to start with the shared values needed to drive this environment. Biber's (1984) goals for children, just noted, draw together a superordinate philosophy for all the people in the early childhood program—directors, teachers, other staff, parents, and children. Here they are in brief:

(1) becoming competent, as a body and a mind . . . and feel one's self a doer and maker in the world; (2) building personal and interpersonal strength [toward] making choices . . ., taking the initiative . . ., problem solving . . ., a code of ethics; and (3) [developing] an open, expanding system of sensitivity and responsiveness [leading to] multiple modes . . . for action. (p. 128)

Director as Role Model

As a role model, the director lives the guiding principles of the program, and demonstrates the people/child orientation, for instance, by showing a caring concern for the staff, the children, and the parents. A concern for the staff may be shown in a variety of ways—by hearing the ideas, interests, and concerns of staff members and by listening carefully enough to comment on the content of staff members' statements and leading them, perhaps, to further questioning. It may also be shown by being available, physically and emotionally, formally and informally. An orientation to people may be modeled by sharing responsibilities through delegation, not of trivial tasks, but of true decision making by empowered staff members. When there is a problem in the delivery of food, for example, the staff member who is in closest proximity to the deliverer (physically, practically, or even emotionally) might be responsible for the resolution of the problems between the program and the food service. Similarly, the teacher who is most concerned with the particulars of an order of supplies might make the call to and form a relationship with the particular supply house.

The director may role model people-oriented values by tolerating mistakes—that is, by not accepting sloppy work, but by seeing mistakes made in the effort to accomplish a task as opportunities for learning. Finally, he or she may role model the people orientation by genuinely including staff in long-term decision making and the development of goals. When establishing an instrument for staff evaluation, the director might have the staff brainstorm the goals they have for children and evolve ideas about the consequent critical aspects of a teacher's work. In developing plans for the future, the director may include the whole staff in a way that would encourage them to picture evolving roles for themselves.

Directors can be occasional role models in the classroom as well. They may demonstrate the value of asking searching questions by reading a story about a hospital and leading the ensuing discussion. They may squat or sit down, thereby showing their respect for children by meeting them eye to eye. Directors should listen with respect and struggle for understanding with children. They may role model the empowerment of children by waiting patiently for the child who really needs to do his or her own zippering (helping only when the child shows visible frustration). They can interact with children on many levels, extending a child's drawing by asking, "Would you like me to write something about your work?" or inviting a child to the office for a "meeting."

The director also can provide a role model in attitude toward parent "customers" by listening caringly (and nondefensively) to the comments a parent may have about the program, about the director, or about a staff member. Respect for and caring about parents may be conveyed by eliciting written comments through an open-ended parent-feedback form. It seems obvious, but the best way the director can role model caring is by caring—demonstrating concern in everyday comments ("the holidays are sure a difficult time for children"), by holding meetings with the parents that focus on the parents' concerns in which he or she elaborates in clear language how the program helps children learn, and by facilitating conferences with parents that focus on helping the family to resolve problems and to grow. A caring director would avoid defending the program at the parents' expense.

Beyond the concern for parents, children, and the staff, the director needs to role model the action orientation of the program. By being active, by looking for practical answers to problems presented by parents and staff members, by taking appropriate action quickly and efficiently when it is possible to do so, and by encouraging others to take action at their level of responsibility, the director can help personify a bias for action.

Director as Facilitator/Enabler

There are two primary components to this aspect of the director's role: (1) fostering the existence of the program itself and (2) nurturing and stimulating the development of staff.

The director is responsible for preparing the organizational environment, in much the same way as the early childhood teacher prepares the classroom environment. In this regard, the director's first responsibility is to ensure the practical existence and stability of the program. Doing so entails working with the board of directors, and the larger organizational community. It entails funding and advocacy with funding and regulatory agencies, so the program remains true to its guiding principles, appropriate staff/child ratios are maintained, and qualified, well-trained staff are hired.

Preparing the environment includes providing sufficient supplies, materials, and equipment to stimulate children's exploration and to ensure their safety. It involves allocating the space, hiring the staff, and ensuring that the space is painted, cleaned, locked, and repaired. It also includes ensuring that the center is a safe and secure, yet stimulating, environment for children and staff members alike.

But the director must be a facilitator on more than this practical level. He or she must be a facilitator for staff as well. To be nurturers of children, the staff members also need to be nurtured at times. They need opportunities for training, both within the program and through payments for courses in colleges and other learning environments, and time to attend these courses. In addition, they should have the opportunity to learn from other programs, through visits and shared workshops.

Staff members need to be encouraged to grow within the program and eventually, if there is no opportunity for advancement, to be encouraged to develop the skills that eventually may take them to leadership positions elsewhere. Although it is sometimes painful to encourage skilled staff to move on, in the long run, such encouragement is a protection against resentment and burnout. Because early childhood programs are small, perhaps this career-long view of staff development will help to maintain the kind of enthusiasm and commitment that lifetime employment encourages in Japan.

Staff need to be provided with the space, time, and materials, such as typewriters, copiers, textbooks, and workbooks, to be able to innovate genuinely—to develop their own quality skunk-works. But the director must enable them through his or her attitude as well. The manager must empower the staff on a day-to-day level so that the staff are not second guessed, but, rather, are encouraged to explore and develop trains of thought and new ideas. The director needs to enable through a true comfort with delegation and shared decision making. Additionally, he or she must empower the professional evolution of staff members based on a root caring for them as individuals and collectively as members of the program.

Director as Tone Setter

Some of the preceding discussion addressed the director's tone-setting role—enabling and role modeling. However, in the following discussion, the term *tone-setting* is used in a larger sense in that the director's role more closely resembles the role of a theater or film director or that of an orchestra conductor.

In their chapter on excellence in school leadership, Peters and Austin (1985) pointed to "showmanship" as one important characteristic. Although superordinate goals are the values that drive the program, it is the director's responsibility to ensure that they emanate from the organization's very walls. In their examination of the leadership by principals from schools across social and economic strata, Peters and Austin found in each principal a compulsion for orchestration. They quoted one principal who stated, "I want to set a tone that is permeating the environment" (p. 472). For the early childhood or day care director, tone setting might occur on two fronts, the internal and the external.

Within the program, the director might help to choreograph the program's philosophy by displaying artwork, photographs, and posters throughout the building. Children's artwork, which reflects the whole range of developmental and individual competencies (from the 2-year-old's initial scribbles to the elaborate work with accompanying stories of the 5-year-old), should be respectfully and prominently displayed. Photographs of children building, pondering, climbing, talking, listening, crying, running, and sleeping should help focus attention on the "whole child." For example, NAEYC publishes posters that emphasize child-centered learning: "Trust Children to Learn," states one poster; another, depicting a child high on a climber, proclaims, "Childhood's Challenge, Mastering Skills"; still others counsel, "Listen to Children with Respect" and "Discovery *is* Learning" (NAEYC, 1986a). In the Borough of Manhattan Community College Early Childhood Center, with which the author is affiliated, the children come from various cultural backgrounds. The center has a huge world map with colored pins indicating family roots in 31 countries and many cities in the United States. Across the top is the statement, "Families from All Over the World." A handmade sign and accompanying article from the *New York Times* states, "Play, Too Serious to Be Left to Experts" (Hechinger, 1980, p. C4). After the New York Mets won the World Series, the center posted a photograph of Darrel Strawberry warmly holding his 3-year-old son, but the photograph was mounted and placed in a display case with the title, "All Parents Are Heroes."

Steps that are taken to dramatize a program *externally* are often the most effective. Slide shows of children at play and videotapes of them in interaction with one another not only highlight the program's values and philosophy, they help to attract funding when used as part of legislative or other funding initiatives.

In October 1986, the author attended a legislative forum held by the Child Care Council at the City University of New York. Children and parents from a coalition of 17 college-based programs brought artwork, balloons, newsletters, and posters. The testimony presented by parents, who ran the gamut from especially capable public speakers to shy-voiced students with notes trembling, was always articulate. And the message was simple: Child care helps parents stay in school (and become productive, contributing members of society), and it helps their children to learn and grow. The legislators in attendance were visibly moved.

Like role modeling and enabling, dramatizing a program is largely a matter of attitude. The program director should never miss an opportunity to include the center's newsletter, with children's work, parents' statements, teachers' commentaries, and appropriate slogans in any important mailing or as a handout to visitors. The director should remember to bring examples of the children's work to board meetings or to have parents who are excited about the program accompany him or her on legislative, board, or funding forays. Discussing the time spent on outside showmanship by one excellent principal, Peters and Austin (1985) observed that

> the amount of time he spends is entirely consistent with what we have learned about leadership. The slide show and the "selling" of the school everywhere, not merely in Atlanta, have their greatest impact not on the outside world, but on the school itself, as generators par excellence of pride and self-confidence. (p. 471)

MANAGEMENT BY WANDERING AROUND

If shared values are the energy source that powers modern management companies and the role-modeling, facilitating, and tone-setting roles of the director are the artful support, management by wandering around is the practical technique that is used most frequently by modern managers. Pascale and Athos (1981) referred to this technique as "visible management" and quoted Ed Carlson, head of United Airlines: "I think it is important for me to know what is going on and for [the employees] to know that I care about what's going on" (p. 158). Alston (1986) described the use of "walk-around management" in Japanese companies "as a technique used to decrease the feeling of separation which exists between . . . levels" (p. 100) and that "develops familiarity between management and worker and encourages a feeling of mutual involvement in the company's success" (p. 102). Peters and Waterman (1982) called management by wandering around a "technology of keeping in touch" (p. 123). However, Peters and Austin (1985) devoted two full chapters to management by wandering around. One is subtitled "The Technology of the Obvious" (pp. 9–42) and the other "Doing MBWA" (pp. 447–464). What, then, does management by wandering around mean to the director of a day care or early childhood program? It means, obviously, getting up from behind the desk, stepping out of the office, and entering the broader world of the day care center and its organizational environment. It means that he or she should physically place his or her body, mind, and soul in close proximity to the real people who are and who relate to the early childhood program—the staff, the children, the parents, the founders, and even the suppliers—the program's inner and outer environments.

But the process involves more than simple movement. Three activities are in operation, usually at the same time—(1) listening; (2) teaching (coaching, role modeling); and (3) direct facilitating. Management by wandering around enables the director to hear firsthand about the problems and successes of the program, and the technique provides the director with the opportunity to be of concrete service (Peters & Austin, 1985).

As obvious as the technique of management by wandering around may seem, Peters and Waterman (1982) pointed out that "management by wandering around ain't as easy as it may sound" (p. 447). Peters and Austin (1985) elaborated on particular approaches to this form of leadership—approaches that provide the framework for the remaining portion of this chapter. One mark of successful management by wandering around is whether the "space" has been left reduced or enhanced after the director's departure. Are those with whom the director has wandered stronger and more self-confident for his or her having been there? Has the process been one of empowerment?

One way that a director might discern how the staff experiences his or her effect on their space is to ask the staff members whether the last visit or staff meeting was helpful. It will take time for teachers and other staff to develop confidence to respond openly, but they will be encouraged to do so by the director's openness. Here, from Peters and Austin (1985) are some other ideas:

(a) talking last, not first; (b) consciously using "What do you think?" and avoiding "Why don't you try X, Y, Z?"; (c) pushing [the staff] to give you a detailed narrative, so that they expose their line of reasoning, ... with [the director] interjecting "And then what did you try?" rather than "Why didn't you try thus and such at that point?"; (d) not forcing them to blame others, . . . [Did maintenance forget to clean again?]; (e) leading them to generate next steps with indirect [at most] guidance, with queries [such as, "If we know that about Johnny and his relationship to his mother, what might it mean for us at pick time?"]; and (f) asking them to stop by and tell you what was tried, or to give you a call when the next step is taken. (p. 451)

These questions should help the director to enhance the space through which he or she has wandered.

Frequency of wandering is another consideration. If management by wandering around is not a regular experience for those wandered to, the experience will be more reminiscent of a sneak visit or, worse, a "state visit" (Peters and Austin, 1985, p. 451). To ensure a natural and productive interchange, management by wandering around must happen all the time. Peters and Austin (1985) had some ideas for directors on this topic as well: (1) keep a checklist on hand (with a copy to the secretary, if appropriate) with the names of parents, children, staff members, and others with whom you need to wander, (2) meet at "their place" rather than yours—in the classroom, in the parent's area, or at the agency in question, (3) mark "don't book" across portions of your appointment calendar, (4) check to see if other "walk throughs" might be coupled with visits that have already been planned. A workshop given by the licensing agency may provide the chance to speak to other directors about staffing needs, the resurfacing of the playground, or the particulars of the new regulations for fingerprinting the staff.

Having discussed the importance of management by wandering around and a few of the how-tos, the question arises, Where does the director wander? The answer is, "anywhere and everywhere having to do with the program." The director needs to wander with the staff, children, parents, other directors, bureaucracies, funders, and regulators.

Doing management by wandering around with the staff means going into the classroom and interacting there—commenting on the quality of play in the block area, noting the work displayed, asking "How are things going?" or "Can I be of some help?" and meaning it. It means sitting with teachers at casual times to challenge and stimulate them with questions or supporting them with sympathy and concrete assistance.

Teachers are, of course, not the only members of the staff. By placing themselves in proximity to office staff, for instance, directors gain a first-hand sense of the complex skills involved in typing a letter, taking in fees, providing accurate information to a phone caller, and warmly greeting a parent and child—all at the same time. Food service and maintenance staff may be wandered among as well, allowing the director to comment on the clever arrangement the cook has developed for coping with limited storage space or providing the evening custodian with the opportunity to communicate through the director to early morning teachers. These contacts enable the director to feel the interpersonal pulse of the program, to continue to support smooth operations, and to take steps to work through difficulties.

Management by wandering around with parents also means meeting them on their "turf"—a coffee shop, play yard, or their homes, and asking *them* how they are doing. More important, it means asking them how the director and program are doing in meeting their needs and the needs of their children. What more could be done? Management by wandering around in this regard means listening and asking the next logical question, avoiding quick answers, and helping the parents to clarify their concerns or the aspects about which they are pleased.

Management by wandering around with children is, in some ways, similar to the role modeling mentioned previously, but it differs from the management by wandering around experience with adults because children tell about their experiences with the program through their actions. How children are playing, how they look, and how they interact with one another tells us the most about the extent to which our program is meeting their needs. The director's personal experience with children is essential when he or she is trying to help a teacher work through particular issues. The director's frustration with a child immediately intercepts the inclination to give pat answers that sometimes leave the teacher's space diminished rather than enhanced.

Management by wandering around with other directors, in the community, and with bureaucracies and licensing and legislative bodies is different from work in the center, but only because the director is less in the position of a facilitator. Opportunities for productive listening, however, abound. Other directors, when plumbed for their expertise through the same leading questions a director might use with the staff, prove to be far more valuable colleagues than they may seem when competed with in a demonstration of who knows best.

Leading questions, attentive listening, and a genuine concern for what might be *their* concern may prove valuable in work with agencies and governmental bodies as well. All people are eager to demonstrate their skill and understanding, to show the importance of their work. A visiting director's appreciation is often remembered. Knowing individuals, stopping in to say hello, and talking about the ball game or the family helps those who might otherwise be no more than a signature on a form or the voice on the other end of a telephone establish human contact with the director and the director's program. Such relationships can make the difference between a threatening memorandum and a friendly, reminding telephone call.

As a final note on management by wandering around, it may be valuable to look once again at NAEYC's (1986b) position paper and at its description of appropriate practice for teachers:

> Teachers move among groups and individuals to facilitate children's involvement with materials and activities by asking questions, offering suggestions, or adding more complex materials or ideas to a situation. Teachers accept that there is often more than one right answer (p. 24).
>
> . . . . .
>
> The correct way to teach children is not to lecture or instruct them. Teachers of young children are more likely guides or facilitators. They prepare the environment so that it provides stimulating, challenging materials and activities for children. Then, teachers closely observe [listen] to see what children understand and pose additional challenges to push their thinking further. (p. 21)

The excellence management tenets of management by wandering around—listening, teaching, and facilitating—are reflected in and flow throughout this statement on appropriate practice with young children.

In this chapter, some of the key principles of Japanese and American excellence-oriented management have been explored and then related to parallel concepts in developmental, interactive day care and early childhood education. Finally, these parallels have been concretized in the form of specific attitudes and actions for early childhood managers. Perhaps the trust in people, action orientation, and strong belief in quality represented by these two usually disparate fields will help directors to further vitalize programs for parents and children.

REFERENCES

Alston, J. (1986). *The American samurai: Blending American and Japanese managerial practices.* New York: Walter de Gruyter.

Biber, B. (1969). *Challenges ahead for early childhood education.* Washington, DC: National Association for the Education of Young Children.

Biber, B. (1984). *Early childhood education and psychological development.* New Haven, CT: Yale University Press.

Biber, B., & Franklin, M. (1967). The relevance of developmental psychodynamic concepts to the education of the preschool child. *Journal of the American Academy of Child Psychology, 6,* 5–24.

Cohen, D., Stern, V., & Balaban, N. (1983). *Observing and recording the behavior of young children.* New York: Teacher's College Press.

Cuffaro, H. (1984). Dramatic play—The experience of block building. In E. Hirsch (Ed.), *The block book* (rev. ed.; pp. 121–151). Washington, DC: National Association for the Education of Young Children.

Hatvany, N., & Pucik, V. (1981). Japanese management practices and productivity. *Organizational Dynamics, 9,* 5–21.

Hechinger, F. (1980, October 21). About education: Experts call a child's play too serious to be left to adults. *New York Times,* p. C4.

Lowenfeld, M. (1967). *Play in early childhood.* New York: Wiley.

National Association for the Education of Young Children. (1986a). *Early childhood resources and services.* Washington, DC: Author.

National Association for the Education of Young Children. (1986b). Position statement on developmentally appropriate practice in early childhood. *Young Children, 6,* 4–29.

Ouchi, W. G. (1981). Organizational paradigms: A commentary on Japanese management and theory Z organizations. *Organizational Dynamics, 9,* 36–43.

Pascale, R., & Athos, A. (1981). *The art of Japanese management.* New York: Simon & Schuster.

Peters, T., & Austin, N. (1986). *A passion for excellence: The leadership difference.* New York: Warner Books.

Peters, T. J., & Waterman, R. H., Jr. (1982). *In search of excellence: Lessons from America's best-run companies.* New York: Warner Books.

Plato. (1941). *The Republic of Plato.* (Cornford, Trans.). New York: Oxford University Press. (Original work published in 378–368 BC).

Rudolph, M., & Cohen, D. (1984). *Kindergarten and early schooling.* Englewood Cliffs, NJ: Prentice-Hall.

Stone, J., & Church, J. (1973). *Childhood and adolescence.* New York: Random House.

14
▲

The Management of Services to Older Americans

Lennie-Marie P. Tolliver

AGING IS A GENERAL WORD that can be defined in terms of physiology, behavior, psychology, sociology, or chronology. In this chapter, older persons are defined in some instances as those who are aged 60 or over and in other instances as those who are aged 65 or over.

PROFILE OF OLDER AMERICANS

The U.S. Bureau of the Census (1984b) reported that the older population—persons aged 65 or older—would represent 12 percent of the population in 1985, or a total of 28.5 million persons. About one in eight Americans is aged. The aged are expected to continue to grow in the future, especially at the turn of the century, when the baby-boom generation reaches age 65. According to the U.S. Bureau of the Census (1983), between 2020 and 2030, one in six persons will be an older person and between 2025 and 2030, one in four persons will be elderly.

Who are the older persons of today, and what can be expected of tomorrow's older persons? According to data from the U.S. Bureau of the Census (1982), in 1985, the average life expectancy for females would be 83.7 years and for males, 80 years. Persons aged 75 and over and, within that group, persons aged 85 and over, would be the fastest growing segment of the older population. In 1983, 32,000 people would be 100 years or older; this number is expected to double by the turn of the century.

In recent years, the elderly minority population has been growing at a faster rate than has the elderly white population (U.S. Bureau of the Census, 1982). This trend is expected to continue. In 1987, over 3.5 million elderly persons, or 10 percent of the population aged 65 and over, were nonwhite (American Association of Retired Persons, 1988). By 2025, it is projected that 15 percent of the elderly population will be nonwhite, and by the year 2050, 20 percent are likely to be nonwhite (U.S. Bureau of the Census, 1984b).

The life expectancy of women continues to increase faster than that of men. Therefore, the male/female imbalance is expected to continue to grow. By the year 2000, 73 percent of the population aged 85 and over may be female (U.S. Bureau of the Census, 1984b). In 1985, half of the older women were widows. The majority of older persons lived in a family setting and 30 percent lived alone; about 5 percent lived in long-term care facilities, such as nursing homes and institutions.

The U.S. Bureau of the Census (1984a) reported that about one in six families headed by an elderly person had an annual income of less than $10,000, and 35 percent had an annual income of $25,000 or more. The poverty rate for elderly whites was 11 percent; for elderly blacks, 32 percent; and for elderly Hispanics, 24 percent. The major source of income for older families was social security, followed by asset income, public and private pensions, and "transfer" payments, such as Supplemental Security Income and veterans' payments. The educational level of elderly people has been increasing. Almost half the older population has completed high school and about 9 percent have had four or more years of college. About 11 percent were in the labor force, half of them part time, or were seeking employment actively.

In 1984, 32 percent of all older persons and 50 percent of older black persons assessed their health as fair or poor. The U.S. Department of Health and Human Services (1984) estimated that 14 percent of those aged 65 to 74, 26 percent of those aged 75 to 84, and 48 percent of those aged 85 and over need the assistance of another person in the areas of personal care or home management.

SOCIAL WORK MANAGERS

The demographic information just presented suggests that, perhaps more than in any other field, social work managers in programs for the aging require specialized information about and skills for serving older adults. In a study on the need for education and training in geriatrics and gerontology, the U.S. Department of Health and Human Services (1984) estimated that 300 social work faculty members need to be trained in gerontology by 1990 and 1,000 need to be trained by the year 2000 if the United States is to have a sufficient cadre of professional trained social workers to work with the elderly population. It identified the following as other actions that need to be taken:

■ Entry-level and mid-career education in geriatrics and gerontology for social work faculty.

■ The further development of curriculum materials for basic, graduate, and continuing education programs.

■ The development of practice sites that would provide role models for outstanding social work practice and research.

■ Increased social work participation in interdisciplinary training programs.

■ A conference of leaders among social work educators and researchers in geriatrics and gerontology to develop future education, training, and research strategies.

In 1983, the Council on Social Work Education received a grant from the U.S. Administration on Aging to develop model curricula, faculty development, and continuing education materials for social work educators. These materials were distributed to all social work education programs. Since their distribution, an International Association of Social Work Educators in Gerontology has been formed (Schneider, 1984).

The data collected by the U.S. Bureau of the Census on the professions does not have a specific category for social workers who identify themselves as administrators or managers; these persons are counted in a general category with other disciplines. Chess, Jayartne, and Norlin (1986) found that about 43 percent of their sample of members of NASW identified themselves as caseworkers or group workers in 1981 but 31 percent in 1985. About 38 percent of the respondents engaged in administration, supervision, and policy analyses in 1981 and about 46 percent in 1985. The study revealed that many of the social workers who engaged in management activities had a private clinical practice. The findings seem to support the view of many social work educators that a generalist base for the practice of management in social work is important. The study also highlighted the fact that many clinicians who move into mangement positions retain their interest in clinical practice.

The need for additional social work practitioners at all levels is supported by the demographics and the staffing projections of several national organizations. The Veterans Administration (1984), for example, estimated that in 2000, it will need 7,000 social workers to work with the large number of aged veterans it anticipates in that year—more than double the 3,000 social workers it employed in 1984 (*see also* Greene, 1986). Social work education has taken a step forward with its development of model curricula and continuing education documents. Each year, the number of educational programs offering gerontological courses is increasing and can be expected to increase in the future.

ADMINISTRATION OF SERVICES TO OLDER PERSONS

In most ways, the management of aging programs does not vary significantly from the management of other social work activities. Thus, the principles suggested in other parts of this book about modern approaches to management are equally applicable here. The one area of special significance is the structure of aging programs, which is somewhat different from that of other public and private services. The following is a description of how those services are organized and delivered. Knowing about the special structure of these services is crucial for effective management.

The Administration on Aging (AOA) is the largest social agency serving older people. AOA was created by Congress with the passage of the Older Americans Act (OAA) of 1965. The preamble to the act has been called the Bill of Rights for Older Americans. Succinctly stated, the agency is mandated to promote opportunities for older persons, aged 60 and over, to live independently and to continue to be contributing citizens in our society. The organization is embedded in a larger social system—the U.S. Department of Health and Human Services, Office of Human Development Services. Quality-of-life needs are to be met through the provision of services by AOA's network of state and area agencies on aging and through mobilizing others to provide these services (Ficke, 1985, p. 113).

Thus, there is a legislative mandate for services ranging from social change and advocacy through restorative, developmental, and preventive services. There is a legislative mandate to develop model demonstration projects, to engage in research, and to educate and train people to work in the field of aging and to provide training opportunities for older people.

About 50 percent of the funds come from appropriations earmarked by the OAA, with the balance coming from state and *general-purpose governments*, those municipal, county and regional units within states, such as economic development and planning districts; other federal sources, such as the Urban Mass Transportation Authority; and private sources, such as the United Way and contributions from recipients of services. Planning is done at the federal, state, and local levels. OAA's provisions require the involvement of older persons and technical experts in the identification of the needs of older persons, the resources and potential resources available to meet those needs, and the mechanisms for meeting those needs. Advisory committees exist at the federal, state, and local levels.

States are encouraged to work in areas of national attention, such as long-term care and intergenerational programming. OAA mandated only a few services: nutrition programs (congregate and home-delivered meals); access services, such as information and referral and transportation; legal services; ombudsmen in long-term care facilities; and a wide variety of supportive services. Under the supportive services category, states and area agencies on aging have considerable discretion in their allocation of resources. These services can range from homemaker–home health aid services to the support of senior centers. OAA has minimal enforcement provisions. Thus, compliance with the initiatives and direction of the AOA are sought through education, persuasion, dissemination of the best practice models and of research findings, and capacity-building activities.

A state prepares a state plan that encompasses the major features of plans submitted by the state's area agencies on aging, which are based on assessments of their needs and resources. Public hearings are held on the plan at the area and the state levels. After the state plan is approved by the governor, it is forwarded to the regional office of AOA for review and then to the commissioner on aging for approval. A review of the state plans may lead to the identification of trends in needs or technological approaches to problem solving, advocacy, or programming that may result in the development of a national initiative.

The value-oriented mission is stated explicitly in OAA. The AOA uses regulations, program instructions, technical assistance, monitoring, and reporting actions to ensure that there is adherence to the basic mission.

In 1981, federal staff were asked to compile data on the needs of the older population. On the basis of these data, the mandates of OAA, and the operating principles of AOA, they were to identify those areas in which AOA and its network should direct their attention and the means by which AOA could exercise its leadership and support the network. A four-year plan of action was developed and circulated, for review and comment, to various constituencies, such as members of Congress, the state and area agencies on aging, gerontological organizations, membership organizations of older persons, and professional associations whose members serve a large number of older people. The blueprint for action became the plan by which AOA systematically attempted to provide leadership (Tolliver, 1982).

The plan of action guided program instructions and technical assistance materials issued to the states and area agencies on aging, relationships with other federal agencies, relationships with organizations in the private sector, the award of discretionary grants, and the activities of staff members at all levels of government. A well-formulated written plan that had been subscribed to by multiple constituencies changed the planning process in AOA.

After the plan was issued to the states, the states were encouraged, on the basis of their assessment of needs and the actual and potential resources that were available to them, to identify areas in which they would be active. There were minimal direct reporting requirements. The assumption was that if a state developed a state plan that identified specific areas in which it would direct its efforts, the state would follow through on its plan and that persons at the state and local levels would be monitoring the outcomes of its efforts. There were, however, opportunities for feedback, usually through regional office staff and direct contact by the U.S. commissioner on aging and AOA staff through various meetings and on-site visits. Modifications were made in the techniques for implementation and in activities. The basic policies, however, were not changed.

One of AOA's basic principles was the establishment of partnerships between the public and the private sectors. The following example illustrates the successful development of such a partnership.

A reporter doing a story on the elderly in New York City asked an 80-year-old woman how she managed to get food, since she lived alone and was unable to leave her small apartment. She told the reporter that she received a home-delivered meal Mondays through Fridays. When asked what she ate on weekends, the woman replied, "Mostly, I don't." Today, that story has changed. As a result of the successful collaboration between a citywide area agency on aging and the private sector, thousands of homebound elderly persons in this community receive meals on weekends and holidays.

Noted food authorities in the community read the article. One of them called the City of New York department for the aging to ask if the agency would make sure that the money went for meals to the elderly if they could get contributions from their colleagues. The director assured them that the money would go to the elderly and assigned a staff member to work with them.

The department assumed the role of broker between the voluntary and the private sectors. The city, the Chamber of Commerce, a foundation, national corporations headquartered in the city, restaurants, and food-industry companies soon became involved. A retired public relations person offered to provide services. The press was contacted and responded by telling the story of the homebound elderly and covering various fund-raising events.

To ensure that the donations would be tax deductible, a separate non-profit corporation was set up to receive them. Three committees were established, each of which was staffed by a member of the Department for the Aging. A city Meals-on-Wheels committee, composed of food-industry leaders, developed financial resources, contacted the business community, and set a policy for the use of contributions on the basis of recommendations made by the voluntary agencies. A providers committee, consisting of representatives of the voluntary agencies that delivered services in the local community, was also formed. Its primary responsibility was to recommend priorities for using the contributions and to highlight unmet needs. A third committee, the staff committee, made up of staff of the Department for the Aging, had primary responsibility for ensuring the accountability and effective implementation of the program. This model became a best-practice model for the aging network and has been replicated, sometimes with differences, in various programs throughout the country.

The private sector has become more aware of the needs of older persons in recent years and has shown a willingness to become involved in providing services and in supporting the efforts of others to provide services. In the foregoing example, the lead in developing resources was assumed by persons in the private sector, and staff of the public agency supported and augmented their efforts.

Another basic principle of the AOA was the restoration of decision making and authority to state and general-purpose governments. In implementing this principle, the AOA undertook the development of an indirect services approach to policy development. An organization received a discretionary award to help the network devise policy options through changes in laws and city ordinances, zoning regulations, and by increasing the use of volunteers. Following the development of model policies, awards were given to the U.S. Conference of Mayors, the

National Association of Counties, and the National Governors Association to support and encourage their efforts at their governmental levels to discern what changes could be made to benefit older people. The network was involved in capacity building so its staff would be able to work effectively with representatives of the various governmental entities. As Gollub, Henton, and Waldhorn (1983) stated, these approaches emphasize the powers of other levels of government to govern rather than simply to spend.

Other Service Delivery Systems

There is no coherent national policy on aging. Over 125 departments in the federal government and numerous agencies at the state level have programs that are designed to serve the elderly. Some examples are the Urban Mass Transportation Authority, the U.S. Department of Housing and Urban Development, the U.S. Department of Energy, and the Health Care Financing Agency. In the mid-1980s, the cost of services to older persons, including social security payments, was about 28 percent of the total federal budget (Tolliver, 1983). Yet, in the continuum of care, there is an unevenness in services (for example, city residents have a greater access to services than do surburban and rural residents), and many older people who are eligible for services do not receive them. In some instances, older people are unaware of services; in other instances, such as the Food Stamp program, some older people associate services with "welfare" and do not apply for them.

In response to the gaps in services, a wide range of programs have been established. One innovation is the location of several services at the same place, so that older people can gain access to more than one service at a time. Another trend is the use of mobile equipment for delivering information and referral services, dental services, eye care services, and general health services, and the growth of alternative health care systems, such as health maintenance organizations. An additional development has been the growth of proprietary home health agencies that enable older people to remain in the community.

In some cases, these programs are part of the national network of aging services, regardless of whether they are public programs, private not-for-profit programs, or private for-profit programs (Ficke, 1985, p. 113). An example of such a network is as follows:

In a review of the types of cases handled by a private family agency, the administrator noted that a large number of older persons had been referred by local public housing officials to the agency's satellite office for alcohol and substance abuse problems. The officials were interviewed, and a survey of needs was conducted in the two public housing units. The results of the survey documented this population's need for services.

The agency administrator shared the results of the survey with the agency's board of directors, director of services, and director of the satellite facility. They agreed that a new position for an outreach worker should be created.

Although the worker's focus was on individuals with alcohol and substance abuse problems, the worker noted that many of the elderly people in the public housing units could use mental health services. The worker's primary roles were to provide information and referral services and, when time permitted, supportive casework services. Within six months, a sufficient number of potential clients had been identified to warrant discussion of creating a second position.

In this instance, an alert administrator who was engaged in a routine review of the agency's caseload believed that a trend in the population could be verified. The service staff had a full caseload, so the administrator decided to hire a new staff member, after involving key persons in the process who supported this decision. The services were offered to and accepted by a sufficient number of older persons to confirm the original decision that was made.

In these programs, successful administrators have demonstrated their basic knowledge about the elderly in their community and of the current and projected demographics, as well as their skills in developing and managing service delivery systems. They have the capacity to take action on the basis of assessments of demographics and needs; involve older consumers as partners; foster leaders and innovators among the elderly, their representatives, and staff of agencies; encourage practical risk taking; articulate and manage the values inherent in serving older persons; have open and frequent communications; set clear and reasonable expectations of staff members and grant them practical autonomy to do the job; be willing to shift and add resources; and be willing to be oriented to people. The example that follows illustrates many of these skills:

As a result of participation in a statewide coalition focused on the health needs of older people, a large southwestern private medical center began to consider its role in this regard. The center conducted a needs survey of its catchment areas to determine the demographics, the willingness of older people to use the center, and the types of services that would be of interest to them.

The top-level administrators supported the idea of developing a program. An advisory committee, composed of older people, advocates for older people, aging services personnel, and medical personnel, was formed. Ideas for programs were generated in brainstorming sessions, and a consultant was brought in to help formulate the ideas into discrete but interrelated programs.

A center for persons aged 55 and over was started in 1986. Among its services are free membership, life-enrichment courses, a physical fitness program, and discounted medical services. Over 4,000 people joined the center in the first year. Members of the nursing services staff and a public relations staff member were the initial personnel of the center. Physical space in the medical center was set aside for the program, and before the end of the year, a section of the medical center was renovated for the program.

MANAGEMENT TOOLS AND TECHNOLOGY

In recent years, the aging network has focused on the efficiency and effectiveness of its services and on using technology to improve them. Management information systems have been designed to facilitate the in-depth evaluation of programs. The National Data Base on Aging, containing information about clients' characteristics; staffing, including volunteers; programs and services, and the allocation of resources, has been developed by the National Association of State Units on Aging and the National Association of Area Agencies on Aging. A national sample of one-third of the states and area agencies is surveyed annually to update the information base. The data are used by the network, policymakers, and researchers in planning, monitoring, and decision making.

Many programs have instituted performance-based contracting, which holds contractors and practitioners accountable for the results. The number of service units, the unit costs, and the administrators' and clients' satisfaction with the services are monitored. When appropriate, contracts are renegotiated (Wedel, 1983).

Computerized systems, such as word processing and data processing, are becoming commonplace. Among the uses for these systems are the planning of meal services, transportation routes, and communication with other service providers and planners. Outcome-oriented objectives for the development and performance of systems and changes in clients are becoming an important concern of management as well as of the funding sources.

PRACTICE, EDUCATION, AND RESEARCH ISSUES

The present and projected needs and characteristics of older people suggest a wide range of practice issues. The following are a few examples:

■ What are the effects of caregiving on family members?

■ Do differences in quality of care exist when long-term facilities operate under different auspices, with various mixes of personnel and types of care?

■ With the declining population of entry-level workers and the increasing population of elderly people, what technologies and employment policies will be needed to provide for an adequate work force?

■ Can a balance be achieved in the expenditure of health care dollars so that freedom of choice, equity, effectiveness, and efficiency are at acceptable levels?

■ How should day care for elderly people and respite care for their caregivers be developed in the future?

Schools of social work recognize that there is a limit to the time that can be devoted to new or expanded content in their curricula. Whenever changes are made, all parts of the system are changed. Students need an increased understanding of the skills that are required to function in a bureaucracy, such as a more creative use of self, policies, rules, and procedures, and their advocacy skills need to be developed. Decision-making theory and its application, along with management, economics, and political science theories, would be useful. In addition, a greater emphasis should be placed on the role of internal and external politics, including the delineation of the various forms of political activity. Students should be taught how to use power judiciously and effectively and how to combine this skill with resources, such as staff and money.

The evaluation of outcomes should be accorded more attention. Better ways of communicating successes must be found, and managers need to be more familiar with the use of various technologies not only to improve management but to communicate more effectively.

As Parham (1982) said, "If your taste is for a dynamic field with lots of ambiguity and flexibility, you are in the right place if you have chosen social services as your occupation. Opportunities are unlimited. You can be a public servant, private entrepreneur, or a combination somewhere between. You can pursue perspectives that are micro, mezzo, or macro" (p. 92). You can be a combination of all three approaches. The future of social work education and management are inextricably intertwined with the state of professional social work practice, the institutionalized social service system, and emerging trends. It is imperative that social work managers be able to function effectively and efficiently so they can provide the highest quality of life for the persons about whom they care.

REFERENCES

American Association of Retired Persons. (1988). *A profile of older Americans: 1987*. Washington, DC: Author.

Chess, W., Jayartne, S., & Norlin, J. (1986). *A study of work satisfaction and job strain among professional social workers in the United States, 1981 and 1985*. Unpublished manuscript.

Ficke, S. C. (Ed.). (1985). *An orientation to the Older Americans Act*. Washington, DC: National Association of State Units on Aging.

Gollub, J. O., Henton, D. C., & Waldhorn, S. A. (1983). Nonservice approaches to social welfare: A local perspective. In R. Agranoff (Ed.), *Human services on a limited budget* (pp. 91–105). Washington, DC: International City Management Association.

Greene, R. (1986). *A discussion on the need for social work services for the aged in 2020*. (Position paper prepared for the U.S. Department of Health and Human Services). Silver Spring, MD: National Association of Social Workers.

Parham, T. M. (1982). Social service issues and challenges in the 1980s. *Administration in Social Work, 6*, 91–105.

Peters, T., & Waterman, R., Jr. (1982). *In search of excellence: Lessons from America's best-run companies*. New York: Harper & Row.

Schneider, R. (1984). *The integration of gerontology into social work educational curricula*. Washington, DC: Council on Social Work Education.

Tolliver, L. M. (1982). *Administration on aging's policies and program directions for 1982–84*. Washington, DC: U.S. Department of Health and Human Services, Office of Human Development, Administration on Aging.

Tolliver, L. M. (1983). [Fiscal data collected and analyzed by Administration on Aging staff for U.S. Commissioner on Aging; for transmittal by internal memorandum to the Secretary of Health and Human Services.] Unpublished raw data.

U.S. Bureau of the Census. (1982). Population estimates and projections. In *Current Population Reports* (Series P-25, No. 922). Washington,

DC: U.S. Government Printing Office.

U.S. Bureau of the Census. (1983). *America in transition: An aging society* (Series P-23, No. 128, pp. 3–6). Washington, DC: U.S. Government Printing Office.

U.S. Bureau of the Census. (1984a). *Demographic and socioeconomic aspects of aging in the United States* (Series P-23, No. 138, pp. 101–110). Washington, DC: U.S. Government Printing Office.

U.S. Bureau of the Census. (1984b). *Projections of the population of the U.S. by age, sex and race: 1983 to 2050* (Series P-25, No. 952, pp. 7–9). Washington, DC: U.S. Government Printing Office.

U.S. Department of Health and Human Services, National Institute on Aging. (1984). *Report on education and training in geriatrics and gerontology.* Washington, DC: U.S. Government Printing Office.

Veterans Administration. (1984). *Caring for the older veteran.* Washington, DC: U.S. Government Printing Office.

Wedel, K. (1983). Purchase of service contracting in human services. In R. Agranoff (Ed.), *Human services on a limited budget* (pp. 185–194). Washington, DC: International City Management Association.

15

Social Work Management in Health Care

Jesse J. Harris and James R. David

THE CHANGES IN MANAGEMENT that have affected all organizational life, including social work, have had a great impact on social work management in health care. In fact, the health care industry and social work's role within it have changed even more rapidly than have management principles in recent decades.

BACKGROUND

Revolution in Technology

For much of the second half of the twentieth century, health care has made enormous strides in its ability to correct health problems and to preserve life. The recent innovations, which were, not long ago, the subject of science fiction, are now routine procedures that are performed constantly throughout the world. These innovations include open-heart surgery and bypasses; heart transplants; liver, lung, and kidney replacements; the reconnection of severed limbs; and the use of newly developed and discovered chemicals to save thousands of lives. In addition, infant mortality has been reduced through such public health measures as improved sanitation, better procedures for prenatal and postnatal care and for delivery of babies, and through the development and widespread use of vaccinations. Developments in health care have been so effective that many people believe that all health care problems can be eliminated, which is a major reason for the concern and fear about AIDS, for which no cure has been found.

Health Care Financing

In addition to the massive developments in health services, the United States has undergone major changes in the ways in which health care is financed. In the 1960s, the government took over much of the financing of health care for the economically disadvantaged and the aged, replacing the often unpredictable charitable services previously provided by hospitals and physicians. Medicare guarantees that the basic health care needs of aged persons are paid for through the social security system. Medicaid, a federal–state program, pays for health services for low-income people, including recipients of public assistance.

The advent of Medicaid and Medicare caused the exponential growth in the long-term care, or nursing home, industry, which began to care for millions of aged and disabled people who were too ill to live in their own homes. Other voluntary and governmental innovations followed. For example, new forms of delivering health care were developed, such as health maintenance organizations (HMOs), which combined not only the health insurance that had been a part of American private health care financing for generations but prepaid care delivered by a specific group of health providers, including hospitals, physicians, and auxiliary services, such as laboratories and rehabilitation facilities.

As the medical technology developed and the costs of providing services increased, it seemed that no realistic limits would be placed on the amount of money that could be spent on medical care in the United States. There was always something else to do and that something else always required more resources. However, because the cost of health care was becoming a greater and greater portion of the gross national product, limits began to be set in the early 1980s.

Today's social work manager in health care has a dual responsibility and problem. The first is to organize and deliver the social work components of the new developments in health care. The second is to deal with the major changes in the administration and management of health care services that have resulted from the technological advances.

Clearly, the most important new developments in health care are less closely related to technological advances and the delivery of health care services than to the effective administration of services. That is true of all the professions in the health care field, including social work. In this chapter, a selected few of the modern management necessities in the field are examined.

A SYSTEMS APPROACH

Although managers may plan sequentially in linear terms, reality is much more complex and demanding. Many social work managers in health care have discovered that it is inappropriate to think in terms of steps in the management process (Ackoff, 1974). In fact, all the activities of management in the health care setting are interrelated and interdependent. Managers plan to assess the system, nurture the staff, develop linkages with other units, maintain the program, develop additional and new programs, and reassess the system. They also must be aware that all these steps may occur simultaneously.

The linear, circular, and contemporaneous views of the major managerial steps are depicted in Figure 1. Several competing requirements generally demand attention at any given time. If a manager does not take time to think, plan, and set priorities, the never-ending process of recurring and competing demands may become overwhelming.

The Clinician as Manager

Often, chiefs of social work departments are chosen because they excelled as clinicians. The challenge to these managers is to use the qualities that enable them to excel as clinicians while they meet the broader goals and expectations of their new roles. The health care industry is undergoing radical changes and intense competition for survival among several factions. Health care facilities are seeking department chiefs who understand the reality of the struggle to provide the best possible care at the most competitive price.

Social work managers are expected to subscribe to the facility's overall mission and vision. They must ask themselves if the facility's values are compatible with their own and if they have the sense of urgency and determination to make the department excel. From a management standpoint, excellence may entail growth or the achievement of greater productivity with the same or fewer resources.

Managers are expected to continue to have the high level of tolerance for ambiguity, frustration, and uncertainty that they had as clinicians (Abramczyk, 1980). A key difference is that their vision must now be broader. Managers must be collegial with managers of other departments

Figure 1.
Linear, Circular, and Contemporaneous Processes

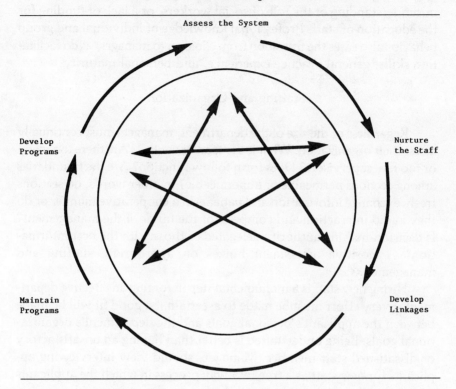

Assess the System

Develop
Programs

Nurture
the Staff

Maintain
Programs

Develop
Linkages

but maintain intradepartmental relationships; they must be team players, ready to emphasize the common good over the goals of their departments.

There are many possible impediments to moving smoothly from clinician to manager. For example, new managers may be more comfortable doing tasks rather than delegating them. They may be loath to use the power of their position. Furthermore, they may be so accustomed to autonomous practice that they find it difficult to move from a focus on the individual patient to a departmental or organizational point of view. It can be agonizing to be responsible for work outside one's immediate control.

Although there are discontinuities between direct practice and management, there are also similarities. A pivotal similarity is the ability to discern, simultaneously, content issues and organizational processes. For example, the content issue may be the facility's refusal to fund continuing health education for the social work staff. The process issue may be ignorance of social work training requirements, a general misunderstanding of the role of social workers, or a lack of funding for the education of staff. Professional knowledge of individual and group behavior also eases the transition from clinician to manager, as do facilitation skills, general practice experience, and personal maturity.

Staffing and Organization

Regardless of the size of the department, managers must continually assess their organization. What is the span of control? Are there too many or too few supervisors? Does form follow function? Are the boundaries among sections permeable or impermeable? In other words, do sections freely exchange information and patients in a cooperative manner or do they avoid interaction and compete for the favor of the management? Is decision-making authority delegated to those with the best information? A positive assessment hinges on appropriate staffing and management.

Hiring new staff is a monumental step in forging an effective department. Every effort must be made to ascertain if a good fit will be made between the applicant's personal goals and the department's organizational goals. Being understaffed is better than having an unsatisfactory or dissatisfied staff member. Managers should view interviewing applicants for new staff as a true two-way process in which the applicants screen the potential employer while they are being assessed.

Managers not only must deal with some inescapable differences between their values and methods of operation and those of their staff members, they must become skilled in understanding and motivating different personality styles. The personal behavior, approaches to clinical practice, and communication styles of staff members vary. The better a manager is at recognizing and weaving these differences into an effective, organizational whole, the more fulfilled and succesful he or she will be.

Helping staff to make decisions and solve problems at the lowest possible organizational level is an important role for managers and one that is difficult to implement. Some workers and middle-level supervisors tend to avoid making decisions. They may either ask the manager what to do or think that it is quicker for the manager to decide. Nonetheless, successful managers must establish the responsibility for problem solving as far down on the hierarchical chain as possible. If the work team has the wherewithal to implement a decision, its members should do so without further consultation. If implementation requires resources or the approval of policies that are beyond the authority of the work unit, recommendations should be formulated and the decision made at the organizational level that has the authority to decide. In this regard, the manager's role parallels that of the clinician. Clinicians are trained not to make decisions for clients but to facilitate the clients' identification of and choice among alternatives. Trusting staff members and empowering them to make decisions and solve problems requires the same professional skill, training, judgment, discipline, and patience.

Goal setting is another aspect of staff development that is necessary for effective organizations (Deegan & O'Donovan, 1982). Establishing goals can be difficult because staff members may correctly interpret the setting of new goals as an inducement to change and hence may be resistant. To maintain purposeful and goal-oriented social work departments, managers must be firm in requiring that individual goals and departmental goals and objectives be formulated with the participation of the staff. If the staff members are not involved in a semiannual examination of where the department is going and how it is going to get there, it is as though they are putting together a jigsaw puzzle with no completed picture to guide them.

Once goals are set, they must be reinforced by rewards and punishments. Many managers find it easier to reward and recognize accomplishments than to deal with unacceptable behavior. Considerable assertiveness, skill, and courage are needed to counsel wayward staff members. Nevertheless, incompetency cannot be overlooked, or it will spread. Managers must set their standards high and allow no deviation from them.

Rewards are particularly important for social work in health care because the work is intense. Positive feedback and appreciation from patients and their families, physicians, nurses, administrators, and others is infrequent. The managerial challenge is to keep staff productive in an environment in which burnout is common. The first step is for the manager to communicate approval, support, and enthusiasm for the staff's work. The next step is to train staff thoroughly. Relevant training, a reward in itself, is not only a requirement of the Joint Commission on the Accreditation of Hospitals, it is a basic insulator against burnout.

In addition to routine rewards, such as time off, letters of appreciation, and the celebration of birthdays, managers may want to consider some of the rewards used in the private for-profit sector. Gain sharing, for example, involves monetary bonuses for increased productivity. Small group incentives and pay for performance may be viable options, depending on the setting. Another path to excellence is additional pay for increased knowledge, a common reward in teaching.

The major key to managing the staffing and organization of an effective department is communication. Managers may not need or want to know everything that goes on in the department, but they do need to forge an environment that encourages open communication. By supporting each clinician's identity, integrity, and freedom, managers not only support the goal of open communication, they accomplish the feat of harnessing autonomous practitioners into a potent organizational force.

INTERDEPARTMENTAL ISSUES

Life in a health care bureaucracy is political and hierarchical. Social work, as a nonmedical discipline in a medical world, must epitomize excellence to merit acceptance and respect. Social work managers who remember their family systems theory will recognize that hospital families are just like regular families. Each family member, that is, clinical department or administrative directorate, has its own role and place in the hierarchical order.

Cooperation is essential. Managers must learn what the decision-makers in their line of supervision value the most and be responsive to those values. If they do not serve their supervisory chain well, their chances of implementing social work goals and values will be impeded. It is important for managers to make the needs and priorities of the institution an integral part of their strategic agenda. When managers think and function as hospital managers as well as social work managers, they can shift readily from being parochial advocates for the needs of their department to team players who see the total needs of the institution.

Good managers often employ the principle of management by wandering around (Peters & Waterman, 1982). They believe that one of the essential activities of an effective manager is to move around the organization to find out what is going on, to identify and deal with problems, and to be visible. Managers should wander around the health care facility not only to supervise their own operations but to get to know others. Direct contact with other units is important in developing the kinds of personal relationships on which solid professional relationships are built and in helping colleagues understand what social workers do and how they do it. In addition, it is important for the manager to learn about and develop an appreciation for the roles and functions of other organizational units.

Knowing the organization and how the social work department fits into the total structure is essential for the manager who wants to introduce innovation and growth. The fastest way to achieve growth is to state the case effectively to those with power so they are motivated to advocate for increases in the social work staff. Some chiefs of social work departments never ask for more staff; instead, they articulate what could and should be done to address the psychosocial dimensions of the care of patients. The social work department alone may have relatively little power in a hospital system, but those who want, need, and value its services may have the power that is needed.

Health care managers must never think that they have a given function in perpetuity. In addition to looking at innovative programs, they must pay critical attention to maintaining the quality of established services. If the social work department trains front-desk clerks for the entire facility and there are repeated complaints about the clerks' lack of responsiveness and courtesy to patients, the department will lose not only the opportunity to establish new programs but the territory it has.

Social workers in a health care facility are always challenged to work as comfortably with the administrative staff as with the clinical staff. Although it is sometimes a difficult chore, they routinely are expected to master both clinical and administrative tasks. Undoubtedly, the best route to a good relationship with the institution as a whole is to develop and retain a good staff.

MARKETING HEALTH SERVICES

Health care facilities have discovered the need to market their services to a broader public. Today, unlike the past, many hospitals are offering care in the same communities, and private and public hospitals are competing for patients. Therefore, those hospitals that want to succeed financially must persuade people to use their facilities. Because of some of the measures designed to reduce the excessive use of hospital care, there is a surplus of hospital facilities in many places. Hence, hospitals are using radio and television advertising, billboards, direct mail, and other devices to induce potential patients to use their facilities.

Similarly, HMOs have found it necessary to promote their services to specific populations. Many potential members of HMOs have several options to consider. Although some employers require their employees to receive health care services through a specific HMO, many others offer a variety of plans. Hence, the HMOs find that they must work to ensure that their organization is chosen over the others.

Social work managers are finding that they, too, must market their services, even though that marketing rarely is done directly to consumers. Instead, the audience for social work marketing is often the hospital administrator or the physician. Some social work managers have created new or different services for clients that become indispensable for the effective performance of the hospital or other health care facility in which they may be employed. Others have described programs, developed them, and proved their effectiveness in achieving some of the objectives of the health care facility, such as reducing costs. An effective social work service can help patients move more rapidly out of the health care facility; may reduce the need for physicians' services, which typically are more costly than other services; and may help locate financial resources to make a patient who might otherwise be dependent on the health care facility self-supporting. The lesson that social work managers in health care facilities have learned is that one must do more than carry out these activities. One also must show how the services work to meet the objectives of the larger organization. It cannot be assumed that others will understand or appreciate the social work service without it being marketed to them.

THE IMPORTANCE OF BUSINESS PRINCIPLES

Because health care has become so expensive that formal limits are now placed on it by various public-planning regulations, social workers, like other professionals in the health care field, have had to become more aware of and conversant with various business-management kinds of activities. Perhaps the most important development in recent years has been the establishment of diagnostic-related groups (DRGs). This system assigns a number of days and various cost-and-service factors to each specific medical condition. Medicare will not pay for more than the specified cost of a particular condition, including any complications and associated conditions contained in DRG. Therefore, if the hospital or health care program spends less on the patient's care than DRG would permit, the health care facility can earn a profit or bonus. However, if it spends more by keeping a person as an inpatient for longer than was planned or by otherwise exceeding the authorized expenditures, Medicare will not reimburse the facility. Therefore, social workers, like other health professionals, have had to manage their activities in such a way that expenditures per patient are held to those permitted by the DRG or less. Effective goal-oriented management can make all the difference in such situations. Discharge planning, in which the patient is released rapidly from the hospital back to the community, is often the responsibility of the social work service. An effective manager can ensure that the social work service responds quickly and can inculcate cost consciousness and a DRG orientation into the staff's attitudes.

APPLICATIONS OF PRINCIPLES

For much of the work of the social work manager in the health care facility, the principles already enunciated in this book are highly applicable. That is, the principles of excellence suggested by Peters and Waterman (1982), some of the concepts of Japanese management that have been discussed (Drucker, 1981; Ouchi, 1981), and other concepts that have been suggested for social work managers, in general, also apply to the practice of social work in health care settings. However, it is clear that health care facilities have to be even more cognizant of and concerned about effective management than do most other services because of the increasing demand for the application of sound management to the delivery of services. All social workers are being held to higher standards of accountability and measurable performance. However, the rapid increase in requirements for effective management in health care has probably made greater demands on social workers in that field to increase their knowledge of management and to improve their managerial performance more immediately and with less time for preparation than may be the case for social workers in other fields. Because health care is such an important part of the U.S. economy and because of the emphasis on containing the cost of that care, it is probable that effective social work health care will continue to require better management than will other settings in which social workers practice.

REFERENCES

Abramczyk, L. W. (1980). The new MSW supervisor: Problems of role transition. *Social Casework, 6,* 83–89.

Ackoff, R. L. (1974). *Redesigning the future: A systems approach to societal problems.* New York: Wiley.

Deegan, A. X., & O'Donovan, T. R. (1982). *Management by objectives for hospitals.* Rockville, MD: Aspen Systems.

Ouchi, W. G. (1982). *Theory Z: How American business can meet the Japanese challenge.* New York: Avon Books.

Peters, T., & Waterman, R. H., Jr. (1982). *In search of excellence: Lessons from America's best-run companies.* New York: Harper & Row.

Specht, H. (1985). Managing professional interpersonal interactions. *Social Work, 30,* 225–230.

16

▲

The Imperative of Professional Leadership in Public Service Management

Joseph J. Bevilacqua

IN THE FUTURE, public services, particularly those services that involve social work, will be facing a new set of challenges. The traditional roles of family, community, and health care, for example, will have to assume new patterns of assistance in dealing with the interdependence of generations, with profound diseases such as acquired immune deficiency syndrome (AIDS), with homelessness, and with the structural poverty brought on by economic dysfunction (Wilkinson, 1987).

These issues will push the human services systems into greater political ferment and, consequently, affect future practice. The question of professional leadership will have to go beyond the confines of any one profession or discipline.

Because the public sector is so large and so comprehensive, it will play a continuing role in managing all these aspects of life. To meet the challenge, governmental service will have a need for stronger advocates and for professionals who are well trained and respected.

It is interesting to note that Paul Volcker, the former chairman of the Federal Reserve Board, plans to devote a significant portion of his retirement to building a stronger base of both support and respect for governmental service (as reported in Hunt, 1987). Additionally, John Gardner, a leading American philosopher and public official, also has focused on the importance of developing leaders who are able to cope with ongoing as well as emerging problems in government (Hechinger, 1987).

It seems that social workers are drifting away from public service and are beginning to emulate models of entrepreneurship in human services. The development of public leaders will require a return to the traditional value of services as opposed to profits. The social work profession must recapture the social ideology that values the sustenance of human beings—an ideology that social workers may have lost by allowing the balance of psychosocial concerns to tilt toward the psychological and away from the social.

THE DRIFT

This trend, as the author has observed in the role of a public official for many years, is away from traditional social work values. Social workers cannot allow themselves to develop into a profession whose mission is simply to avoid doing harm nor can they afford to condone the idea that the state cannot be trusted and that litigation is the only way to make the state behave.

It seems that in programs of government service and education, discussions of some real and continuing problems in the practice of social work are avoided. Professional social work education teaches far too little about the chronic mentally ill and provides far too little professional labor for their care (Davis, 1987). Apparently, social workers focus less on public issues than on the microproblems of individuals and families—those who are more likely to be able to pay for the services they receive. This a paradox in that as more community care is required for people, social work is moving away from its traditional role as a participant and leader in community care. At a time when care is increasingly home based and as other voluntary and informal groups are moving into community caregiving, social work is becoming more office based and emulating the professional models of medicine and law. Skills that are necessary for group work and planning, which are central to good psychosocial programs for the mentally ill and for helping the chronically mentally ill become employable, are becoming less identified with social work, even though the concepts emerged from the social work tradition. Private practice is becoming the goal and the occupation of many professional social workers, which poses a problem because too much of private practice is unavailable to the indigent. However, this does not mean to imply that public service is the easy path to take.

THE ENVIRONMENT OF PUBLIC SERVICE

The environment of public services has become less attractive to new and developing professionals. Although there is a tradition of lifelong employment in the civil service positions of many human service agencies, the tenure in office for top leaders is brief. State commissioners of mental health, for example, average 2 years on the job. In 1987, 22 states changed mental health commissioners, according to the National Association of State Mental Health Program Directors ("The Editors Interview Harlan Cleveland," 1982). That pattern is replicated in departments of social services and other human services programs.

The Management Environment

Working with chief executive officers—governors—is also a new kind of challenge for top leaders in the human services. Once they are elected, politicians assume centrist positions; they are not as free to take risks. Human services issues are unpopular with governors and have only minimal clout with voters. What a governor achieves in the area of human services rarely has a positive impact on his or her career. Frequently, however, it has a negative impact, when human service programs are seen primarily as problems and not solutions.

The problems in public agencies are so diverse and so complex that they can be mind boggling. The typical governor, in a single day, may have to deal with major issues of architecture and finances involving millions or even billions of dollars, as well as individual case matters that affect only a few people. All that work takes place in a glass bowl, with the press, the legislature, clients' families, staff, and all the other constituencies of a public official watching closely.

In this era of declining real resources for the government, there is also great competition for the funds that are available. The competition with highway programs, education, and other services makes it difficult for governments to allocate funds on the basis of need, particularly to the human services. In many states, lawsuits have been filed to bring programs of mental health and support services to needful citizens.

Importance of the Public Sector

Despite all its problems, the public sector remains the keystone of all other human services. It does so because of several reasons. For example, only the public sector can and must treat people in need equitably and insist on their right to equal treatment. Because the services are designed to alleviate poverty and hunger, as is the case with social services, or to treat problems of physical or mental illness, as is often the case with public health and mental health programs, equality of treatment is an absolute in governmental service. All people have a right to treatment, and anything less is a legitimate basis for litigation. The government remains the one sector of human services systems that cannot say no to people who are eligible for help.

The public sector also can promote and enforce standards in such fields as education, child care, and health care. Only the government has the sanction and the resources to ensure that adequate standards are met. And were it not for those standards, which even today are not as fully enforced as they should be, the treatment of people who have social and emotional problems would be even less adequate than it is.

The government is able to deal with need in a variety of other ways as well. For instance, it can, and generally must, serve as the organization of last resort for dealing with individuals who have nowhere else to turn. In doing so, individual and group needs emerge. Governmental agencies can and do conduct research to identify trends in needs and developments; they are able to fund demonstration models that develop efficient approaches to helping others in ways that can be replicated by larger systems, as well as by voluntary agencies. Perhaps what is most important, the public sector serves as a forum for policy discussions within the agencies themselves, within legislative bodies, and within the court systems. As Thomas Jefferson said, "The care of human life and happiness, and not their destruction, is the first and only legitimate object of good government."

THE ROLE OF SOCIAL WORK

The profession of social work is a facilitator of leadership in public service. Traditionally, social work has provided the link among services and the services themselves to those people who need them. Social work has provided that same link among service providers, so that together, they can make the best care available at the lowest possible cost. Social workers are a profession of organizers and planners, not just treatment providers.

Social work also plays a crucial role in the development of services because it works with people as they relate to the environment in which they live. Problem solving takes place most effectively when it occurs within the context of the larger environment.

Social workers also are oriented toward working through systems; they recognize the impact of working in an interdisciplinary fashion. By working together with people as they solve problems in an effective way, they build on their own capacities to solve problems.

Social workers are optimistic; for example, they view the cup as half full, rather than half empty. They value self-determination, which they express in work toward enhancing clients' strengths, rather than focusing on weaknesses and pathology. This model is increasingly important in public service. As a profession, social workers have a long tradition of working with the community at large—with lay citizens, volunteers, and boards. Social workers are dedicated more to service and action than they are to study and analysis. That is, social workers have a bias for doing rather than for simply thinking or projecting solutions.

LEADERSHIP

Many are beginning to say that the essence of leadership for the future will be the skill of pulling together expertise, not in developing more expertise ("The Editors Interview Harlan Cleveland," 1982). Expert information already is available in many areas, including the technical areas of human services. What is needed now is the ability to blend that expertise so that social workers will be better able to implement good programs. Social workers recognize more and more that the real problems are interdisciplinary—that no one discipline has all the answers. The profession of social work has no need to feel threatened by that awareness.

Indeed, social workers are situated ideally to work in an interdisciplinary world. Their focus on consultation, information and referral, and case management is a good indicator of how committed they are to the interdisciplinary approach.

They also have focused on similar concepts that are important for the development of leadership in the future. Social workers practice what they know about maximizing strengths. They know about helping people develop self-confidence and the will to improve before they try to change those people. All these factors point to leadership, and the factors will be influential in making social work prominent in public service in the future.

PERSONAL BELIEFS

The author, throughout many years in public service, has developed several beliefs about the necessary conditions of leadership. They are as follows:

■ Believe in what you are doing and have the vision to understand its importance.

■ Assume and understand that risk is part of the game and that effective leaders lose as well as win their battles.

■ Recognize that there are no secrets in public service—that anything one does or says may become public knowledge almost immediately.

■ Get out into the public and be known on the street and in the community. Do not be a shadowy, isolated figure.

■ Do not wear green eye shades. You have specialists in accounting, so you do not need to be one yourself.

■ Recognize that ambiguity is part of the job. Many more situations are ambiguous than are clear and precise.

■ Have a good personal support system of family, friends, and colleagues.

■ Search for and employ able people who are loyal and who share your values. They are important to your success.

■ Encourage celebrations of success but avoid bureaucratic rituals. That is, honor devoted employees but do not let these honors become ritualistic. Celebrate milestones in the agencies; work to make them genuine celebrations in which people want to participate.

■ Develop a broad base of support to lead effectively.

■ Work for, obtain, and use political support.

■ Pay attention to the consumer—both listen and respond. The recipient of services may know more about what your agency does and should be doing than anyone else.

■ Develop and maintain a connection with institutions of higher education. Universities have the objectivity and the information to help you succeed in ways that would not be possible without such connections.

■ Work for significant and visible success early in your tenure on the job. You will be able to build on that success.

■ Do not take the credit—not all or even most of it. Defer to others and spread the credit around. Everyone will assume that you are largely responsible for what happened, but others will appreciate your willingness to let them share in the glory.

■ Do not be caught in a corner with a dogmatic position. Have convictions, but understand that there are many ways to achieve the same fundamental objectives.

■ Communicate in a straightforward way. Do not dodge the truth or use complex terminology to avoid saying what you mean. Everyone needs to hear from you in a straight and direct manner.

■ Love your job, but recognize that you are only a temporary occupant and will some day have to give it up. Be willing to be totally dedicated and willing to drop out when the time comes.

REFERENCES

Davis, K. E. (1987). *The challenge to state mental health systems and universities in Virginia: Preparation of mental health professionals for work with the chronic mentally disabled: Final report.* Unpublished manuscript. Virginia Commonwealth University, School of Social Work, Richmond.

The editors interview Harlan Cleveland. (1982). *New England Journal of Human Services, 2,* 8.1

Hechinger, F. M. (1987, August 18). Help wanted: Leaders [About Education]. *New York Times,* p. 20.

Hunt, A. R. (1987, July 24). Paul Volcker: The ultimate public servant. *Wall Street Journal,* p. 20.

Wilkinson, G. (1987). National Planning Assumptions and Select Key Implications for United Ways. Paper presented at the National Professional Symposium, National Association of Social Workers, New Orleans, LA.

17

Management Insights for the American Workplace

Larry Crump

MANY AMERICAN MANAGERS AND ACADEMICS respond positively to the apparent humanistic nature of the Japanese style of management, but do not think it will work in the United States. U.S. executives show a particular distaste for "Japanese style management," reported Kim Clark of the Harvard Business School. "In seminars you can just see it. They roll their eyes and sort of turn off. The questions I do get are more strident and bitter" ("Japan's Strategies," 1983, p. 3).

Yes, the United States and Japan are different, and management style is truly a mirror image of culture. However, praising or questioning the application of the Japanese style of management in the United States is beyond the stage of intellectual curiosity. Japanese subsidiaries are a "growth industry" in the United States, which is a polite way of saying that Japanese corporations will be employing Americans in large numbers.

Within the manufacturing sector, 640 Japanese companies or affiliated firms employed 160,000 American workers in 42 states and Puerto Rico as of 1987. Although this may not be a significant number, it is worth noting that 60 percent of these factories have been operating since 1980—50 percent of them only since 1985. It was estimated that from May to December of 1987, Americans working for Japanese manufacturers would increase 20 percent, to 200,000 employees (Dai-Nanakai, 1987).

One could discuss the advantages of and concerns that many Americans might have about this circumstance. But, for a moment, imagine that a 30- to 50-year-old Japanese *salaryman* (manager) is about to leave Japan for a 2–5-year assignment in the United States. Of course, most of his work force will be American. How would he effectively conduct organizational life with Japanese managers and American workers? Given the American culture and social structure, what advice might you offer the Japanese salaryman? What Japanese management concepts, principles, and techniques should he "pack in his bag" and what should he leave in Tokyo? And, what concepts might be transferred to receptive American social welfare administrators or business managers?

A FUNCTIONAL STRUCTURE

A functional approach to management will be most effective for conducting this analysis. Management is "the process of achieving organizational goals through the coordinated performance of five specific functions: (1) planning, (2) organizing, (3) staffing, (4) directing, and (5) controlling" (Mauser & Schwartz, 1982, p. 98).

Given the opportunity to participate in both American and Japanese management systems, one could observe each of these functions. However, the application of these functions would be different in each nation. In this chapter, the author considers these differences and their significance for the application of Japanese management in an American organizational context in relation to management issues pertaining to personnel, supervision, human relations, and the organizational culture. Concurrently, the important differences that exist between Japanese and American structural factors are noted, such as financing policies and tax laws, the organization–stockholder relationship, the labor market structure and industrial relations, and the political and legal system. These structural factors have a direct influence on what is popularly known as "Japanese management."

However, one structural factor merits analysis: the role of educational systems in shaping the management philosophies toward American or Japanese workers. Generally, American management still is unable to move beyond Taylor's style of "scientific management" (Taylor, 1911). Management students continue to receive a technical education. Certainly, managers of the future will require analytical problem-solving skills, but what American schools of management lack is a serious and sincere commitment to teach the knowledge and skills of human relations.

The American management style generally includes the attitude that workers do not have useful knowledge and motivation. This philosophy becomes even more apparent when American and Japanese management are compared. In turn, the American labor movement has pursued and continues to pursue a strategy that makes it difficult for American managers to reflect on their philosophy.

In sharp contrast, the Japanese philosophy of management communicates a strong feeling of confidence in the employees' motivation to work and in their ability to contribute intelligently to the organization. Furthermore, the Japanese educational system is not a structural factor that is a primary force in shaping a person's management philosophy. The Japanese manager learns his or her management philosophy and skills on the job. This difference in philosophy serves as a cornerstone to understanding the American and Japanese styles of management. The functions of management are analyzed as follows.

Directing and Controlling

The functional definition of management cited by Mauser and Schwartz (1982, p. 98) is from an American textbook on business. Japanese managers do not direct or control, at least they would never admit to doing so. The American manager would probably use terms like "conferring" or "reciprocal consultation" to describe the work of a Japanese supervisor. Yet, these words fall short. Many concepts and techniques are utilized to provide motivation and leadership in the Japanese organization. Beyond the Japanese management philosophy, the one factor that is of greatest significance is the relationship between the manager and the worker.

To understand this supervisory relationship, one must consider a Japanese term that has no equivalent English translation. As Reischauer (1981) stated, the noun *amae* involves the action of looking for affection by being enveloped in the group and receiving its approval. In Japan, the child first develops a psychic dependency for gratification on the mother, expecting understanding indulgence from her, but at the same time, completely accepting her authority (p. 141). When Japanese children mature, they transfer their need for dependence and this style of relating to the social group, the workplace, and Japanese society.

The Japanese style of relating certainly represents a different social and psychological structure from what is found in the West. In an American context, the skills that a social worker might use to develop a client–counselor relationship appear much like the relationship skills used by the Japanese manager and worker, with two exceptions. First, in the Japanese relationship, both parties perform continuous acts that are intended to cause mutual feelings of obligation and dependence (Doi, 1977). Second, the American social worker would not experience the intensity of feeling that is represented by the concept *amae*, although some clients might do so through the Western concept of transference. What is of additional interest is that Japanese managers perceive that they are responsible for counseling their workers (Crump, 1987). In this regard, the author found in interviews with Japanese managers and workers that formal Japanese employee evaluations are of the "total person." Thus, it is not unusual for managers to discuss issues that are related to their workers' personal lives, and some managers have even met with workers and their wives during times of marital crises. One of Japan's first industrial counselors (and one of the few who has a formal education in social welfare) reported to the author that 20 years ago, it was difficult to convince supervisors to refer emotionally disturbed workers to the company's counselor because they believed that the management would question their supervisory competence if they could not help the workers themselves.

The author has provided training to hundreds of Japanese managers before their overseas assignments. He always teaches them to pack their relationship skills in their bag when they move to the United States but to use caution in asking workers questions that are of a personal nature. The inability of Japanese supervisors to manage cultural differences might produce misunderstandings initially. Specifically, American workers could feel smothered in a typical Japanese supervisory relationship. However, they might find the general supervisory style to be refreshing if they have become accustomed to an autocratic style of leadership. The Japanese style encourages self-esteem and positive relationships in the workplace—factors that have been known to contribute to the productivity of employees since the Hawthorne studies of 1927 (Mayo, 1960).

However, Japanese communication skills may not contribute to positive relationships in the workplace. Western people accuse Japanese people of communicating in a vague manner. It is true that "trust, understanding and open but subtle communication are important organizational values in Japan" (Crump, 1986, p. 57). Thus, the Japanese manager who is about to leave for the United States is advised to unpack his communication skills and leave them in Tokyo. His skill at being vague will only become of value once he learns how to communicate assertively and directly. Then, he will be in a position to use these communication skills selectively.

Ambiguity, diplomacy, or information management can be a useful management tool—one that American managers would be wise to develop and use selectively in human relations. As Pascale (1978) observed:

> To watch a skilled manager use ambiguity is to see an art form in action. Carefully selecting his words he picks his way across difficult terrain. In critiquing a subordinate's work, for example, the executive occasionally finds it desirable to come close enough to the the point to ensure that the subordinate gets the message but not so close as to "crowd" him and cause defensiveness. (p. 47)

This technique is much like the methods that a skilled counselor sometimes uses with vulnerable clients.

Control is another functional area of management. Written policies and human relationships are primary tools for organizational control, both of which are used in American and Japanese organizations. However, Japanese organizations have a distinct preference for human relationships, as can be imagined, while U.S. organizations place their trust in the written word. The 100-page American legal contract and the Japanese contract of 1 or 2 pages are excellent examples of the difference in values (Graham & Sano, 1984).

Although the hypothetical Japanese manager has been advised to take his relationship skills to the United States, he will learn that these skills are less effective in controlling an American organization. However, he, unfortunately, must be told to duplicate the American strategy of written organizational policies. He will not need these policies on a day-to-day basis (he has the human relationship for this purpose), but the American legal system will demand to see these tools if serious management problems develop.

Staffing

The Japanese method of selecting, training, compensating, and evaluating employees may have the least relevance in the American workplace, primarily because American norms and policies would dominate. However, Japanese methods should not be discounted, because they offer productivity benefits to the organization and welfare benefits to workers. At issue is the radical difference between "economic organizations" (a Western model) and "work communities" (a Japanese model) as the economic strategy of society.

Work communities are highly motivated and, hence, more productive than are economic organizations. Although workers may be confronted with repetitious or boring tasks, their level of alienation from life and work decreases because of the community orientation to work life. Of course, the supervisory relationship is a primary factor in the development of this social phenomenon.

Ishida (1986) identified 15 human resource management practices that would constitute the Japanese style. These practices are as follows: (1) the recruitment and employment only of graduating students (high school or university), not of experienced workers; (2) continuous on-the-job training; (3) open promotion from within; (4) employment security; (5) information sharing; (6) participation; (7) sex discrimination; (8) the extensive rotation of workers from one job task and skill area to another; (9) the evaluation of the total person; (10) a seniority/ability-based wage and promotion system; (11) early retirement; (12) systematic overtime; (13) low levels of vacation; (14) company welfare facilities; and (15) unions organized by enterprise, rather than trade. After a comparative analysis of organizational models, Ishida made the following conclusion: If a Japanese philosophy of management were a guiding principle, the first six employment practices could be transferred to a heterogeneous class society with an individualistic culture and an economic labor market, with political and legal factors similar to the United States.

Ishida indicated that a number of organizational outcomes might be expected if these employment practices were properly implemented. These possible outcomes include the development of employees' skills, motivation, teamwork, and flexible behavior on the job; the low turnover of employees; and labor–management cooperation. He did not expect, however, the American work force to develop a commitment to their employing organizations or the type of discipline that is found in Japanese organizations.

After 200 years of interaction between social welfare and economic organization, the general state-of-the-art practice model in the American economy includes pension programs, medical insurance, EAPs, and corporate philanthropy. Social workers must recognize that the work community is a philosophical and structural economic system that is different from anything social workers have considered or confronted. The social work profession would be wise to give serious thought to this difference, identifying ways that a work-community model might become an arena for social work practice.

Planning and Organizing

What work will be done and how will it be conducted? These functional questions require a discussion of the issues of leadership, delegation of responsibility, and decision making.

Japanese management is most famous for a participatory style of leadership and decision making. This philosophy is different from the general American style, in which authority is delegated to a specific organizational position.

American managers have defined areas of responsibility and power to make certain decisions. The organization offers some policy direction regarding how this authority might be exercised, but usually no policy or norm regarding the style of leadership that should be presented. As a result, there is a range of American patterns, from an autocratic style to one that is as participatory as the organizational structure will tolerate.

This range of styles is not found in Japanese organizations, at least not in Japan. Negandhi, Eshghi, and Yuen (1985) indicated that an autocratic style of management, or a "facade of participation," may be observed in Japanese subsidiaries outside Japan. These researchers offered convincing data but did not explain what might cause this management paradox. This author suggests that two factors contribute to this phenomenon. The Japanese experience provides members of work communities with a shared and homogeneous culture. In addition, the culture does not teach Japanese managers to respond effectively to workers who express their own ideas and directly question the ideas of others. The Japanese manager, unskilled in this type of social dialogue, responds in a fearful manner. Outside Japan, this fear is expressed as an autocratic style of management, even though organizational norms provide for the participation of members.

To understand the nature of "participatory management" in Japan, one must recognize the importance of amae. It is also of value to recognize four other concepts of almost equal value: (1) hitonami is the attitude that one must be like the group; (2) haji is an uncomfortable feeling that occurs if a Japanese person senses that he or she is different from others. Hitonami and haji regulate the behavioral patterns of nine out of 10 Japanese people (Hitonami: Keeping up with the Satos, 1983). They are expressed with two verbal behaviors, tatemae (a statement required to maintain harmony) and honne (true feelings or thought). Generally, Japanese social norms expect a tatemae response. It should be noted, however, that a nonverbal message might provide information about a person's true feelings—even though such a response would be unintelligible to non-Japanese people.

Now, imagine the nature of a Japanese staff meeting in which *wa*, or harmony, is the primary goal. Or, imagine the amount of *nemawashi* (literally "preparing the roots," but generally like unobserved organizational lobbying in a Western context), which must occur before a new idea is presented to the group (Christopher, 1983). In the following discussion of Japanese "participatory management" these concepts, social norms, and behaviors should be kept in mind.

It is rare to find an autocratic leader in Japan. Participation and consensus are the official organizational norms. This participatory style exists in a number of organizational structures and relationships.

Generally, Japanese unions probably are manipulated on a regular basis by management. But, when Japanese and American industrial relations are compared, the Japanese model stands out as a superior example of productivity. It is also the most significant example of Japanese participatory management. This relationship has the appearance of a business partnership; it exists primarily because management recognizes its importance.

It must be noted that Japanese work communities do not experience the same pressure for profits and dividends that American stockholders place on their economic organizations. This is a significant structural factor that usually is not identified when discussing Japanese management and industrial relations, but one that the author has spent considerable time investigating through interviews with people in the Japanese financial and banking industries and through a review of the literature (Abegglen & Stalk, 1987).

Comparisons of industrial relations in Japan and the United States usually consider several factors. One primary difference is organizational. U.S. unions are organized by trade. It is possible that one U.S. company could have as many individual unions as national organized trade groups. Japanese unions are organized on the "one company–one union" concept, or enterprise unions (Cole, 1979). This single factor contributes to some of the differences in the dynamics of U.S. and Japanese industrial relations and may contribute to the establishment of a work community. Other factors include a system of paying workers that generally is based on employees' seniority, rather than trade union power, skill, or profession. Also, management is strongly committed to act on all alternatives before laying off employees. Finally, management and labor prefer to avoid confrontation, and most companies have joint labor-management consultation committees in which all matters of company business may be discussed (Labor–Management Relations in Japan, 1983).

Although the quality control circle is an American invention, it never took root. However, the Japanese developed the quality circle to an art form. Quality circles comprise workers who are concerned about the quality of products and efficiency and effectiveness in the workplace. As Kume (1985) noted, the quality circle is a "procedure to problem-solving" (p. 192). Japanese quality circles are built on their management philosophy, workplace relationships, staffing policies, and industrial relations. The Japanese quality circle represents an extension of the partnership between management and labor. Its introduction naturally is more successful in a work community than in an economic organization.

Finally, there is the *ringi* decision-making system, which generally is considered the major tool of Japanese bottom-up management and for the participation of workers. A *ringisho* is a document that includes the statement of a problem and a solution, a proposal, or a new organizational concept. In theory, this document may be drafted and submitted by any individual in the organization, but it is more likely that a group of individuals would contribute to the development of the ringisho, probably after a fair amount of nemawashi. This document must receive the approval of any person affected by the proposal, regardless of his or her power in the organization. As the document is passed from person to person, from department to department, and from one level of management to another, modifications are negotiated. The top management will not consider the ringisho before organizational consensus has been reached.

The author had a personal experience with ringisho at a Japanese government-sponsored training center. He conducted a workshop on American and Japanese industrial relations for managers from developing countries in Asia, South America, and Africa. When it was time to receive payment, the training coordinator offered him only 75 percent of the agreed-on fee, with a sincere apology, indicating that the center had never employed a non-Japanese trainer before. It seems that the training coordinator had made the mistake of offering a contract without first conducting nemawashi. He had been forced to submit a ringisho quickly, proposing that a non-Japanese be allowed to conduct a training workshop at the center. The author imagines that the lost 25 percent was part of a compromise—a way of teaching the training coordinator not to develop organizational policies on his own.

The Japanese manager who is on his way to the United States would be wise to learn how to respond to the Western style of disagreement. Cooperative industrial relations, quality control circles, a decentralized organizational structure, and the ringi method of decision making are all possible in a non-Japanese work community. Some of these concepts might even be effective in a traditional American economic organization under the correct conditions. But, if the Japanese manager is to implement such concepts in an American context, he must be able to respond to social norms.

BENEFITS TO SOCIAL WORKERS AND JAPANESE WORK COMMUNITIES

Eventually the Japanese manager will learn how to respond directly and assertively to open disagreement while communicating information in a manner that a Western listener can easily understand. The Japanese have well-developed relationship and communication skills and a consuming desire to learn.

However, the Japanese manager will require some assistance. American social workers would be wise to seek employment opportunities with these Japanese subsidiaries. These potential work communities would also be wise to retain American social workers. In such an arrangement, both parties would benefit. Japanese work communities would come to value social work communication, relationship, and organizational skills, and they also would appreciate learning about American managers who have a philosophy that is similar to their own.

Following extensive research, Japanese–American experts on negotiation report that the American business community would be more successful with Japan if it sent negotiators who demonstrated the following characteristics; "listening ability, interpersonal orientation, willingness to use team assistance, self-esteem, high aspirations, attractiveness (ability to cause others to want to be with you, superior social skills), and influence at headquarters" (Graham & Sano, 1984, p. 39). In a social work context, this advice speaks for itself.

The American social work community also would receive great benefits in such an arrangement. To the benefit of society, American educational institutions would find an increased demand for social work students. But, beyond this, American social workers would continue to develop expertise in management and economics. In addition, social workers would have an opportunity to experiment in a new kind of economic organization, one that values communication, human relationship, and organizational skills. These social workers would reflect on this experimentation and identify methods, processes, and practice models that could integrate the economic sector in the task of preventing and alleviating social problems.

REFERENCES

Abegglen, J. C., & Stalk, G. (1987). *Kaisha: The Japanese corporation.* Tokyo: Charles E. Tuttle.
Christopher, R. C. (1983). *The Japanese mind.* New York: Simon & Schuster.
Cole, R. E. (1979). *Work, mobility and participation.* Berkeley: University of California Press.
Crump, L. (1986). Nihon e no Urikomiseikoho [Selling successfully to the Japanese]. *This Is, 3,* 52–57.
Crump, L. (1987). The economic sector of Japanese society: An exploration for social welfare activities. *International Social Work, 30,* 343–351.
Dai-Nanakai Zaibei Nikkei Seizo Kojo Kakeiei Jittai Chosa [Seventh survey on the actual conditions of management of Japanese-affiliated manufacturing plants in the United States]. (1987). Tokyo: Japan External Trade Organization.
Doi, T. (1977). *The anatomy of dependence.* Tokyo: Kodansha International.
Graham, J. L., & Sano, Y. (1984). *Smart bargaining: Doing business with the Japanese.* Cambridge, MA: Ballinger.
Hakuhodo Institute of Life & Living. (1983). *Hitonami: Keeping up with the Satos.* Tokyo: Author.
Ishida, H. (1986). Transferability of Japanese human resource management abroad. *Human Resource Management, 25,* 103–120.
Japan Productivity Center. (1983). *Labor-management relations in Japan.* Tokyo: Author.
Japan's strategies may need some tuning to work here. (1983, January 23). *Los Angeles Times,* Part 4, p. 13.
Kume, H. (1985). *Statistical methods for quality improvement.* Tokyo Association for Overseas Technical Scholarship.
Mauser, F. F., & Schwartz, D. J. (1982). *American business: An introduction.* New York: Harcourt Brace Jovanovich.
Mayo, G. E. (1960). *The human problems of an industrial civilization.*

New York: Viking.

Negandhi, A. R., & Eshghi, G. S., & Yuen, E. C. (1985). The management practices of Japanese subsidiaries overseas. *California Management Review, 27*, 93–105.

Pascale, R. T. (1978). Zen and the art of management. *Harvard Business Review, 56*, 44–53.

Reischauer, E. O. (1981). *The Japanese.* Cambridge, MA: Belknap Press of Harvard University.

Taylor, F. W. (1911). *Scientific management.* New York: Harper & Bros.

Contributors

▲

EDITORS

Paul R. Keys, PhD, is Professor and Chair, Administration Sequence, Hunter College School of Social Work, New York; former Deputy Administrator, State of Wisconsin Division of Community Services; and Management Consultant. He conceived the Institute on Administration at the 1985 NASW Professional Symposium that led to this book and the National Network for Social Work Managers/NASW "The Management Conference" for which he was co-chair. He has published extensively on human service management issues and his book *Groups in Industry: Enhancing Individual and Organizational Performance* will be published soon by Sage.

Leon H. Ginsberg, PhD, has been Carolina Research Professor, College of Social Work, University of South Carolina, Columbia, since 1986. Before 1986, he was a state official in West Virginia, holding positions of Chancellor of the Board of Regents and Commissioner of Human Services. He also served as Dean, School of Social Work, West Virginia University for 9 years; as faculty member, University of Oklahoma; and as visiting professor to several U.S. and Latin American universities. An active member of NASW, he has served as chair of the boards of the Center for Social Policy and Practice, and on the Program Committee, Publications Committee, and eighteenth edition of the *Encyclopedia of Social Work* Committee.

AUTHORS

Joseph J. Bevilacqua, PhD, is Commissioner of Mental Health, State of South Carolina. A nationally published protagonist for reform and innovation in such areas as community mental health and services for the homeless, children, and the chronically mentally ill, he has served as

Commissioner, Virginia Department of Mental Health and Mental Retardation and Director, Rhode Island Department of Mental Health, Retardation, and Hospitals.

Todd Boressoff, CSW, is Chair, Child Care Council of the City University of New York, and Executive Director, Early Childhood Center and Child Care Network, Borough of Manhattan Community College. He plays a leadership role in the Early Childhood Education Council of New York City, the New York City Early Childhood Coalition, and Child Care, Inc.

Larry Crump, MSW, is a self-employed Management and Cultural Consultant serving Japan's business community. He also is Research Fellow, Japan College of Social Work, studying and writing about the integration of economic and social welfare systems. Before he went to Japan in 1985, he was active in NASW and Washington state's occupational social work movement.

Anthony A. Cupaiuolo, DSW, is Associate Professor and Director, Edwin G. Michaelian Institute for Sub/Urban Governance, Pace University, White Plains, New York. Formerly Special Assistant to the Commissioner of the New York State Department of Social Services, he has lectured and written extensively on the legal and community relations issues affecting the establishment of group homes and on management of the public sector. His current professional memberships include NASW and the American Society of Public Administration.

Col. James R. David, PhD, is Assistant Chief, Social Work Service, Walter Reed Army Medical Center. He also is Clinical Member and Approved Supervisor, American Association of Marriage and Family Therapists; Adjunct Associate Professor, The Catholic University of America; and Clinical Assistant Professor, The Uniformed Services University of Health Sciences.

Richard L. Edwards, PhD, is Dean and Professor, Mandel School of Applied Social Sciences, Case Western Reserve University, Cleveland, Ohio. His major areas of research are organizational and managerial effectiveness. The current President-elect of NASW, he also has served as national Treasurer, member of the national Board of Directors, and chair of a variety of committees and task forces. He has contributed to a variety of edited books and has been published extensively in such journals as *Social Work, Administration in Social Work, Human Services in the Rural Environment, Arete,* and *Journal of Continuing Social Work Education.*

Burton Gummer, PhD, is Associate Professor and Chair, Management Concentration, School of Social Welfare, Rockefeller College of Public Affairs and Policy, State University of New York at Albany. His major areas of interest are the organization and administration of social service organizations. He has published extensively on these topics and his book, *The Politics of Social Administration,* will be published soon by Prentice-Hall. His "Notes from the Management Literature" is a regular feature of *Administration in Social Work.*

Col. Jesse J. Harris, DSW, is Consultant to the Army Surgeon General and Chief, Social Work Service, Walter Reed Army Medical Center. He is responsible for social work policy as it pertains to the Army Medical Department. He also is a member of the Executive Committee, American Board of Social Work Examiners, and Chair, NASW 1988 National Conference. From 1983 to 1987, he was Chair, NASW Clinical Register, and he is a former member, Accreditation Committee, Council on Social Work Education.

Wilburn Hayden, Jr., MSW, is Head and Associate Professor, Social Work Department, Western Carolina University, Cullowhee, North Carolina, and a doctoral candidate, School of Social Work, University of Toronto. He has had management experience in community organization and social planning and has served as director of a human services program, chief of a prison social work unit, and consultant.

James N. Miller, MSW, is President, Family Service Association of Indianapolis. He has had extensive experience in the areas of foster care, adoption, residential care, marriage and family counseling, psychiatric social work, and administration. He has taught at the Department of Psychiatry, University of Cincinnati, Hope College, and the Indiana University School of Social Work; has been a field instructor for five schools of social work, a part-time consultant to Lilly Endowment, accreditation reviewer for the Council on Social Work Education, Council on Accreditation of Services for Families and Children, and National Home Caring Council, and has served as Vice-chair, Indiana Coalition for Human Services, and member, Committee on Governmental Affairs, Family Service America.

Marc L. Miringoff, PhD, Associate Professor and Assistant Dean, School of Social Service, Fordham University, New York, and founder and director of Fordham's Institute for Innovation of Social Policy. He is the author of *American Social Welfare Policy: Reassessment and Reform* and *Management in Human Service Organizations* as well as numerous articles on social policy.

Felice Davidson Perlmutter, PhD, is Professor, School of Social Administration, Temple University, Philadelphia. A consultant and lecturer, she has written extensively in the area of social service administration. In addition, she was instrumental in organizing a graduate social work program in administration, which has received national attention.

Russy D. Sumariwalla, MA, LLM, is Vice President, Community, Agencies, and Programs Market, Strategic Planning and Markets division, United Way of America, Alexandria, Virginia, and Senior Fellow, United Way Institute. Author of numerous books, reports, and studies, including the *National Taxonomy of Exempt Entities,* published by the Independent Sector, he is an advisor to nonprofit organizations in the areas of taxation, charities regulation, and financial accounting and staff director of the project to revise the *Standards of Accounting and Financial Reporting for Voluntary Health and Welfare Organizations.*

Milton Tambor, MSW, is Staff Representative, American Federation of State, County, and Municipal Employees (AFSCME) in Michigan and a doctoral candidate in sociology. He has had extensive experience in the trade union movement and has taught collective bargaining, steward training, and labor issues at the University of Michigan/Wayne State University Labor School. He also has written articles on social work unionization that have appeared in *Social Work, Administration in Social Work,* and *Catalyst.*

Lennie-Marie P. Tolliver, PhD, is Professor, School of Social Work, University of Oklahoma, Norman. A former Commissioner on Aging, U.S. Department of Health and Human Services, she has been a member of the Technical Advisory Committee on Retirement, 1971 White House

Conference on Aging, and a charter member of the Federal Council on Aging.

Joel Walker, DSW, is Associate Professor, Hunter College School of Social Work, New York, where he teaches human behavior and group work and social policy. He has conducted research on social welfare processes in minority communities and currently is studying the use of group work skills in organizations.

Index